W9-ACV-015

COOKIES
ARE MAGIC

Don’t miss these other great books by Maida Heatter:

HAPPINESS IS BAKING

CHOCOLATE IS FOREVER

MAIDA HEATTER

COOKIES ARE MAGIC

CLASSIC COOKIES, BROWNIES, BARS, AND MORE

Illustrations by
ALICE OEHR

Foreword by
DEB PERELMAN

VORACIOUS
LITTLE, BROWN AND COMPANY
New York | Boston | London

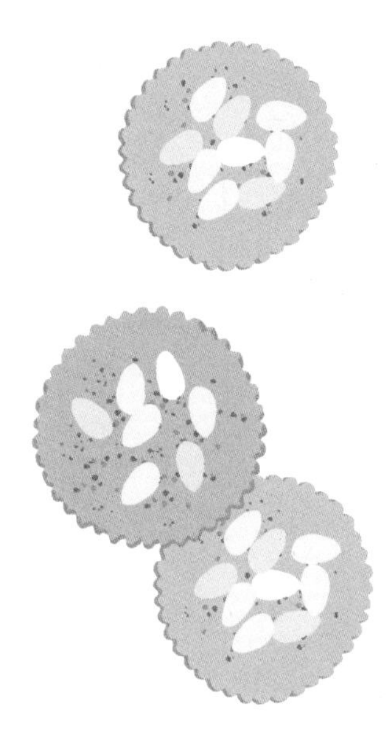

Illustrations by Alice Oehr

Voracious / Little, Brown and Company
Hachette Book Group
1290 Avenue of the Americas, New York, NY 10104
littlebrown.com

First Edition: April 2020

Voracious is an imprint of Little, Brown and Company, a division of Hachette Book Group, Inc. The Voracious name and logo are trademarks of Hachette Book Group, Inc.

The recipes in *Cookies Are Magic* have been assembled from Maida Heatter's previously published books, including *Happiness Is Baking, Maida Heatter's Cakes, Maida Heatter's Cookies, Maida Heatter's Book of Great Chocolate Desserts, Maida Heatter's Book of Great Desserts, Maida Heatter's New Book of Great Desserts,* and *Maida Heatter's Book of Great Cookies*. They have been occasionally updated or modernized from their original forms for consistency, for ease of use, and in instances where the author's personal notes on her books have improved a recipe after its original publication.

Design by Toni Tajima

ISBN 978-0-316-46018-7
LCCN 2019950650

10 9 8 7 6 5 4 3 2 1

WOR

Printed in the United States of America

"I heard a doctor talking on television about the dangers of stress. The doctor listed ways of coping with stress. Exercise. Diet. Yoga. Take a walk.

I yelled, 'Bake cookies.'"

contents

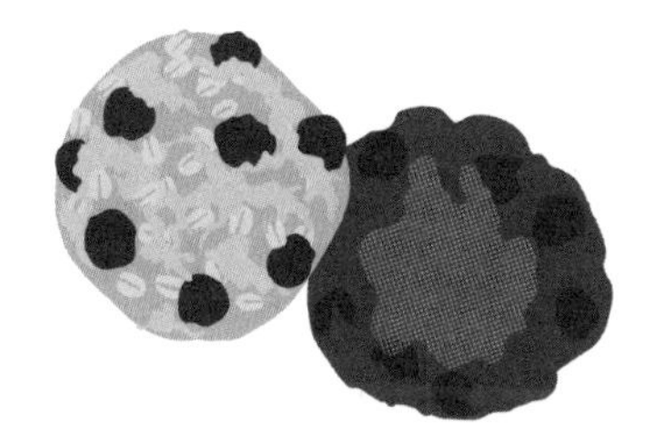

foreword

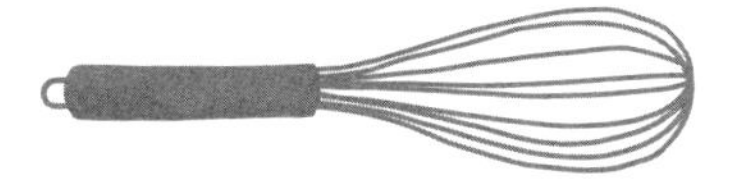

If you ask a home baker, or perhaps a million of them on the internet, about their favorite Maida Heatter recipe, almost all of them will name a cake, a fitting response to a query about the woman known as the Queen of Cake. But despite my affection for her Blueberry Crumb Cake (you'll never need another), I've always had a soft spot for her cookies. They were my first introduction to Maida, twenty years ago on Christmas Eve at my best friend's mom's house. My friend's mother is an excellent baker, and her medley of holiday cookies always included a couple of selections from Maida's repertoire—something featherlight and buttery, something deeply spiced. When I gushed over them and she realized I didn't know who Maida was, she was (politely) appalled. At the time, I was just a baking enthusiast who had no inkling of my future career, but still it would be like not knowing who Dorie Greenspan is today.

Along with a lot of America, my friend's mom learned about Maida in 1968 when she read Craig Claiborne's article about her in the New York Times, and she went on to buy all of her cookbooks as they were released. In Maida she found someone who could really explain baking—what to look for, which oven rack to use, and even which cookies are too fragile to ship well (see: Old-Fashioned Jumbo Lemon Wafers) and which aren't (Chocolate Scotch Shortbread) — in a way that few cookbooks did at the time. Maida's recipes make you feel as though she's in the kitchen with you, coaching you along, encouraging you.

I've been making up for lost time with Maida ever since, baking in particular her Florida Lemon Squares and Johnny Appleseed Squares, a kid favorite. To tune in to Maida Heatter's cookies in the year 2020, some forty-six years after she published her first cookbook, is to instantly notice a few things: She loves walnuts in a way that few contemporary bakers do, where almonds and pecans reign supreme. Her recipes are precise but friendly, and you feel certain she's having fun in the kitchen — how else would a recipe get the title Positively-the-Absolutely-Best-Chocolate-Chip Cookies (she's not wrong). She has a knack for naming recipes, from 24-Karat Cookies to Sour-Cream and Pecan Dreams. Many of my favorites evoke places — East 62nd Street, Savannah, or Palm Beach — ones that were as important to her as they've since become to us.

Maida's recipes feel lighthearted and modern even now. Stuffing candy bars inside baked goods seems straight out of Pinterest, yet it goes straight back to Maida. After you share her thick, craggy, chewy-centered Palm Beach Brownies with your friends, they will never allow you to make anything else.

But above all else, I love Maida's cookie philosophy: Pot roast is mandatory; cookies are not. You make them because they're pure, simple fun. I hope this book brings her baking enthusiasm into a new generation of kitchens. Mine has become unquestionably more delicious since I welcomed Maida into it.

— Deb Perelman

introduction

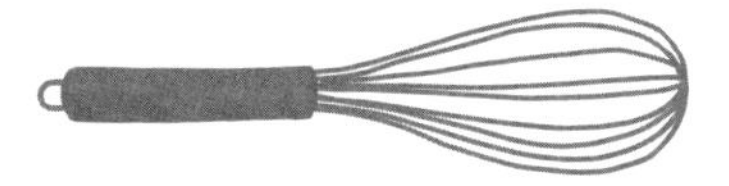

Baking is a great escape. It's fun. It's happiness. It's creative. It's good for your health. It reduces stress.

If you are reading this book, chances are you know what I mean. You have probably baked cookies. You could probably tell me a thing or two about what fun it is. But if you have not baked cookies, then let me tell you. Bake cookies! Happiness is baking cookies.

People often ask me how I started to bake, and I'm startled. It was so natural, part of life. That was because of my mother, a most unusual woman. She could do almost anything and did everything well. She was a great cook and a true gourmet. Every meal was an occasion... the menu planned with care, the table set beautifully and arranged with an artist's eye. Whether or not she had help, she did most of the cooking herself because she loved it. And she imparted that love to me.

Cookies are very special to me. All cooking and baking can be great fun and a wonderful escape, but cookies are in a class by themselves. I feel that one can be especially creative with cookies, actually handling the dough—kneading, shaping, building, designing.

I was talking to a friend who is an excellent cook and I was shocked when she said, "I haven't baked cookies since I was a little girl." Too bad — what fun she's missing.

My philosophy is that cookies are fun — pure, simple fun. You don't make cookies if you're hassled. It's not like pot roast — you don't *have* to make cookies.

Cookies are love, the love of making them and the love of sharing them. (It is so much looser and easier to bring someone a few cookies than a layer cake or chocolate mousse.) Many of the recipes in this book will keep well, travel even better, and are perfect straight out of the freezer when a guest comes around unexpectedly. I keep many cookies on hand in my freezer, individually wrapped in wax paper or plastic, for company. And nothing makes a better gift than some cookies, elegantly packaged in a beautiful box.

One more word about this book — about any cookbook — before you get down to the serious (fun) business of making cookies. A cookbook should be treated like a school textbook. When reading it, or cooking from it, keep a pencil handy for notations. Underline things you especially want to remember, make notes — just don't be afraid to write in it. Write down your experiences with the recipes and any changes you make. In the future you will find that your own notes have added to the book and made it more valuable to you.

I have made each of these recipes many times, and have experienced many moments of pure pleasure and joy at each bite. I am sure that you can make them all, and I am sure you will have fun with them.

Enjoy!

Maida Heatter

before you bake

I have cooked and tested every one of the recipes in this book over and over so that they are worked out perfectly. But in order for these recipes to work for you as they do for me, it is of the utmost importance that you follow every direction exactly. Many instructions may seem trivial, arbitrary, or unimportant, but there really is a practical reason for everything.

If a recipe says to line a cookie sheet with aluminum foil, it is not because I am a fuddy-duddy and care about keeping cookie sheets clean. In some recipes, you would encounter disaster without the foil. With it, if you are like me, you will squeal with joy at the ease, fun, and satisfying excitement of peeling the foil from the smooth, shiny backs of the cookies.

If brownies are not allowed to stand for the specified time after they come out of the oven, they will squash when you cut them into portions.

I could go on and on, but please, take my word for it. Read the recipes carefully and follow them exactly.

before you bake

1. Read the recipe completely. Make sure you have everything you will need, including the correct-size baking pan.
2. Remove butter, cream cheese, and eggs from the refrigerator.
3. Adjust oven racks and preheat the oven.
4. Prepare the pan according to the directions.
5. Grind or chop nuts.
6. Sift flour (and other dry ingredients) onto a large piece of wax paper or baking parchment.
7. Crack open the eggs (and separate them if necessary).
8. Measure all the other ingredients and organize them into the order called for in the recipe.

Ingredients

• BUTTER •

Whenever butter is called for it means unsalted (sweet) butter.

• CHOCOLATE •

Unsweetened chocolate is also called baking chocolate or bitter chocolate.

Sweet, semisweet, bittersweet, and **extra-bittersweet chocolates** are generally interchangeable in cooking and baking, depending on your taste and the availability of chocolates.

Semisweet chocolate morsels, chips, or **bits:** Made by Nestlé, Hershey, and others. I seldom use them (although many people do with excellent results) except in cookies—and for making one of the greatest cookies of all, Toll House Cookies. The recipe for those cookies is printed on the package of Nestlé's Chocolate Morsels. Of course, that did not stop me from including my own Positively-the-Absolutely-Best-Chocolate-Chip Cookies on page 26.

Milk chocolate: I seldom use milk chocolate in cooking or baking. When I do, it is mostly used cut or broken up, like morsels (for chocolate chip cookies).

Compound chocolate or **melting chocolate:** Real chocolate contains cocoa butter. Compound chocolate contains some shortening rather than cocoa butter. Real chocolate should be tempered to prevent discoloring or streaking after melting and cooling—compound chocolate does not need to be tempered and will set up (harden) faster than real chocolate. I use compound chocolate for dipping, as in my Chocolate Chip Coconut Macaroons (page 217).

To Melt Chocolate

When melting chocolate with no other ingredient, the container must be absolutely dry. Even the merest drop of moisture will cause the chocolate to "tighten" or "seize," becoming a pasty, gritty mess. (If it should tighten, stir in 1 tablespoon vegetable shortening for each 3 ounces of chocolate.) Melt chocolate by stirring it slowly in the top of a double boiler over hot, but not boiling, water. The reason for this is that boiling water might bubble up and get into the chocolate. Some people swear by melting chocolate in a microwave oven.

Chocolate should melt slowly—it burns easily. To be sure chocolate doesn't get overheated and burn, it is always advisable to remove it from over the hot water before it is completely melted and then stir it until it is entirely melted and smooth. Milk chocolate should be melted even more slowly than other chocolates.

Unsweetened chocolate will run (liquefy) as it melts; sweet, semisweet, and milk chocolates hold their shape when melted

and must be stirred. Some semisweet chocolates might not melt as smoothly as unsweetened. If the chocolate is not smooth, stir it briskly with a rubber spatula, pressing against any lumps until it becomes smooth. Various chocolates have different consistencies when they are melted. Unsweetened chocolate is the thinnest, and milk chocolate the thickest. When you melt chocolate in or with milk (or when you mix melted chocolate and milk), if the mixture is not smooth and the chocolate remains in little flecks, beat it with an electric mixer, a wire whisk, or an eggbeater until smooth.

• COFFEE •

Instant espresso or coffee in a recipe means dry—powdered or granules.

Instant coffee powder will dissolve more easily than granules. If you happen to have granules on hand, it is easy to powder it yourself. Whirl some in the blender, then strain it and return the coarse part to the blender to grind until it is all powdered. Medaglia d'Oro instant espresso is finely powdered and works very well. It is generally available at specialty food stores and Italian markets.

• CREAM •

To Whip Cream

Heavy cream may be whipped with an electric mixer, a rotary beater, or a large, balloon-type wire whisk. It will whip more easily and give better results if the cream, bowl, and beaters are cold. The bowl should be metal (but not copper), as that gets and stays colder. Place the bowl and beaters in the refrigerator or freezer just before using them; they should be thoroughly chilled. If the room is very warm, the bowl in which you are whipping the cream should be placed in a larger bowl of ice and water.

Do not overbeat or the cream will lose its smooth texture; if you beat even more it will turn into butter. If you use an electric beater, a handy safeguard is to stop beating before the cream is completely whipped and then finish the job with a wire whisk. This allows less chance for overbeating.

• EGGS •

These recipes are all based on the use of large eggs, or occasionally extra-large or jumbo eggs.

If directions call for adding whole eggs one at a time, they may all be cracked open ahead of time into one container and poured into the other ingredients, approximately one at a time. Do not crack eggs directly into the batter—you wouldn't know if a piece of shell had been included.

To Separate Eggs

A new bride, when faced with the direction "separate eggs," placed them carefully on the table about 4 inches apart, and wondered how far they should be from one another...

Eggs separate best (that is, the yolks separate most readily from the whites) when they are cold. Place three small bowls in front of you, one for the whites and the second for the yolks. The third may not be

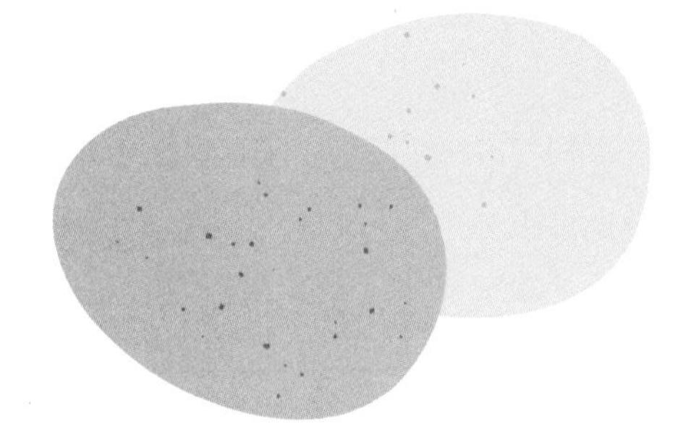

needed, but if you should break the yolk when opening an egg, just drop the whole thing into the third bowl and save it for some other use. When cracking the shell it is important not to use too much pressure or you will break the yolk at the same time.

Some cooks open the egg directly onto the palm of a hand and let the white run through their fingers into a bowl while the yolk remains in their hand. But the most popular method is to tap the side of the egg firmly on the edge of a bowl to crack the shell. Then, holding the egg in both hands, separate the two halves of the shell, letting some of the white run out into the bowl. Now pour the yolk back and forth from one half of the shell to the other, letting all of the white run out. Drop the yolk into the second bowl.

To Beat Egg Whites

Egg whites may be beaten with an electric mixer, a rotary eggbeater, or a large balloon-type wire whisk. Both the bowl and the beater must be perfectly clean and dry. Just a bit of oil, egg yolk, or grease will prevent the whites from inflating properly.

If you use an electric mixer or a rotary beater, be sure not to use a bowl that is too large, or the whites will be too shallow to get the full benefit of the beater's action. Also, if you use an electric hand mixer or a rotary beater, keep moving it around in the bowl. If you use a mixer on a stand, use a rubber spatula frequently to push the whites from the sides of the bowl into the center. If you use a wire whisk and a bowl, an unlined copper bowl is best, though you may use glass, china, or stainless steel. Do not beat egg whites in an aluminum or plastic bowl.

The beaten whites will have a better—creamier—consistency if you beat some of the sugar into the whites as they begin to hold a shape.

Do not beat egg whites ahead of time. They must be folded in immediately after they are beaten.

Do not overbeat the whites or they will become dry and you won't be able to fold them in without losing the air you have beaten in. Beat only until they hold a shape or a point—"stiff but not dry."

• FLOUR •

With only a few exceptions, these recipes call for *sifted* flour. This means that it should be sifted immediately before it is measured. If the flour is not sifted, or if it is sifted long before it is used, it packs down and 1 cup is liable to contain a few spoonfuls more than 1 cup of flour that has been sifted immediately before measuring.

To Sift Flour

If you have one, use a double or triple sifter (which forces flour through multiple layers of fine mesh); otherwise sift the flour twice using a fine-mesh sieve. Sift onto a piece of wax paper or baking parchment, sifting a bit more than you will need. Use a metal measuring cup. Spoon the sifted flour lightly into the cup. Do not shake the cup or pack the flour down; just scrape any excess off the top with a metal spatula or any flat-sided implement. It is not necessary to wash a flour sifter; just shake it out firmly and store in a plastic bag.

• SUGARS •

When sugar is called for in these recipes, unless otherwise stated, it means granulated white sugar.

Sugar should be measured in the same metal cups as those recommended for flour. If granulated sugar is lumpy it should be strained before use. Brown sugar and confectioners' sugar are best strained also. (Hard lumps in brown sugar will not disappear in mixing or baking.) Unlike flour, sugars may all be strained ahead of time and you may do several pounds at once. Use a very large strainer set over a large bowl and press the sugar through with your fingertips.

Brown Sugar

Most brown sugars are made of white granulated sugar to which molasses has been added. Dark brown has a slightly stronger flavor than light brown sugar, but they may be used interchangeably.

You can make your own brown sugar by blending together ½ cup granulated sugar with 2 tablespoons unsulphured molasses. The yield is equivalent to ½ cup brown sugar.

Brown sugar is moist; if it dries out it will harden. It should be stored airtight at room temperature. If your brown sugar has hardened, place a damp paper towel or a slice of apple inside the bag and close the package tightly for 12 hours or more.

Confectioners' Sugar

Confectioners' sugar and powdered sugar are exactly the same. They are both granulated sugar that has been pulverized very fine and has had about 3 percent cornstarch added to keep it in a powdery condition. Of these, 4X is the least fine and 10X is the finest; 10X is now the most common. They may be used interchangeably. Store it airtight.

• NUTS •

I've given weights as well as volume measure for nuts weighing over 2 ounces. If only volume is given, the weight is under 2 ounces.

To Store Nuts

All nuts should be stored in the freezer or refrigerator. Always bring them to room temperature before using, and smell them and taste them – rancid nuts would ruin an entire batch of cookies.

To Blanch Nuts

To blanch almonds: Cover almonds with boiling water. Let them stand until the water is cool enough to touch. Pick out the almonds one at a time and squeeze each one between thumb and forefinger to squirt off the skin. As each one is skinned, place it on a towel to dry. Then spread the almonds in a single layer in a shallow baking pan and bake in a 200-degree oven for half an hour or so, until they are dry. Do not let them brown. If the almonds are to be split or sliced or slivered, cut them immediately after removing the skin and bake to dry as above.

To blanch hazelnuts: Spread the hazelnuts on a rimmed baking sheet and bake at

350 degrees for 15 minutes, or until the skins parch and begin to flake off. Then, working with a few at a time, place them on a large coarse towel (I use a terrycloth towel). Fold part of the towel over to enclose the nuts and rub firmly against the towel. Or hold that part of the towel between both hands and roll back and forth. The handling and the texture of the towel will cause most of the skins to flake off. Pick out the nuts and discard the skins. Don't worry about the few pieces of skin that remain. This is not as quick and easy as it sounds.

To Grind Nuts

When the instructions say to grind nuts, it means that the nuts should be reduced to a powder, the consistency of coarse flour. *Chopped* nuts are much less fine and are left in visible pieces. To grind nuts in a food processor, use the metal chopping blade; you can also use a nut grinder or blender. If possible, always add some of the flour called for in the recipe. It will help to prevent the nuts from becoming oily. If the recipe does not have any flour, add some of the sugar called for. And do not overprocess.

• DATES AND RAISINS •

Raisins and dates must always be fresh and soft—baking will not soften them. They may be softened by steaming them in a vegetable steamer or strainer over boiling water, covered, for about 5 minutes. Dates and raisins should be stored in the refrigerator or freezer.

• ORANGE AND LEMON ZEST •

When grating orange or lemon zest, if your grater has a variety of shaped openings, it is best to grate the zest on the side with the small, round openings, rather than the diamond-shaped ones.

• OATS •

All cookie recipes that call for oats mean uncooked. There are many varieties of oats and they give different qualities to cookies. Instant oats should not be used in cookies; they are too fine, too absorbent, and do not give any of the crunchy quality you want. The recipes in this book call for old-fashioned or quick-cooking oats, and I suggest you use those if you can. Steel-cut oats (cooking directions are generally to simmer for 20 to 25 minutes) may be used for cookies but the oats will remain rather hard and will give an even crunchier texture.

Equipment

• COOKIE CUTTERS •

Obviously it is not necessary to use exactly the same size or shape cutter that the recipe calls for; that is just a guide. Cutters should be sharp with no rough edges. If the cutter sticks to the dough, dip it in flour each time. Always start cutting at the edge of the dough and work toward the center, cutting the cookies as close to each other as possible.

• COOKIE SHEETS •

A cookie sheet should be flat, not warped. Shiny, bright aluminum sheets are the best. Cookie sheets should be at least 2 inches narrower and shorter than the oven so the heat will circulate around them and the cookies will bake evenly. Generally 12 x 15½ inches is the most practical size.

Many of these recipes call for placing the cookies on sheets of aluminum foil and then sliding a cookie sheet underneath for baking. The foil is not called for in order to keep your cookie sheets clean (although it will, and if you do a lot of baking you will be delighted with not having to wash and dry them). It will keep the cookies from sticking, and some of the really thin wafer-type cookies, which would be a problem without the foil, will be easy and fun if you use it. I also find that in many recipes the cookies hold their shape better on foil than they do on buttered sheets; often the butter makes them run too thin and become too brown on the edges.

Another reason is mathematics—if you have only two sheets, and if you need four or five for a recipe, by using the foil you can prepare all of the cookies for baking, place them on the foil, and then just slide a sheet under the foil when you are ready to bake them. (You do not have to wait for the cookie sheet to cool.)

Therefore, the recipes say to cut the foil, place the cookies on it, slide a sheet under, and bake. I find this system works very well.

• COOLING RACKS •

You should have several cooling racks. Almost all cookies should be removed from the cookie sheet immediately or soon after baking (unless the recipe specifies otherwise) and cooled with air circulating around them. Many racks are not raised enough for air to circulate underneath, which causes the bottoms of the cookies to be damp and soggy instead of dry and crisp (there should be ½ inch for crisp, thin wafers, 2 inches for large cookies). To raise the racks (especially if the cookies are large and/or thick), simply place the rack on a right-side-up cake pan or bowl.

• DOUBLE BOILER •

Since it is essential to melt chocolate slowly it is generally best to do it in a double boiler, and many of these recipes specifically call for one. If necessary, you can create a double boiler by placing the ingredients in a heatproof bowl over a saucepan of shallow hot water. The bowl should be wide enough so that its rim rests on the rim of the saucepan and the bowl is supported above the water.

• ELECTRIC MIXER •

Mixing and beating in these recipes may be done with different equipment—an electric hand mixer, any type of stand mixer, or by hand. I use a stand mixer. Susan, my mother's cook for thirty-five years, beat egg whites with a tree branch, in spite of a fantastically well-equipped kitchen. In the country she picked a fresh one as she needed it; in the city, she always washed it carefully and put it away.

Because I use a stand mixer, I have given directions for beating times based on this type of mixer; a handheld mixer might take longer. If you are not using a stand mixer, when directions call for "small bowl of electric mixer," use a bowl with a 7-cup capacity. When directions call for "large bowl of electric mixer," use one with a 4-quart capacity.

Some of these recipes would be too much work without a mixer. Others may be made using your bare hands for creaming and mixing. Don't be afraid to use your hands.

• MEASURING EQUIPMENT •

Oven Thermometer

Success in baking depends on many things. One of the most important is correct oven temperature. I suggest that you buy an oven thermometer, preferably a good one. Hardware stores and quality cookware stores sell them. All oven temperatures in this book are in Fahrenheit.

Measuring Cups

Glass measuring cups with the measurements marked on the sides are only for measuring liquids. With the cup at eye level, fill carefully to exactly the line indicated. To measure dry ingredients, use the cups that come in sets that include at least four sizes: ¼ cup, ⅓ cup, ½ cup, and 1 cup. Fill to overflowing and then scrape off the extra with a flat spatula or large knife. If you are measuring flour, do not pack it down—but do pack down brown sugar.

Measuring Spoons

Standard measuring spoons must be used for correct measurements. For dry ingredients, fill to overflowing and then scrape off the excess.

• PASTRY BAGS •

A few of these cookies are shaped with a pastry bag. Though most bakers prefer the convenience of disposable pastry bags, canvas bags are still available online and at high-end kitchen shops. If you use canvas bags, they should be washed in hot soapy water after use, then just hung up to dry.

It is easier to work with a bag that is too large rather than one that is too small. When filling a pastry bag, unless there is someone else to hold it for you, it is generally easiest if you support the bag by placing it in a tall and wide glass or jar.

It is easier to work with a pastry bag if you work at table height instead of kitchen-counter height. The table is lower and you have better control of your work.

• PASTRY BRUSHES •

There are different types of pastry brushes. Use a good one, or the bristles will come out while you are using it. Sometimes I use an artist's watercolor brush in a large size; it is softer and there are times when I prefer it.

• PASTRY CLOTH •

A pastry cloth is most important for preventing cookie dough from sticking when you roll it out. Buy the largest and heaviest cloth you can find. Always wash it after using. The butter in the dough soaks into the cloth, and unless it is kept very clean it will smell rancid. It may be ironed or not. I've tried it both ways and it works the same. If you do not have one or wish to buy one, you may flour your work surface well instead—but I've always used a cloth and find it works wonderfully.

• ROLLING PINS •

If you have many occasions to use a rolling pin (and I hope you will), you really should have different sizes and shapes. Sometimes a very long, thick, and heavy one will be best; for other doughs you will want a smaller, lighter one. The French style, which is extra-long, narrow, and tapered at both ends, is especially good for rolling dough into a round shape, as for a pie crust, while the straight-sided pin is better for an oblong shape.

However, in the absence of any rolling pin at all, other things will do a fair job. Try a straight-sided bottle, tall jar, or drinking glass.

• RUBBER SPATULAS •

Rubber spatulas are almost indispensable—do not use plastic; they are not flexible enough. Use rubber spatulas for folding, for some stirring, for scraping bowls, pots, etc. I suggest that you have several. Most spatulas manufactured now are synthetic and heatproof.

Techniques

• FOLDING •

Some recipes call for folding beaten egg whites and/or whipped cream into another mixture. The egg whites and/or cream have air beaten into them, and folding rather than mixing is done in order to retain the air.

This is an important step and it should be done with care. The knack of doing it well comes with practice and concentration. Remember that you want to incorporate the mixtures without losing any air. That means handling them as little as possible.

If one of the mixtures is heavy, first actually stir in a bit of the lighter mixture. Then, with a rubber spatula (or occasionally on the lowest speed of an electric mixer), gradually fold the remaining light mixture into the heavier mixture as follows:

Place some of the light mixture on top. With a rubber spatula, rounded side down, cut down through the center to the bottom, then toward you against the bottom of the bowl, then up against the side, and finally out over the top, bringing the heavier ingredients from the bottom over the top. Rotate the bowl slightly with your other hand. Repeat, cutting with the rounded side of the spatula down, rotating the bowl a bit after making each cut. Continue only until both mixtures are combined. Try to make every motion count; do not handle any more than necessary.

Using Ingredients

• TO BRING INGREDIENTS TO ROOM TEMPERATURE •

In individual recipes I have indicated the very few times I actually bring ingredients to room temperature before using. Otherwise they may be used right out of the refrigerator. If butter is too hard, cut it into small pieces, and let it stand only until it can be worked with.

• TO ADD DRY INGREDIENTS ALTERNATELY WITH LIQUID •

Always begin and end with dry ingredients. The procedure is generally to add about one-third of the dry ingredients, half the liquid, the second third of the dry, the rest of the liquid, and finally the last third of the dry.

Use the lowest speed on an electric mixer for this. After each addition, mix only until smooth. If your mixer is the type that allows for a rubber spatula to be used while it is in motion, help the blending along by using the rubber spatula to scrape around the sides of the bowl. If the mixer does not have the room, or if it is the handheld kind, stop it frequently and scrape the bowl with the spatula.

Timing

It is important to time cookies carefully. Set a timer for a few minutes less than the recipe specifies, and check the cookies to be sure you aren't overbaking them.

When directions say to reverse the position of cookie sheets during baking, wait until the baking is at least half or three-quarters finished. Then work quickly—do not keep the oven door open any longer than necessary.

When you bake only one sheet at a time instead of two, cookies bake in a little less time.

Storing Cookies

With few exceptions, these cookies are best when fresh. Even the ones that will last for weeks are best when fresh. So, unless I know that there will be people around to eat them, I freeze almost all cookies in plastic freezer boxes (after reserving at least a few for unexpected company and for my husband's usual daily cookie party). And even in the freezer they do not stay fresh forever—a few weeks, a month or two, but after that they lose their extra-special goodness. Although most charts say that cookies may be frozen for up to twelve months, as far as I'm concerned that only means they will not spoil. I don't believe that they taste as good after many months in the freezer. (Thaw frozen cookies before removing them from their containers or they might sweat and become soggy or wet. Usually an hour or so at room temperature will do it, but it depends on the size of the container.)

For short-term storage at room temperature, do not mix soft cookies with crisp cookies in the same container or the crisp ones will soon become soft.

To add moisture to soft cookies that have begun to dry out (or that you might have baked too long), place half an apple, skin side down, or a whole lemon or orange, depending on the flavor you want, on top of the cookies in an airtight container (you may use a plastic bag). Let stand for a day or two and then remove the fruit.

But I'm putting the cart before the horse. Enough of what to do with the cookies once they're baked. Before baking, check on your equipment and ingredients, then go for it.

DROP COOKIES

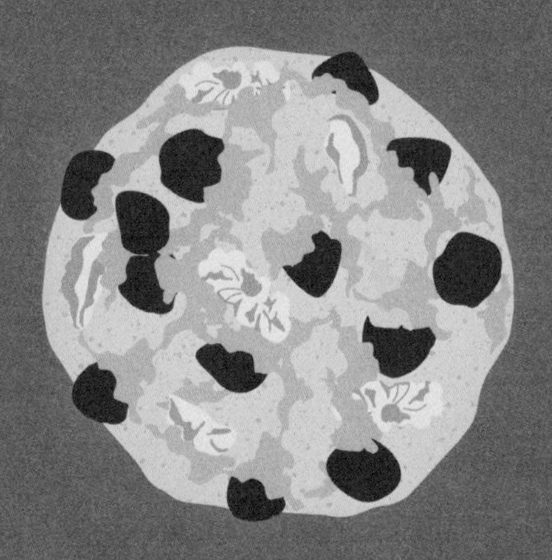

Drop cookies are probably the easiest of all cookies to make. But the dough should not be dropped (or slopped) onto the cookie sheet. It should be placed carefully, gently, and neatly. The mounds should all be the same size and they should be as round and evenly shaped as possible. Use two spoons (not measuring spoons), one for picking up the dough and another for pushing it off.

POSITIVELY-THE-ABSOLUTELY-BEST-CHOCOLATE-CHIP COOKIES

About 50 (3-inch) cookies A poll taken among food editors at newspapers and magazines found that chocolate chip cookies were the number one favorite of all homemade cookies in America. (That's not news.)

Well, this recipe is the mother of all chocolate chip cookie recipes.

The following recipe is closely based on the original Toll House recipe. But I make a few changes: I use 2 teaspoons vanilla instead of 1. And I use 16 ounces of chocolate instead of 12. Also, instead of using morsels, I use semisweet or bittersweet chocolate bars, cut into pieces.

Do not sift the flour before measuring it! Just stir it a bit to aerate it.

- 8 ounces (2 sticks) unsalted butter
- 1 teaspoon salt
- 2 teaspoons vanilla extract
- ¾ cup granulated sugar
- ¾ cup firmly packed light brown sugar
- 2 large eggs
- 2¼ cups *unsifted* all-purpose flour
- 1 teaspoon baking soda
- 1 teaspoon hot water
- 8 ounces (generous 2 cups) walnuts, cut or broken into medium-size pieces
- 16 ounces (2 cups) semisweet or bittersweet chocolate bars, chopped into pieces

NOTES

I was told that this is a big secret: Mrs. Fields refrigerates her chocolate chip cookie dough before shaping and baking. (Actually, Ruth Wakefield, who created the original Toll House recipe in the 1930s, did also.) The dough should be cold when the cookies go into the oven. The cookies have a much nicer and more even golden brown color.

This method of dissolving the baking soda before adding it is the way Mrs. Wakefield did it. The Nestlé Toll House recipe sifts the soda with the flour. I do not know which method is better. I only know these are delicious this way.

You may think 16 ounces of chocolate is too much to be incorporated into the dough. Just be patient. It's not too much.

Adjust two racks to divide the oven into thirds and preheat oven to 375 degrees. Line cookie sheets with baking parchment or with aluminum foil shiny side up.

In the large bowl of an electric mixer, beat the butter until soft. Add the salt, vanilla, and both sugars and beat to mix. Add the eggs and beat well. On low speed, add about half of the flour and, scraping the bowl with a rubber spatula, beat only until incorporated.

In a small cup, stir the baking soda into the hot water to dissolve it (see Notes), then mix it into the dough. Add the remaining flour and beat only to mix. Remove the bowl from the mixer. Stir in the walnuts and the chocolate.

Spread out a large piece of aluminum foil next to the sink. Use a rounded large spoonful of the dough for each cookie and place the mounds any which way on the foil. Wet your hands with cold water and shake off excess, but do not dry your hands. Pick up a mound of dough and roll it between your wet hands into a ball, then press it between your hands to flatten it to about a ½-inch thickness.

Place the cookies on the lined sheets about 2 inches apart.

Bake two sheets at a time, reversing the sheets top to bottom and front to back as necessary to ensure even browning.

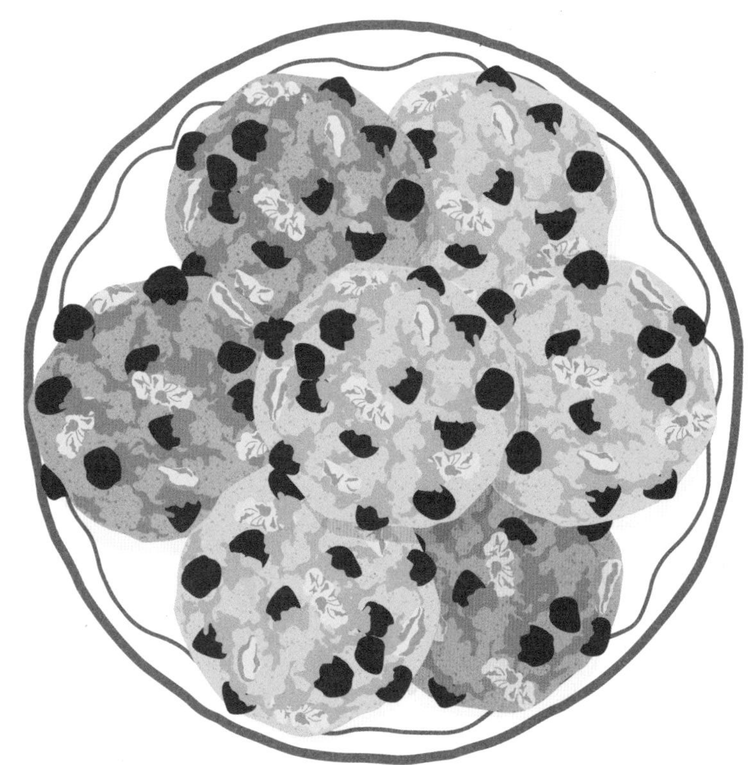

continues ↘

(If you bake one sheet alone, bake it on the upper rack.) Bake for about 12 minutes, until the cookies are browned all over. The cookies must be crisp; do not underbake.

Let the cookies stand a few seconds, then transfer with a metal spatula to racks to cool.

Store in an airtight container.

VARIATIONS

Cooks have varied the above recipe in just about every way possible. Some use whole-wheat flour for all or half of the flour, or less flour to make thinner cookies, or more flour to make thicker cookies. Or more sugar. Some add 2 cups of raisins or chopped dates, or coconut, either with or in place of the nuts. Some cooks add grated orange zest or chopped candied orange peel. Or chopped candied ginger. Or pumpkin seeds and/or wheat germ. Or 1 teaspoon cinnamon. Some add about 1 cup of peanut butter to the basic recipe and use peanuts in place of walnuts. (If you use salted peanuts, shake them vigorously in a large strainer to remove as much salt as possible; then use slightly less salt in the ingredients.) And a popular cookie that I have seen in many places across the country is what appears to be the basic recipe but probably has more flour; it is formed into extra-large cookies that are 6 to 8 inches in diameter.

The quickest way of shaping and baking the dough is to bake it in a pan for bar cookies. Butter a 10½ x 15½ x 1-inch rimmed baking sheet and spread the dough smoothly in the pan. Bake in the middle of a 375-degree oven for 20 minutes. Cool in the pan. Use a small, sharp knife to cut into 35 squares and use a wide metal spatula to remove the cookies.

CHOCOLATE AND PEANUT BUTTER RIPPLES

About 30 cookies **A chocolate dough and a peanut butter dough, baked together, make a rather thin, crisp, candylike cookie.**

CHOCOLATE DOUGH

- **2 ounces unsweetened chocolate**
- **4 ounces (1 stick) unsalted butter**
- **1 teaspoon vanilla extract**
- **¼ teaspoon salt**
- **¾ cup granulated sugar**
- **1 large egg**
- **1 cup *sifted* all-purpose flour**

PEANUT BUTTER DOUGH

- **2 tablespoons unsalted butter**
- **¼ cup smooth (not chunky) peanut butter**
- **½ cup firmly packed light brown sugar**
- **2 tablespoons *sifted* all-purpose flour**

Adjust two racks to divide the oven into thirds and preheat oven to 325 degrees. Line cookie sheets with baking parchment.

FOR THE CHOCOLATE DOUGH

Melt the chocolate in the top of a double boiler over hot water on moderate heat. Set the chocolate aside.

In the large bowl of an electric mixer, cream the butter. Add the vanilla, salt, and granulated sugar and beat well. Beat in the egg and then the melted chocolate, scraping the bowl as necessary with a rubber spatula. On low speed, gradually add the flour and mix only until smooth. Transfer the dough to a small shallow bowl for ease in handling and set aside.

FOR THE PEANUT BUTTER DOUGH

In the small bowl of the electric mixer, cream the butter with the peanut butter. Beat in the brown sugar until well mixed. Add the flour and beat to mix. Transfer to a small shallow bowl for ease in handling.

Now shape the cookies: Divide the chocolate dough in half and set one half aside. By level or barely rounded spoonfuls, drop the remaining half on the cookie sheets, placing the mounds 2 inches apart. You will need two to three cookie sheets and will end up with 30 mounds of the dough.

Top each mound with a scant spoonful of peanut butter dough. And then top each cookie with another spoonful of the chocolate dough. Don't worry about the

continues ↘

doughs being exactly on top of each other. Flatten the cookies slightly with a fork, dipping the fork in granulated sugar as necessary to keep it from sticking.

Bake for 15 minutes, reversing the cookie sheets top to bottom and front to back once to ensure even baking. (If you bake only one sheet at a time, use the higher rack.) Do not overbake. These cookies will become crisp as they cool.

Let the cookies cool briefly on the sheets, only until they are firm enough to transfer with a wide metal spatula to racks. When cool, handle with care. Store in an airtight container.

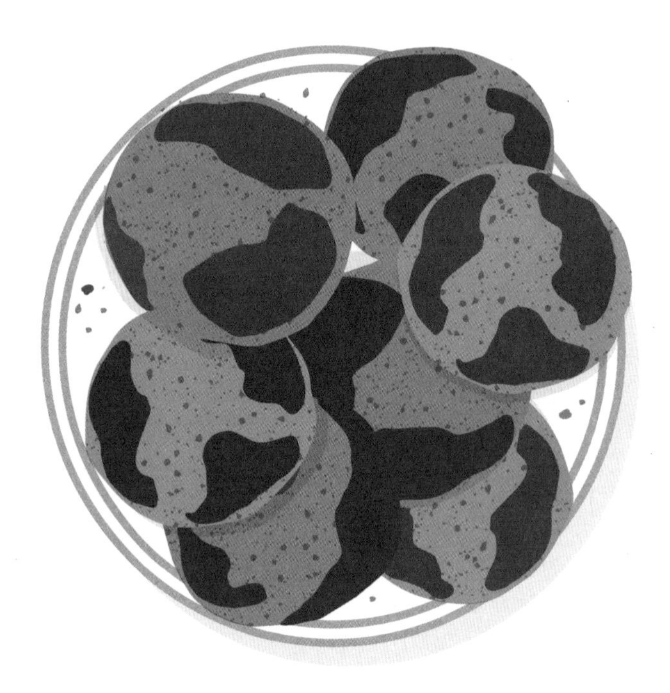

BROWNIE COOKIES

About 28 cookies **These delicious drop cookies (actually they are dropped, but then rolled into balls between your hands) are made with brownie ingredients. They are semisoft and chewy, very dark, dense, fudgy, not-too-sweet chocolate cookies. Quick and easy, they are mixed in a saucepan.**

- 2 ounces unsweetened chocolate, broken into pieces
- 4 ounces semisweet chocolate, broken into pieces
- 4 ounces (1 stick) unsalted butter
- ½ teaspoon salt
- ½ teaspoon vanilla extract
- 1 cup sugar
- 2 large eggs
- 1½ cups *sifted* all-purpose flour
- 6 ounces (generous 1½ cups) walnuts, cut or broken into medium-size pieces

Adjust two racks to divide the oven into thirds and preheat oven to 375 degrees. Line two cookie sheets with baking parchment or with aluminum foil shiny side up and set aside.

In a 3-quart heavy saucepan over low heat, melt both of the chocolates and the butter, stirring frequently with a heavy wooden spoon. Remove from the heat. Add the remaining ingredients, in order, stirring briskly after each addition.

Place a long piece of aluminum foil next to the sink. Use two teaspoons (not measuring spoons), one for picking up the dough and one for pushing it off. Use a heaping spoonful of dough for each cookie. Place the mounds any which way on the foil.

Wet your hands with cold water and shake off the water but do not dry your hands. Pick up a mound of the dough, roll it between your hands into a ball, and place it on one of the lined cookie sheets. Continue to roll the balls of dough and place them about 1 inch apart. Wet your hands again if dough begins to stick.

With the bottom of a fork, press each ball of dough lightly to flatten it to about ½- or ⅗-inch thickness (no thinner).

Bake for 10 to 12 minutes, reversing the sheets front to back and top to bottom once during baking. Bake only until the tops of the cookies lose their shine and become dull: They should feel dry but soft when pressed gently with a fingertip. The cookies become firmer as they cool.

With a wide metal spatula, transfer the cookies to racks to cool. Store airtight.

CANDY COOKIES

24 large cookies **The narrow dividing line between candy and cookies becomes even narrower with this dessert. The recipe is a combination of two American favorites, chocolate chip cookies and candy bars. The candy bars (crisp toffee covered with milk chocolate) are coarsely cut up and used in place of chocolate chips (the candy does not melt during baking). Fabulous!**

- **9 ounces Heath bars**
- **4 ounces (1 stick) unsalted butter**
- **½ teaspoon salt**
- **½ teaspoon vanilla extract**
- **⅓ cup granulated sugar**
- **⅓ cup firmly packed dark brown sugar**
- **1 large egg**
- **1¼ cups *unsifted* all-purpose flour**
- **½ teaspoon baking soda**
- **½ teaspoon hot water**
- **4 ounces (generous 1 cup) walnuts, broken into large pieces**

Adjust two racks to divide the oven into thirds and preheat oven to 375 degrees. Line cookie sheets with baking parchment.

Cut the Heath bars into ½-inch pieces and set aside.

In the large bowl of an electric mixer, beat the butter until soft. Add the salt, vanilla, and both sugars and beat to mix. Then beat in the egg. On low speed, add the flour, scraping the bowl as necessary with a rubber spatula and beating only until incorporated.

In a small cup, combine the baking soda and water and beat into the dough. Remove the bowl from the mixer, then add the walnuts and the cut-up Heath bars and stir with a heavy wooden spoon until evenly mixed.

Use a rounded large spoonful of the dough for each cookie. Place them 2 inches apart on the lined sheets.

Bake two sheets at a time for 13 to 15 minutes, reversing the sheets top to bottom and front to back as necessary to ensure even browning. Bake until the cookies are lightly browned all over.

Let the cookies stand on the sheets for about 5 minutes. Then use a wide metal spatula to transfer the cookies to racks to cool. Store airtight.

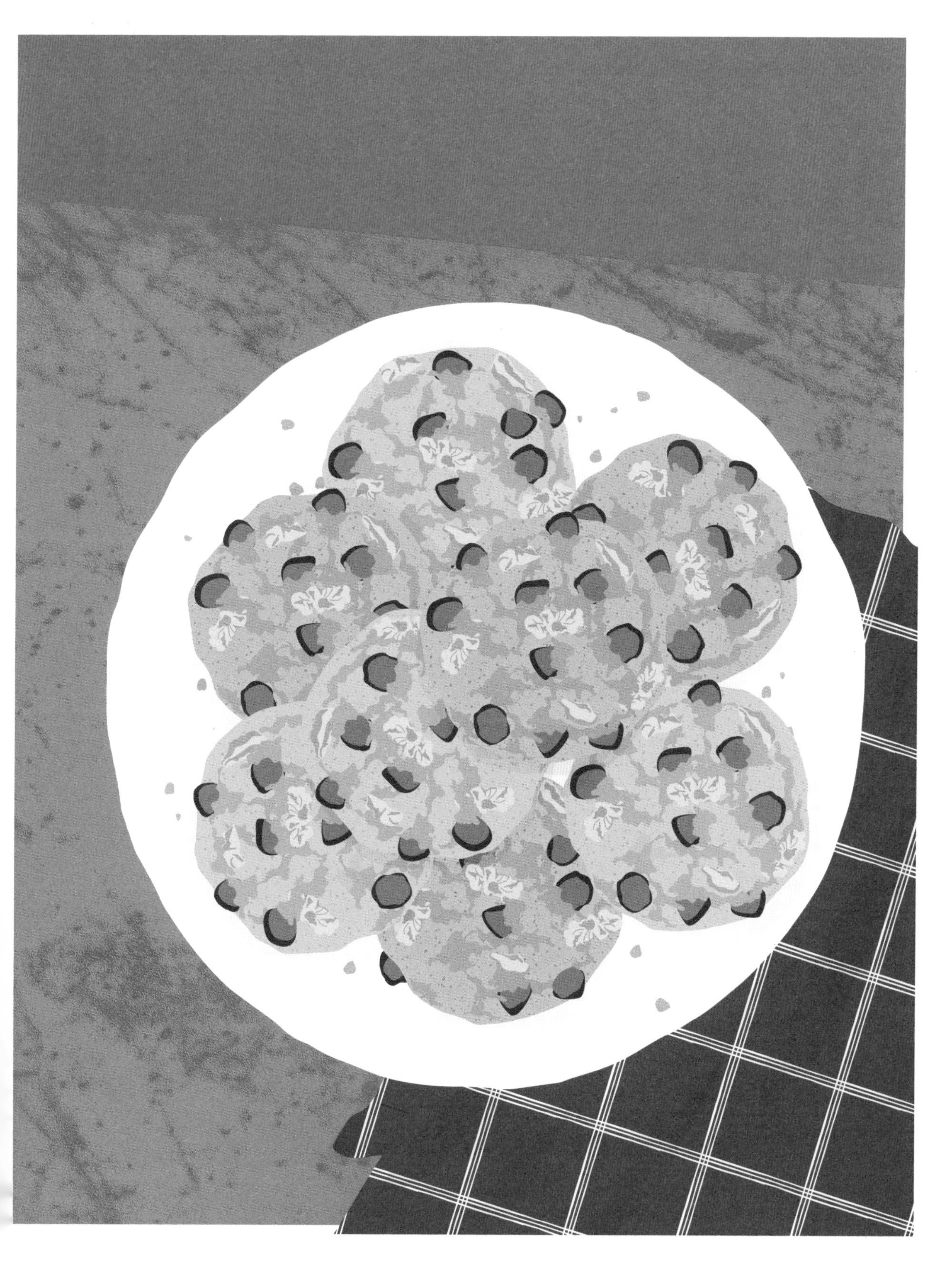

MRS. L.B.J.'S MOONROCKS

48 large cookies **These are large and thick spice cookies with crisp, chewy edges and semisoft centers—real old-fashioned "down home" cookie-jar fillers. In our home, and surrounding territory, everyone loves them. While they are baking, they perfume the house with an irresistible sweet-and-spicy aroma.**

- **4 cups *sifted* all-purpose flour**
- **1 teaspoon baking soda**
- **⅛ teaspoon salt**
- **1 teaspoon ground cloves**
- **1 teaspoon ground cinnamon**
- **1 teaspoon ground allspice**
- **1 teaspoon ground nutmeg**
- **8 ounces (2 sticks) unsalted butter**
- **1½ cups sugar**
- **3 large eggs**
- **½ cup dark corn syrup**
- **3½ ounces (1 packed cup) shredded coconut (sweetened or unsweetened)**
- **5 ounces (1 cup) raisins (dark, light, or half of each)**
- **8 ounces (1 cup) pitted dates, each cut into about 4 pieces**
- **7 ounces (2 cups) walnuts, broken into large pieces**

Adjust two racks to divide the oven into thirds and preheat oven to 350 degrees. Line cookie sheets with baking parchment.

Sift together the flour, baking soda, salt, cloves, cinnamon, allspice, and nutmeg and set aside.

In the large bowl of an electric mixer, beat the butter until it is soft. Beat in the sugar. Then add the eggs one at a time, beating until incorporated after each addition. Beat in the corn syrup. On low speed, add the sifted dry ingredients and beat until incorporated.

Remove from the mixer and, with a large, heavy wooden spoon or rubber spatula, stir in the coconut, raisins, dates, and nuts.

Use a well-rounded large spoonful of the dough for each cookie. Place the mounds of dough 2 inches apart on the sheets.

Bake two sheets at a time, reversing the sheets top to bottom and front to back as necessary to ensure even browning. Bake for 18 to 20 minutes, until the cookies are golden all over.

With a wide metal spatula, transfer the cookies to racks to cool. Store airtight.

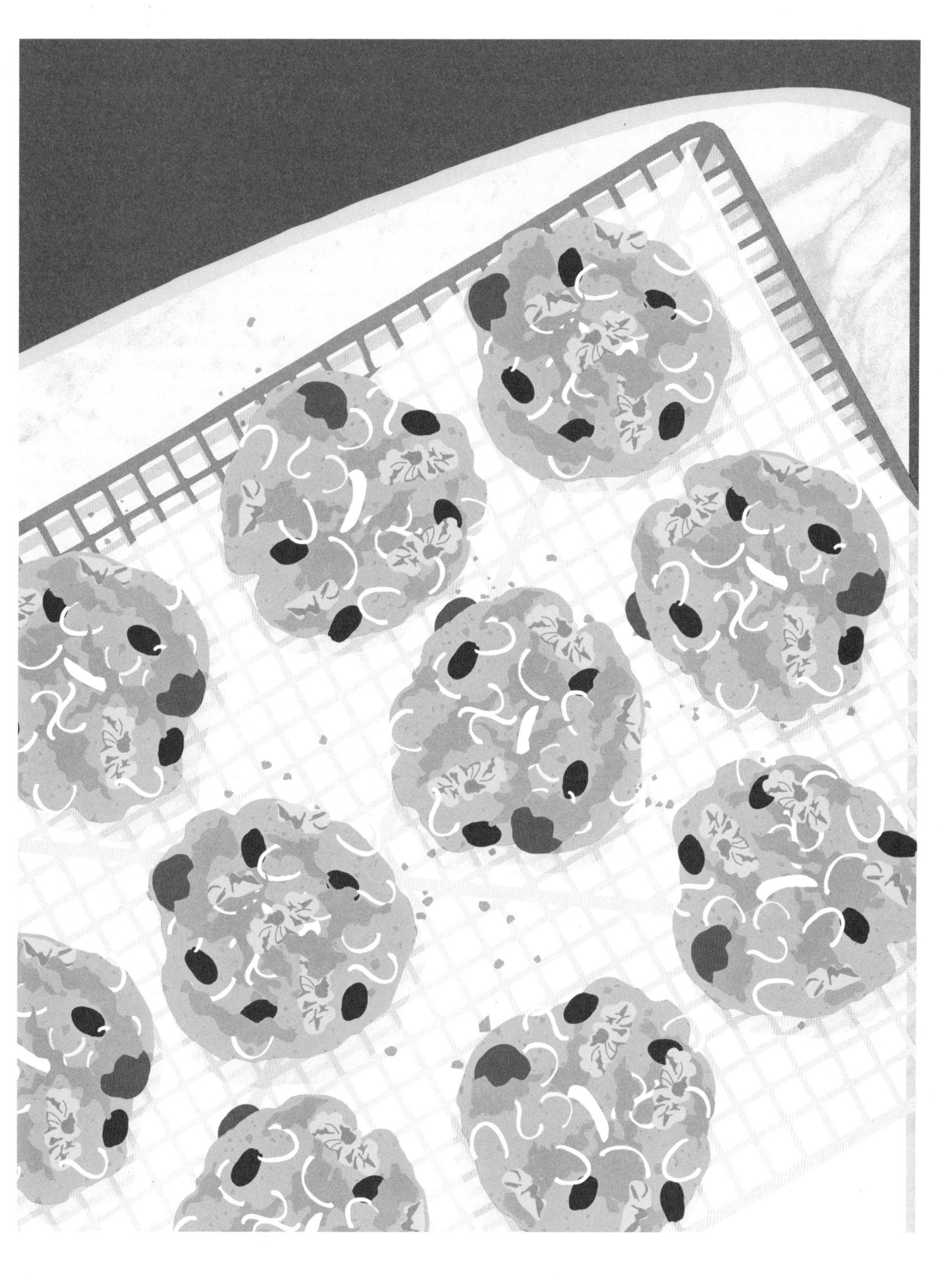

PRALINE WAFERS

28 wafers **This is an old recipe from New Orleans. These fragile wafers are similar to praline candy—made without a mixer.**

- **3 tablespoons unsalted butter**
- **1 cup firmly packed light brown sugar**
- **1 tablespoon vanilla extract**
- **1 large egg**
- **2 tablespoons (must be exact) *sifted* all-purpose flour**
- **3½ ounces (1 cup) pecans, chopped medium fine**

Adjust two racks to divide the oven into thirds and preheat oven to 350 degrees. Line cookie sheets with aluminum foil shiny side up.

Melt the butter in a 1½- to 2-quart saucepan. Remove from the heat and stir in the sugar. Add the vanilla and the egg and stir until smooth. Then stir in the flour and finally the nuts.

Place well-rounded spoonfuls of the dough 2½ to 3 inches apart (no closer, these spread) on the lined sheet. With the back of a spoon, move the nuts around gently so they are spread out all over the cookie and not piled on top of each other.

Bake for 7 to 10 minutes, reversing the cookie sheets top to bottom and front to back as necessary to ensure even browning. (If you bake only one sheet at a time, place the rack in the center of the oven.) The cookies are done when they are completely colored, including the centers—the nuts will remain light.

Let the cookies stand on the foil until they are completely cool and the foil may be easily (but gently) peeled away. If the foil does not peel away easily, the cookies have not baked long enough.

As soon as these are removed from the foil they must be stored airtight in order to remain crisp. If they are not to be served soon, they may be frozen.

GIANT GINGER COOKIES

28 extra-large cookies **These won first prize in a New England county fair. They are huge, soft, and spicy—and enough for filling a large cookie jar (or two).**

4¾	cups *sifted* all-purpose flour	8	ounces (2 sticks) unsalted butter
1	tablespoon baking soda	1	tablespoon instant coffee powder
½	teaspoon salt	1	cup sugar
2	teaspoons ground cinnamon	1	cup molasses
2	teaspoons ground ginger	1	extra-large or jumbo egg
1	teaspoon ground cloves	¾	cup milk
1	teaspoon mustard powder	6¼	ounces (1¼ cups) currants (see Note)

NOTE

If the currants are not especially soft and fresh they should be softened before using. Do this before starting with the rest of the recipe. Cover the currants with boiling water, let stand for a few minutes, and drain them in a strainer. Or steam them for a few minutes in a vegetable steamer. Then spread them out on several layers of paper towels and pat the tops with more paper towels. Let the currants stand on the paper until you are ready for them.

Adjust two racks to divide the oven into thirds and preheat oven to 350 degrees. Line cookie sheets with baking parchment.

Sift together the flour, baking soda, salt, cinnamon, ginger, cloves, and mustard and set aside.

In the large bowl of an electric mixer, cream the butter. Add the coffee powder and beat well. Then beat in the sugar. Add the molasses and beat until smooth. Add the egg and beat well; the mixture will look curdled—it's OK. On low speed, add the sifted dry ingredients in three additions alternately with the milk in two additions, scraping the bowl as necessary with a rubber spatula and beating only until smooth after each addition. Stir in the currants.

Use a heaping large spoonful of the dough for each cookie. Make these extra-large—use as much dough as you can reasonably pile on the spoon. Place the cookies 2½ to 3 inches apart on the lined sheets, keeping the cookies as round and as even as possible.

Bake for 20 to 22 minutes, reversing the sheets top to bottom and front to back a few times to ensure even baking. Be careful that the bottoms of the cookies on the lower sheet do not burn; if the bottoms of the cookies seem to be turning too dark, change the position of the lower sheets often or raise the rack, or slide an extra cookie sheet under the lower one. (If you bake only one sheet at a time, use the higher rack.) Bake until the tops of the cookies spring back sharply when lightly pressed with a fingertip.

With a wide metal spatula, transfer the cookies to racks to cool. Because these are such large cookies, they will form steam as they cool and the steam will make the bottoms moist. To prevent that, raise the cooling racks by placing them on right-side-up cake pans or mixing bowls.

Giant Ginger Cookies (page 37)

OLD-FASHIONED JUMBO LEMON WAFERS

14 (4½-inch) cookies **This is a very old recipe from Connecticut for old-fashioned drop cookies. They are wide, flat, semisoft, crisp, and brown on the edges, and they have a gorgeous lemon and mace flavor. Because these are so large and fragile, do not choose them for mailing or packing as a gift.**

- 1¼ cups *sifted* all-purpose flour
- ¼ teaspoon salt
- ½ teaspoon baking powder
- ½ teaspoon ground mace
- 6 ounces (1½ sticks) unsalted butter
- ½ teaspoon lemon extract
- ¾ cup granulated sugar
- 1 large egg plus 1 egg yolk
- Finely grated zest of 2 or 3 lemons
- Coarse or sanding sugar, or additional granulated sugar, to sprinkle on the tops

Adjust two racks to divide the oven into thirds and preheat oven to 350 degrees. Line cookie sheets with baking parchment or with foil shiny side up.

Sift together the flour, salt, baking powder, and mace and set aside.

In the large bowl of an electric mixer, beat the butter until it is soft. Add the lemon extract and then the granulated sugar and beat well for 2 to 3 minutes. Add the egg and yolk and beat for 2 to 3 minutes more. Then, on low speed, add the sifted dry ingredients, scraping the bowl with a rubber spatula and beating only until incorporated. Remove from the mixer and stir in the zest.

Transfer the mixture to a small bowl for easy handling.

Make these very large; use a heaping small spoonful or a rounded larger spoonful of the dough for each cookie. They will spread considerably in baking; do not place more than 5 cookies on a 12 x 15½-inch sheet — one near each corner and one in the center. However, I suggest that you try a sample sheet first with only 3 or 4 cookies so you know just what to expect. (If you bake only one sheet at a time, adjust a rack to the center of the oven.)

Wet a teaspoon in cold water. Press down gently on each cookie with the back of the wet spoon to flatten the cookies to about ¾-inch thickness. Then, with the wet spoon, smooth the edges of each cookie to round it.

Sprinkle the tops generously with coarse or sanding sugar, or granulated sugar.

continues ↘

Bake for about 10 minutes, reversing the sheets top to bottom and front to back once during baking to ensure even browning. When the cookies are done, they will have brown rims and the tops will feel semi-firm to the touch. Do not underbake.

With a wide metal spatula, transfer the cookies to racks to cool.

Store the cookies airtight, preferably in a plastic freezer box, placing two cookies at a time, bottoms together, with wax paper between the layers.

THE FARMER'S WIFE'S PECAN COOKIES

36 (3-inch) cookies **An old Southern recipe, mixed in a saucepan, for thin cookies that are both crisp and chewy.**

- **1¼ cups *sifted* all-purpose flour**
- **¼ teaspoon baking soda**
- **⅛ teaspoon salt**
- **4 ounces (1 stick) unsalted butter**
- **1¼ cups firmly packed light brown sugar**
- **½ teaspoon vanilla extract**
- **1 large egg**
- **2¼ ounces (⅔ cup) pecans, chopped medium fine**
- **36 pecan halves**

Adjust two racks to divide the oven into thirds and preheat oven to 350 degrees. Line cookie sheets with baking parchment.

Sift together the flour, baking soda, and salt and set aside.

Cut the butter into 1-inch pieces and place in a heavy 2- to 3-quart saucepan. Melt slowly over low heat, stirring occasionally. Remove from the heat and, with a heavy wooden spoon, stir in the sugar, then the vanilla and egg. Add the sifted dry ingredients, stirring until smooth. Mix in the chopped pecans. Transfer to a small bowl for ease in handling.

Use a rounded spoonful of dough for each cookie. Place them 2 inches apart on the sheets. Place a pecan half on each cookie, pressing it gently and lightly into the dough.

Bake for 12 to 14 minutes, reversing the position of the sheets top to bottom and front to back to ensure even browning. (When baking only one sheet at a time, use the higher rack.) These will rise during baking and then will settle down. They should be medium brown – do not underbake.

With a wide metal spatula, transfer the cookies to racks to cool.

The Farmer's Wife's Pecan Cookies (page 41)

PUMPKIN ROCKS

48 large cookies **Many cookies from old recipes are called "rocks," not because they're as hard as rocks but because of their shape. These are thick, soft, spicy, and old-fashioned.**

- **2½ cups *sifted* all-purpose flour**
- **2 teaspoons baking powder**
- **½ teaspoon baking soda**
- **½ teaspoon salt**
- **1 teaspoon ground cinnamon**
- **¾ teaspoon ground nutmeg**
- **½ teaspoon ground ginger**
- **¼ teaspoon ground cloves**
- **¼ teaspoon allspice**
- **4 ounces (1 stick) unsalted butter**
- **1 cup granulated sugar**
- **½ cup firmly packed dark brown sugar**
- **2 large eggs**
- **16 ounces (about 1¾ cups) canned pumpkin (not pumpkin pie filling)**
- **5 ounces (1 cup) raisins**
- **7 ounces (2 cups) walnuts, cut or broken into medium-size pieces**

GLAZE

- **2 tablespoons softened unsalted butter**
- **1½ cups confectioners' sugar**
- **Pinch of salt**
- **2 tablespoons lemon juice**
- **1 tablespoon milk**

Adjust two racks to divide the oven into thirds and preheat oven to 375 degrees. Line cookie sheets with baking parchment.

Sift together the flour, baking powder, baking soda, salt, cinnamon, nutmeg, ginger, cloves, and allspice and set aside.

In the large bowl of an electric mixer, cream the butter. Beat in both sugars. Add the eggs one at a time and beat well, then beat in the pumpkin. (The mixture might look curdled—it's OK.) On low speed, gradually add the dry ingredients, beating only until thoroughly mixed. Stir in the raisins and walnuts.

Use a rounded large spoonful of the dough for each cookie, and place them 1 to 1½ inches apart (these do not run in baking) on the cookie sheets.

Bake the cookies for about 18 minutes, reversing the sheets top to bottom and front to back as necessary to ensure even browning. The cookies are done when they are lightly browned and spring back if gently pressed with a fingertip.

FOR THE GLAZE

Place all of the glaze ingredients in the small bowl of an electric mixer and beat until completely smooth. The mixture should have the consistency of soft whipped cream—it might be necessary to add more liquid (either lemon juice or milk) or more sugar. Cover the glaze airtight when you are not using it.

As you remove the baked cookies from the oven—immediately, while the cookies are very hot—brush the glaze generously over the tops. It should be a rather heavy coating that runs unevenly down the sides.

With a wide metal spatula, transfer the cookies to racks to cool. The glaze will dry completely.

COCONUT GROVE COOKIES

44 cookies **These are chocolate cookies with hidden chunks of chocolate and a baked-on coconut meringue topping.**

CHOCOLATE DOUGH

- 2½ cups *sifted* cake flour (see Note)
- 1½ teaspoons baking powder
- ¼ teaspoon salt
- 8 ounces semisweet chocolate
- 4 ounces (1 stick) unsalted butter
- 1 teaspoon vanilla extract
- 2 teaspoons instant coffee powder
- ½ cup granulated sugar
- ¼ cup firmly packed dark brown sugar
- 2 large egg yolks (reserve the whites for the meringue topping)
- ⅓ cup milk

MERINGUE TOPPING

- 2 large egg whites
- Pinch of salt
- ½ cup granulated sugar
- Scant ¼ teaspoon almond extract
- 2 tablespoons *sifted* cake flour (see Note)
- 7 ounces (2 packed cups) finely shredded coconut

NOTE

Cake flour (not cake mix and not self-rising flour) is more finely ground than all-purpose flour and comes in a box. One cup sifted cake flour equals 1 cup minus 2 tablespoons sifted all-purpose flour, so in the dough recipe you could substitute 2¼ cups minus 1 tablespoon all-purpose flour if cake flour is unobtainable.

Adjust two racks to divide the oven into thirds and preheat oven to 375 degrees. Line cookie sheets with baking parchment.

FOR THE CHOCOLATE DOUGH

Sift together the flour, baking powder, and salt and set aside.

Place 4 ounces (reserve remaining 4 ounces) of the chocolate in the top of a small double boiler over hot water on moderate heat. Stir occasionally until melted and smooth, then remove from the heat and set aside to cool.

To cut the remaining 4 ounces of chocolate, use a heavy knife, work on a cutting board, and cut the chocolate into pieces measuring ¼ to ½ inch across. Set aside.

continues ↘

In the large bowl of an electric mixer, cream the butter. Add the vanilla and instant coffee and then both sugars and beat well. Beat in the egg yolks, scraping the bowl with a rubber spatula. Beat in the melted chocolate. On low speed, gradually add half of the sifted dry ingredients, continuing to scrape the bowl with the spatula. Now gradually add the milk and then the remaining dry ingredients and beat only until smooth. Remove the bowl from the mixer and stir in the cut chocolate pieces. Set the chocolate dough aside at room temperature and prepare the topping.

FOR THE MERINGUE TOPPING

In the small bowl of an electric mixer with clean beaters, beat the egg whites together with the salt until the whites hold soft peaks. Gradually add the sugar, 1 to 2 spoonfuls at a time, and then beat at high speed for 3 to 5 minutes, until the meringue is very stiff. Toward the end of the beating, beat in the almond extract.

Remove the bowl from the mixer and fold in the flour and then the coconut.

To form the cookies: Use a rounded spoonful of the chocolate dough for each cookie and place them 2 inches apart on the lined cookie sheets. Then top each cookie with a slightly rounded spoonful of the meringue topping. In order to wind up even, use a tiny bit less of the meringue topping than the chocolate dough for each cookie. Try to place the topping carefully so that it won't all run off the chocolate cookie while it is baking. A little of it will probably run down the side of the cookie, no matter what, but that's OK; it looks nice anyhow.

Bake for 12 to 13 minutes, until the topping is lightly browned. Reverse the cookie sheets top to bottom and front to back once during baking to ensure even browning.

With a wide metal spatula, transfer the cookies to racks to cool.

BLIND DATE COOKIES

30 cookies **Although these came to me from a friend in New York, I am told that the recipe originated over one hundred years ago with a famous pastry shop in Milwaukee. They are semisoft drop cookies with a surprise date and nut hidden inside. Technically these cookies are dropped onto the cookie sheet, but—since each cookie contains a stuffed date—the procedure is slightly different from that of the usual drop cookie.**

- **30 large (about 10 ounces) pitted dates**
- **30 large (1¼ ounces) walnut halves, or about ⅓ cup large pieces**
- **1¼ cups *sifted* all-purpose flour**
- **¼ teaspoon salt**
- **¼ teaspoon baking powder**
- **½ teaspoon baking soda**
- **2 ounces (½ stick) unsalted butter**
- **½ teaspoon vanilla extract**
- **¾ cup firmly packed light brown sugar**
- **1 large egg**
- **½ cup sour cream**

GLAZE

- **2 ounces (½ stick) unsalted butter**
- **1 cup confectioners' sugar**
- **½ teaspoon vanilla extract**
- **2 to 3 tablespoons milk**

Adjust a rack to the top position of the oven and preheat oven to 400 degrees. Line cookie sheets with baking parchment.

For each date, slit one long side, stuff with one walnut half or a few pieces of walnut, close the date around the nuts, and set aside.

Sift together the flour, salt, baking powder, and baking soda and set aside.

In the small bowl of an electric mixer, cream the butter. Add the vanilla and brown sugar and beat to mix well. Add the egg and beat thoroughly. On the lowest speed, gradually add half of the sifted dry ingredients, then all of the sour cream and then the remaining half of the dry ingredients, scraping the bowl with a rubber spatula and beating only until smooth after each addition. Remove the dough from the mixer and transfer it to a shallow bowl for easy handling.

Using two forks, drop each stuffed date into the dough and roll it around until the date is completely coated. There will be enough dough to cover each date with a generous coating, but don't overdo it or you will not have enough dough to go around. Using the forks, place the dough-coated dates 2 to 3 inches apart on the cookie sheets.

Bake one sheet at a time for about 10 minutes, until lightly browned, reversing the position of the sheet once during baking to ensure even browning.

While the first sheet of cookies is baking, prepare the glaze.

continues ↘

FOR THE GLAZE

Melt the butter and mix it well with the confectioners' sugar, vanilla, and milk, using only enough milk to make a mixture the consistency of soft mayonnaise. Keep the glaze covered when you are not using it.

Remove the baked cookies from the oven. With a pastry brush, immediately brush the tops of the hot cookies with a generous coating of the glaze. Then, with a wide metal spatula, transfer the cookies to a rack to cool.

Bake and glaze the remaining cookies. Let them stand until the glaze is dry.

NORMAN ROCKWELL'S OATMEAL WAFERS

18 large wafers **These are large, thin wafers that are crisp, crunchy, and fragile. They were a favorite of Norman Rockwell, the great illustrator of Americana.**

- ½ cup *sifted* all-purpose flour
- ¼ teaspoon salt
- ¼ teaspoon baking soda
- 4 ounces (1 stick) unsalted butter
- ¼ cup granulated sugar
- ½ cup firmly packed light brown sugar
- ½ teaspoon vanilla extract
- 2 tablespoons water (measure carefully)
- 1 large egg
- 1 cup old-fashioned or quick-cooking (not instant) rolled oats
- 2½ ounces (¾ cup) walnuts, chopped medium fine

Adjust two racks to divide the oven into thirds and preheat oven to 350 degrees. Line cookie sheets with aluminum foil shiny side up.

Sift together the flour, salt, and baking soda and set aside.

In the small bowl of an electric mixer, cream the butter. Gradually add both sugars and beat for 2 to 3 minutes. Add the vanilla, water, and egg and beat well. On low speed, gradually add the sifted dry ingredients, scraping the bowl with a rubber spatula and beating only until smooth. Stir in the oats and then the nuts.

Use a rounded large spoonful of dough for each cookie. Place them 3½ to 4 inches apart (these spread a lot) on the lined sheets. With the back of a wet spoon, flatten each cookie until it is ¼ to ⅓ inch thick.

Bake for 13 to 15 minutes, reversing the position of the cookie sheets top to bottom and front to back as necessary during baking to ensure even browning. (If you bake only one sheet at a time, use the higher rack.) Bake until the cookies are completely golden brown. These must be timed carefully; if they are underbaked the bottoms will be wet and sticky and it will be difficult to remove the cookies from the aluminum foil; if overbaked they will taste burnt and bitter.

Let the baked cookies stand until they are completely cool. Then, carefully and gently, peel the foil away from the backs of the cookies. (If you have any trouble, use a wide metal spatula to move the cookies.) Turn the cookies upside down and let them stand for 5 to 10 minutes on the foil to allow the bottoms to dry a bit. These must be stored airtight.

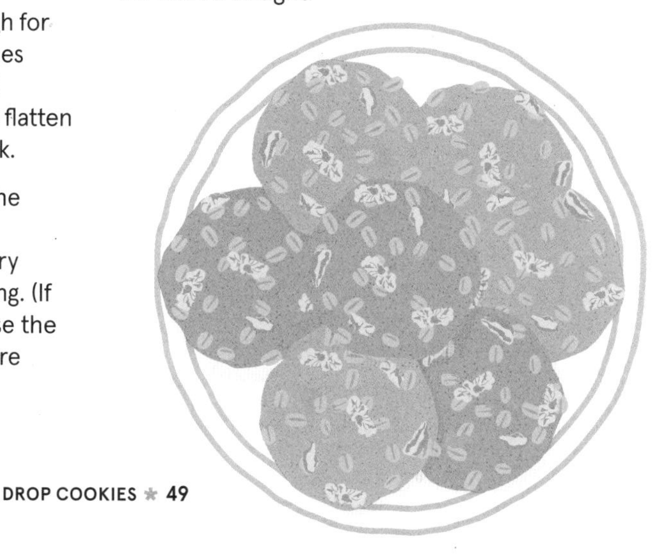

VANILLA BUTTER WAFERS

24 small cookies **These thin, buttery rounds will be brown and crisp on the edges, light and slightly soft on the tops. They are simple, easy cookies to make, but are extremely delicate and fragile. This recipe makes only 24—double it if you wish.**

NOTE

If you make the dough rounds too large or place them too close to each other on the cookie sheets, they will run together.

4 ounces (1 stick) unsalted butter

1 teaspoon vanilla extract

⅓ cup sugar

1 large egg

⅓ cup *sifted* all-purpose flour

Adjust two racks to divide the oven into thirds and preheat oven to 350 degrees. Line cookie sheets with baking parchment.

In the small bowl of an electric mixer, cream the butter. Add the vanilla and the sugar and beat very well for 2 to 3 minutes. Add the egg and beat well again for 2 to 3 minutes more. On low speed, add the flour, scraping the bowl with a rubber spatula and beating only until smooth. Transfer the dough to a shallow bowl for ease in handling.

Use a slightly rounded spoonful of the dough for each cookie (keep these small). If you place the dough neatly and carefully, the cookies will bake into perfect rounds, which is the way they should be. Place the mounds of dough 3 inches apart on the cookie sheets.

Bake for 12 to 15 minutes, until the edges are well browned. Reverse the sheets top to bottom and front to back once to ensure even browning.

With a wide metal spatula, transfer the cookies to racks to cool.

COOKIE KISSES

48 cookies **Hershey's milk chocolate Kisses are about as American as can be. Everybody knows them. These are delicious peanut butter cookies shaped by rolling the dough between your hands. The Kisses are put on top as soon as the baked cookies are taken out of the oven. Fun to make and fun to serve.**

This is a variation of an old American recipe that is sometimes called Sombreros (they do look like them), Blossoms, or Silver-Tipped Blossoms. (Does that mean that they did not remove the foil from the Kisses?)

- **48 Hershey's milk chocolate Kisses**
- **1¾ cups *sifted* all-purpose flour**
- **1 teaspoon baking soda**
- **¼ teaspoon salt**
- **½ cup granulated sugar, plus more for rolling the dough balls**
- **½ cup firmly packed light brown sugar**
- **1 large egg**
- **1 teaspoon vanilla extract**
- **2 tablespoons milk**
- **4 ounces (1 stick) unsalted butter**
- **½ cup smooth peanut butter**

Adjust two racks to divide the oven into thirds and preheat oven to 375 degrees. Line cookie sheets with baking parchment. Remove the wrapping from the Kisses and set them aside.

This dough can be prepared in a food processor or in the large bowl of an electric mixer.

In a processor: Place the flour, baking soda, salt, granulated sugar, and brown sugar in the processor bowl fitted with the metal chopping blade and process on/off quickly 2 or 3 times to mix. Place the egg, vanilla, and milk in a 1-cup glass measuring cup and set aside.

Cut up the butter and add it and the peanut butter to the bowl of the processor. Turn the machine on and pour the egg mixture through the feed tube. Process until the mixture forms a ball and is thoroughly mixed.

Or in a mixer: Sift together the flour, baking soda, and salt and set aside.

Reserve both sugars. Place the egg, vanilla, and milk in a small cup and reserve. Place the butter and peanut butter in the large bowl of the mixer and beat until soft. Add both sugars and beat to mix. Then add half of the sifted dry ingredients, the egg mixture, and the remaining dry ingredients. Beat until thoroughly mixed.

Place a long piece of wax paper or foil on the work surface. Divide the dough into 48 mounds, each one a rounded spoonful. (You can either just pick up the cookie-size mounds and place them on the paper or foil, or roll the dough into a long sausage shape and cut it into 48 even pieces.)

Place additional granulated sugar (about 1 cup) on a wide plate and have it handy. One at a time, roll the mounds of dough between your hands to make balls, roll

continues ↘

them around in the granulated sugar to coat the cookies, and then place them on the lined sheets, placing only 12 cookies on each sheet.

Place one sheet in the oven; wait a few minutes before placing the second sheet in the oven so that they do not come out of the oven at the same time. (If you might forget which sheet went into the oven first, roll up a little bean-size piece of foil and place it in a corner on the first sheet.) Reverse the sheets top to bottom once during baking to ensure even browning. Bake each sheet for 12 to 13 minutes. The cookies will be only lightly colored and will still feel soft to the touch.

Immediately as you remove a sheet from the oven, place a chocolate Kiss, point up, in the middle of each cookie, pressing it down firmly. Then, with a wide metal spatula, transfer the cookies to racks to cool.

The chocolate Kisses will soften from the heat of the cookies and they will remain soft for quite a while. Therefore, if you are packing these or stacking them, be sure that the Kisses have become firm; if necessary, chill the cookies.

OATMEAL MOLASSES COOKIES

72 cookies **These are crunchy and chewy, and you will definitely taste the molasses. Unless you love the flavor of strong, dark molasses, use a light, mild-flavored kind.**

- **3 cups *sifted* all-purpose flour**
- **2 teaspoons baking soda**
- **1 teaspoon salt**
- **1 teaspoon ground cinnamon**
- **¾ teaspoon ground ginger**
- **8 ounces (2 sticks) unsalted butter**
- **1½ teaspoons vanilla extract**
- **2 cups sugar**
- **1½ cups molasses**
- **2 large eggs**
- **2 cups old-fashioned or quick-cooking (not instant) rolled oats**
- **3½ ounces (1 firmly packed cup) shredded coconut**
- **4 ounces (generous 1 cup) walnuts or pecans, cut or broken into medium-size pieces**

Adjust two racks to divide the oven into thirds and preheat oven to 375 degrees. Line cookie sheets with baking parchment.

Sift together the flour, baking soda, salt, cinnamon, and ginger and set aside.

In the large bowl of an electric mixer, cream the butter. Beat in the vanilla and then add the sugar and beat well. Add the molasses and beat to mix. Add the eggs one at a time, scraping the bowl with a rubber spatula and beating well after each addition. On low speed, gradually add the sifted dry ingredients, continuing to scrape the bowl and beating only until mixed. Then add the rolled oats, coconut, and nuts, stirring only until mixed.

Use a well-rounded (but not heaping) spoonful of the dough for each cookie. Place them 2 inches apart on the lined cookie sheets.

Bake for about 15 minutes, reversing the cookie sheets top to bottom and front to back as necessary during baking, until the cookies are lightly colored. The cookies will still feel slightly soft and underdone, but do not overbake. (If you bake only one sheet at a time, use the upper rack; it will take less time to bake than two sheets.)

Remove from the oven and let the cookies stand on the sheets for a minute or so and then, with a wide metal spatula, transfer to racks to cool.

SAVANNAH CHOCOLATE CHEWIES

12 large cookies **In Savannah, Georgia, we went to one of America's great bookstores, E. Shaver. As soon as I introduced myself, the lovely ladies who ran the store—and loved to cook—screamed and giggled and swooned (just thinking about delicious desserts). They asked me if I knew how to make Chocolate Chewies, a Savannah specialty, and a deep, dark secret. I was told they were made at Gottlieb's, a hundred-year-old local bakery. When they phoned Isser Gottlieb at the bakery, he rushed right over, picked us up, drove us to the bakery, showed us the kitchen, fed us tastes of everything, and gave me this recipe. Talk about Southern hospitality!**

The cookies are large, very dark, very chewy, and, since they have egg whites and no yolks (and no butter), they are a sort of meringue, a decidedly chocolate meringue.

NOTE

At Gottlieb's, they told me that if these are not served the day they are made, they should be frozen or they will dry out. I packed them in a freezer bag and let them stand on the counter overnight (just to test) and they were still moist and delicious. I also let some stand uncovered overnight (just to test) and they were still just as wonderful. (Maybe there's something in the air.) Incidentally, this is Gottlieb's number one best-selling cookie.

- 8 ounces (generous 2 cups) pecans
- 3 cups confectioners' sugar
- 2/3 cup *unsifted* unsweetened cocoa powder (preferably Dutch-process)
- 1 teaspoon instant coffee or espresso powder (not granular)
- 2 tablespoons *unsifted* all-purpose flour
- Pinch of salt
- 3 large egg whites (they may be whites that were frozen and thawed)
- ½ teaspoon vanilla extract

Adjust a rack to the middle of the oven and preheat oven to 350 degrees. Line cookie sheets with baking parchment or with aluminum foil shiny side up.

The pecans should be chopped rather finely. If you do it in a food processor fitted with the metal chopping blade, process on/off 10 quick times (10 seconds), or chop the nuts on a board using a long chef's knife. Some pieces will be larger than others, but none should be larger than a pea, and some will be smaller. Set aside.

Place the sugar, cocoa, coffee or espresso, flour, salt, egg whites, and vanilla in the small bowl of an electric mixer. Beat slowly at first until the dry ingredients are moistened, and then beat at high speed for 1 minute. Remove the bowl from the mixer and stir in the nuts.

It is important now to spoon out the cookies as soon as possible. Once they are spooned out they can wait before baking, but if they remain in the mixing bowl for any length of time, they will not be beautifully shiny when baked. Use a spoon for spooning out the cookies (not a measuring spoon) – make each cookie one rounded large spoonful of the dough – and use another spoon for pushing off the mounds of dough. Place the cookies at least 1 inch apart on the prepared sheets.

I think these bake best if you bake only one sheet at a time. Bake for 15 minutes, reversing the sheet front to back once during baking to ensure even baking. When done, the cookies should be dry and crisp on the outside, wet and chewy inside.

If you have used baking parchment, the cookies may be removed from the paper with a wide metal spatula as soon as they are done and transferred to a rack to cool. If you have used foil, the cookies will have to stand on the foil until they can then be lifted easily with your fingers (or, if you have trouble, peel the foil away from the backs of the cookies).

Store these airtight.

24-KARAT COOKIES

32 cookies **These are made with grated raw carrots. Probably no one will recognize the taste, but the carrots will keep the cookies soft and moist.**

NOTE

It is not necessary to peel the carrots, just clean them with a brush under running water. Grate them on the medium-fine side of a grater. Two medium-large carrots will make ¾ cup when grated.

- **1 cup *sifted* all-purpose flour**
- **1 teaspoon baking powder**
- **1 teaspoon baking soda**
- **¼ teaspoon salt**
- **4 ounces (1 stick) unsalted butter**
- **1 large egg**
- **½ cup honey**
- **¾ cup firmly packed grated raw carrots (see Note)**
- **½ cup old-fashioned or quick-cooking (not instant) rolled oats**
- **½ cup raisins**
- **2½ ounces (¾ cup) walnuts, cut or broken into medium-size pieces**

Adjust two racks to divide the oven into thirds and preheat oven to 350 degrees. Cut aluminum foil to fit cookie sheets.

Sift together the flour, baking powder, baking soda, and salt and set aside.

In the large bowl of an electric mixer, cream the butter. Add the egg and beat to mix. Beat in the honey and then the carrots. On low speed, add the sifted dry ingredients and then the oats, scraping the bowl with a rubber spatula and beating only until thoroughly mixed. Stir in the raisins and the walnuts.

Place the dough by rounded spoonfuls about 2 inches apart on the cut aluminum foil. Slide cookie sheets under the foil.

Bake for about 15 minutes, reversing the position of the cookie sheets top to bottom and front to back as necessary to ensure even browning. The cookies are done when they are golden-colored and the tops spring back if lightly pressed with a fingertip.

With a wide metal spatula, transfer the cookies to racks to cool.

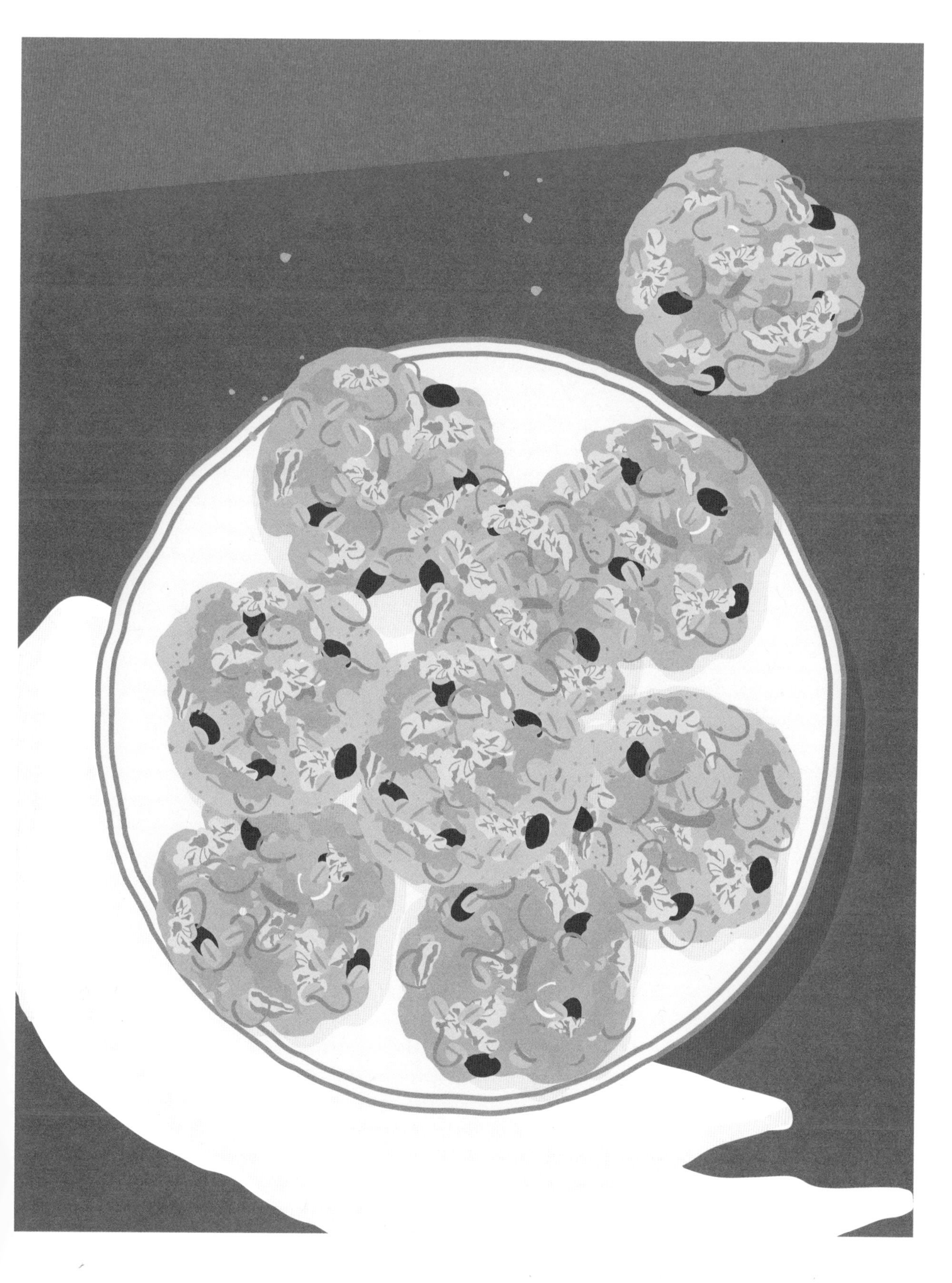

OATMEAL SNICKERDOODLES

54 cookies **Snickerdoodles are Early American; there are many different versions. These from Connecticut are plain old-fashioned—thin, crisp, and crunchy.**

- **2 cups *sifted* all-purpose flour**
- **1 teaspoon baking soda**
- **½ teaspoon salt**
- **1 teaspoon ground cinnamon**
- **8 ounces (2 sticks) unsalted butter**
- **1 teaspoon vanilla extract**
- **¾ cup granulated sugar**
- **¾ cup firmly packed light brown sugar**
- **2 large eggs**
- **1½ cups old-fashioned or quick-cooking (not instant) rolled oats**

CINNAMON SUGAR

- **2 tablespoons granulated sugar**
- **2 teaspoons ground cinnamon**

Adjust two racks to divide the oven into thirds and preheat oven to 400 degrees. Cut aluminum foil to fit cookie sheets.

Sift together the flour, baking soda, salt, and cinnamon and set aside.

In the large bowl of an electric mixer, cream the butter. Add the vanilla and both sugars and beat well. Add the eggs one at a time and beat well. On low speed, gradually add the sifted dry ingredients, scraping the bowl with a rubber spatula and beating only until mixed. Stir in the oats.

Place by rounded spoonfuls 2 inches apart on the cut foil.

FOR THE CINNAMON SUGAR

Stir the sugar and cinnamon together well. With a spoon, sprinkle it generously over the cookies.

Slide cookie sheets under the foil. Bake the cookies for 10 to 12 minutes, reversing sheets top to bottom and front to back as necessary to ensure even browning. Bake until the cookies are browned all over, including the centers.

Let cookies stand on the sheets for a few seconds until they are firm enough to transfer. Slide the foil off the sheets and, with a wide metal spatula, transfer the cookies to racks to cool. Store airtight.

"I am so lucky—I always have so much to do, even if it's that I'm going to go into the kitchen to bake. When you're busy being creative, the outside world can't compete."

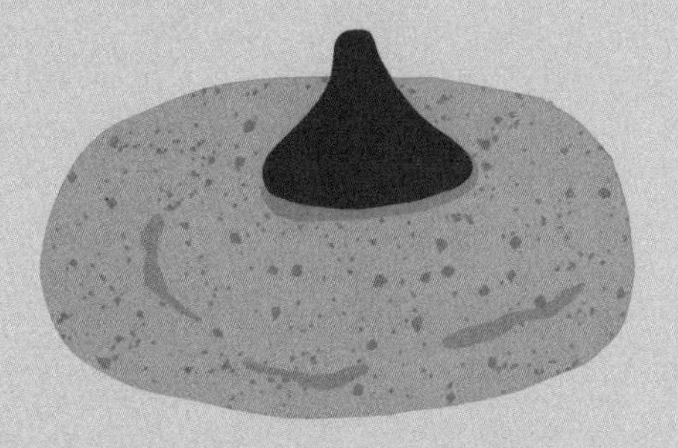

BAR COOKIES

Most of these are made in a shallow pan and then cut into bars after baking.

PENNSYLVANIA SQUARES

32 squares **I met a lady who worked in the test kitchen at the Hershey company. She spent all her time testing chocolate recipes. I asked if she had a favorite. She didn't hesitate and gave me this recipe. They are very thin, brown-sugar cookie squares covered with milk chocolate and chopped walnuts. The result is like a combination of chewy butterscotch and English toffee. Quick, easy, foolproof, wonderfully delicious candylike cookies.**

You need rather small (about 1½-ounce) bars of Hershey's milk chocolate, although I don't see any reason you couldn't use any other brand of milk chocolate, and if those bars are not the same size, approximately the same size will do.

- 8 ounces (2 sticks) unsalted butter
- 1 teaspoon vanilla extract
- ¼ teaspoon salt
- 1 cup firmly packed dark brown sugar
- 1 large egg yolk
- 2 cups *sifted* all-purpose flour
- 8 (1½-ounce) bars Hershey's milk chocolate
- 5 ounces (1¼ cups) walnuts

Adjust a rack one-third up from the bottom of the oven and preheat oven to 350 degrees. Coat a 9 x 13-inch baking pan with butter (additional to that called for) and set aside.

In the large bowl of an electric mixer, beat the butter until soft. Beat in the vanilla, salt, and sugar. Then add the egg yolk and beat well. On low speed, gradually add the flour, scraping the bowl as necessary with a rubber spatula and beating until incorporated. (It might be necessary to finish the beating by hand.)

To make a thin layer of the dough in the buttered pan, it will be best if you first place the dough by rounded spoonfuls over the bottom of the pan. Cover with a length of wax paper and, with the palm of your hand and your fingertips, press down on the paper to press the mounds of the dough together into a rather smooth layer. Remove the wax paper.

Bake for 23 minutes. (During baking the dough will rise and then settle down.)

Meanwhile, as the cake is baking, unwrap the chocolate bars and set them aside. And, on a large chopping board with a long, heavy chef's knife, chop the nuts into rather small pieces. Small is better than large for these cookies. Set the nuts aside.

Remove the baked layer from the oven and immediately, without waiting, place the chocolate bars on the hot cake. Keep them about ¼ inch away from the sides of the pan. Break the bars into pieces wherever necessary and fit them together to cover the cake; a few empty areas — uncovered — will be all right.

continues ↘

In about a minute or two, the chocolate will have softened from the heat of the cake. With the bottom of a spoon, smooth over the chocolate. Then, with your fingertips, sprinkle the nuts all over the chocolate. Cover with a length of plastic wrap or wax paper and, with the palms of your hands and your fingertips, press down gently on the nuts to make sure that they are all embedded in the chocolate. Remove the plastic wrap or wax paper.

With a small, sharp knife, cut around the sides of the cake to release. Let stand until cool. Then refrigerate only until the chocolate is set.

With a small, sharp knife, cut the cake into 32 squares. (Or cut it into 16 squares and, after removing them from the pan, cut each one in half.)

To remove the first 1 or 2 cookies from the pan it might be helpful to use a fork to pry the cookie up; then use a metal spatula to remove the remaining cookies.

Wrap the cookies individually in clear cellophane or wax paper or aluminum foil, if you wish, or place them on a tray and cover with plastic wrap until serving time.

FLORIDA LEMON SQUARES

24 to 32 squares **These are rich layered bars with a baked-in tart lemon filling. They should be refrigerated until serving time.**

- **1½ cups *sifted* all-purpose flour**
- **1 teaspoon baking powder**
- **½ teaspoon salt**
- **1 (14- or 15-ounce) can unsweetened condensed milk**
- **Finely grated zest of 1 large lemon**
- **½ cup lemon juice**
- **5⅓ ounces (1¼ sticks plus 2 teaspoons) unsalted butter**
- **1 cup firmly packed dark brown sugar**
- **1 cup old-fashioned or quick-cooking (not instant) rolled oats**
- OPTIONAL: **confectioners' sugar**

Adjust a rack one-third up from the bottom of the oven and preheat oven to 350 degrees. Butter a 13 x 9 x 2-inch pan.

Sift together the flour, baking powder, and salt and set aside.

Pour the condensed milk into a medium mixing bowl. Add the grated lemon zest and then, gradually, add the lemon juice, stirring with a small wire whisk to keep the mixture smooth. (The lemon will thicken the milk.) Set the mixture aside.

In the large bowl of an electric mixer, cream the butter. Add the brown sugar and beat well. On lowest speed, gradually add the sifted dry ingredients, scraping the bowl with a rubber spatula and beating only until thoroughly mixed. Mix in the rolled oats. The mixture will be crumbly—it will not hold together.

Sprinkle a bit more than half of the oat mixture (2 generous cups) evenly over the bottom of the prepared pan. Pat the crumbs firmly with your fingertips to make a smooth, compact layer. Drizzle or spoon the lemon mixture evenly over the crumb layer and spread it to make a thin smooth layer. Sprinkle the remaining crumbly oat mixture evenly over the lemon layer. Pat the crumbs gently with the palm of your hand to smooth them—it is OK if a bit of the lemon layer shows through in small spots.

Bake for 30 to 35 minutes, until the cake is lightly colored.

Cool the cake completely in the pan. Refrigerate for about 1 hour (or more).

continues ↘

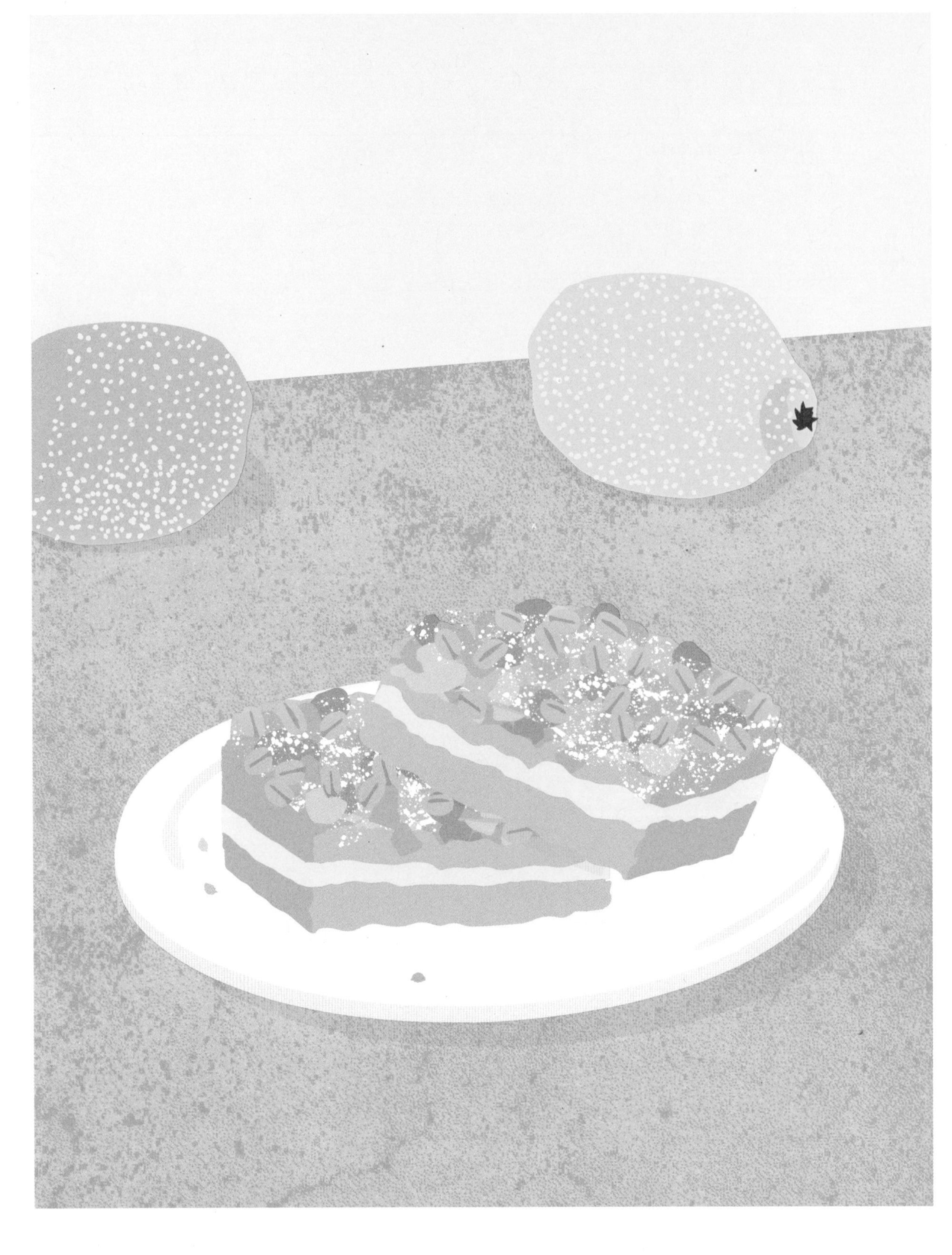

With a small, sharp knife, cut around the sides of the cake to release it. Cut it into small squares. With a wide metal spatula, remove the squares from the pan; transfer them to a serving plate, cover with plastic wrap, and refrigerate.

If you like, just before serving, the squares may be topped with confectioners' sugar. Use your fingertips to press the sugar through a fine strainer held over the squares. (It is best to have the squares on wax paper while coating them with sugar.)

FIG BARS

24 bars **A pastry chef on a cruise ship that sailed from the Port of Miami and cruised through the Caribbean gave me this recipe. He made it frequently for the passengers to have with tea in the afternoon. The cookies are almost solid figs, a few nuts, and just barely enough batter to hold them together — delicious on land or sea. They are homey, old-fashioned cookies — moist, chewy, yummy, not too sweet. Great for a picnic or lunch box, wonderful to mail.**

- **1 pound (2 generous packed cups) dried brown figs (although they are called "dried," they should be soft and moist)**
- **½ cup *sifted* all-purpose flour**
- **½ teaspoon baking powder**
- **½ teaspoon salt**
- **2 large eggs**
- **½ cup firmly packed light brown sugar**
- **1 teaspoon vanilla extract**
- **6 ounces (1½ cups) walnuts, cut or broken into medium-size pieces**
- **Confectioners' sugar (to be used after the cookies are baked)**

Adjust a rack to the center of the oven and preheat oven to 350 degrees. Prepare a shallow 9-inch square cake pan as follows: Turn the pan upside down, cover it with a 12-inch square of foil shiny side down, and fold down the sides and the corners of the foil. Remove the foil, turn the pan right side up, and place the foil in the pan. To butter the foil, place a piece of butter in the pan and place the pan in the oven to melt the butter. Then, with a pastry brush, brush the butter over the bottom and the sides of the pan and set the pan aside.

With a small, sharp knife, cut off and discard the tough stems on the figs. Cut into ¼- to ½-inch pieces; they should not be finely chopped or ground. This can be done with a small, sharp knife or with scissors (I use scissors). Set the prepared figs aside.

Sift together the flour, baking powder, and salt and set aside.

In a mixing bowl, beat or whisk the eggs just to mix well. Beat in the brown sugar and vanilla. Add the sifted dry ingredients and beat or whisk until smooth (if necessary, use a mixer). Then stir in the figs and the nuts.

Turn the batter into the prepared pan and smooth the top. Bake for 35 minutes. Cool in the pan until tepid.

Cover with a rack, turn the pan and rack over, remove the pan, and peel off the foil. Cover with a fresh square of foil or wax paper (these might stick to the rack) and another rack, and turn over again, leaving the cake right side up (on the foil or wax paper) on the rack.

When cool, place in the freezer for about an hour (it is much easier to cut these when they are almost frozen). Transfer to a cutting board and, with a long, sharp, heavy knife, cut into 4 strips. Then cut each strip into 6 bars.

To sugar the cookies, place them on wax paper. Place confectioners' sugar in a strainer and sugar them generously. Then turn them over and sugar the other sides.

Wrap these individually in clear cellophane or wax paper, or package them in an airtight container.

JOHNNY APPLESEED SQUARES

16 to 24 squares **Once, during a beautiful drive through the Appalachian Mountains along the spectacular Skyline Drive in Virginia, we picked up some local literature and learned about John Chapman, better known as Johnny Appleseed. During the early 1800s, Chapman personally planted a veritable forest of apple trees throughout Pennsylvania, Indiana, and Ohio. He later sold the grown trees to early settlers for a penny each—ah, those were the good old days!**

At a local gift shop, we bought some wonderful apple cookies. I had only to ask for the recipe: They had it typed and printed and were so happy I asked.

The recipe consists of a chewy, chunky oatmeal mixture that is spread thinly in a pan, covered with sliced apples, and topped with another layer of the oatmeal mixture. It is unusual for bar cookies to have a layer of juicy apples in the middle. They are extremely, deliciously chewy, and easy and fun to make. The bars may be frozen.

- 1 cup *sifted* all-purpose flour
- ½ teaspoon baking soda
- Scant ½ teaspoon salt
- 1 teaspoon ground cinnamon
- ¼ teaspoon ground nutmeg or mace
- 1½ cups quick-cooking (not instant) rolled oats
- ⅔ cup firmly packed dark or light brown sugar
- 4 ounces (1 stick) unsalted butter, melted
- 1 large egg
- 1 teaspoon vanilla extract
- 2 to 3 firm cooking apples (preferably Granny Smith)
- ½ cup pecans, toasted, cut or broken into medium-size pieces

Adjust a rack to the middle of the oven and preheat oven to 350 degrees. Line a 9 x 1¾-inch square pan as follows: Turn the pan over, center a 12-inch square of foil shiny side down over the pan, and fold down the sides and corners to shape the foil. Remove the foil, turn the pan over again, and place the foil in the pan. With a pot holder, firmly press the foil into place. Butter the pan by putting a piece of butter in the pan and then placing it in the oven to melt. Spread the butter with a pastry brush or a piece of crumpled wax paper over the bottom and sides. Place the prepared pan in the freezer (it is easier to spread a thin layer of dough in a frozen pan).

Into a mixing bowl, sift together the flour, baking soda, salt, cinnamon, and nutmeg or mace. Stir in the oats and sugar. In a small bowl, stir together the butter, egg, and vanilla, and then mix into the oat mixture.

With your fingertips, press about 1 cup of the dough into the prepared pan; it will be a very thin layer. Set aside.

Place the remaining dough between two 12-inch lengths of wax paper and, with a rolling pin, roll over the top piece of paper to roll out the dough into a 9-inch square; it will be very thin. You may remove the top piece of paper, cut off pieces of the rolled-out dough, and place them where you need them, to make the square even. Slide a flat-sided cookie sheet under the dough and the wax paper and transfer it to the freezer for a few minutes.

Meanwhile, peel, quarter, and core the apples, then cut each quarter lengthwise into 5 or 6 slices.

Place the apples in rows, each slice slightly overlapping another, to cover the bottom layer of dough. Sprinkle with the nuts.

Remove the rolled-out square of dough from the freezer and peel off the top piece of paper. Turn the dough over the apples, remove the remaining paper, and press down on the edges of the dough.

Bake for 25 to 30 minutes, reversing the pan front to back once during baking to ensure even browning. About 10 minutes before the cake is done, if the top has not started to brown, raise the rack to a higher position to encourage browning.

Cool in the pan. Then cover with a rack or a cookie sheet, turn the pan and rack or sheet over, remove the pan, and peel off the foil. Cover the cake with a cookie sheet or a cutting board and turn it over again, leaving the cake right side up.

It is best to chill the cake a bit before cutting it into squares, but this has a good texture and will cut well even if it is not chilled.

Cut into squares or bars.

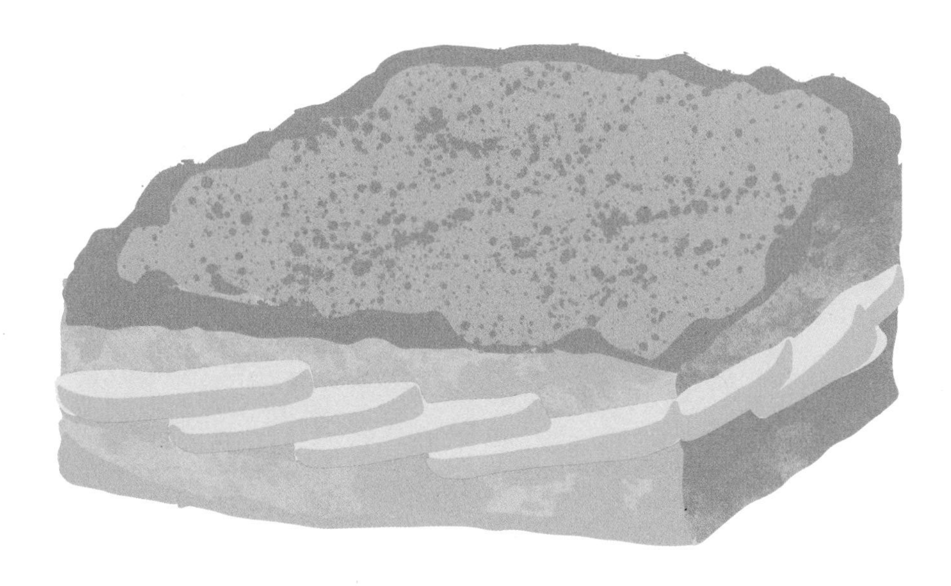

POLISH WEDDING CAKES

16 (2-inch) squares or 32 to 48 small bars **These are called *mazurki* in Polish. There are many versions, all rich and moist. This one has a crunchy crust and tart apricot filling. The pastry is not like American pastry; it will resemble a crumb mixture.**

APRICOT FILLING

- **4 ounces (about 24 halves) dried apricots**
- **½ cup water**
- **2 tablespoons granulated sugar**

POLISH PASTRY

- **1¼ cups *sifted* all-purpose flour**
- **¼ teaspoon salt**
- **1 cup firmly packed dark brown sugar**
- **6 ounces (1½ sticks) cold unsalted butter, cut into ½-inch pieces**
- **1¾ ounces (firmly packed ½ cup) shredded coconut**
- **¾ cup old-fashioned or quick-cooking (not instant) rolled oats**
- **2 ounces (generous ½ cup) walnuts, cut medium fine**

OPTIONAL: confectioners' sugar, for dusting

FOR THE FILLING

In a small, heavy saucepan with a tight cover, bring the apricots and water to a boil, uncovered. Reduce the heat to low, cover the pan, and simmer until the apricots are very tender, about half an hour, depending on the apricots. The fruit should be very soft and the water should be partially but not completely absorbed.

Press the apricots with a potato masher or stir and mash vigorously with a fork. The mixture should be very thick. Add the granulated sugar and stir until it dissolves. Cool to room temperature. (If you wish, the filling may be made ahead of time and refrigerated.)

FOR THE PASTRY

Adjust an oven rack one-third up from the bottom and preheat oven to 325 degrees.

Place the flour, salt, and brown sugar in a mixing bowl. With a pastry blender, cut in the butter until the mixture resembles coarse meal. Stir in the coconut, oats, and walnuts.

Place half (3 cups) of the mixture in an unbuttered 8-inch square cake pan. Press it evenly with your fingertips. Cover with a piece of wax paper and, with the palm of your hand, press against the paper to make a smooth, compact layer. Remove the wax paper.

Spread the apricot filling smoothly over the pastry, staying ¼ to ½ inch away from the edges. Sprinkle the remaining pastry evenly over the filling and repeat the directions for covering with wax paper and pressing smooth. Remove the wax paper.

Bake for 60 to 70 minutes, until the top is barely semi-firm to the touch.

Cool in the pan for 15 minutes. Cut around the sides of the cake to release it. Cover with a rack or a cookie sheet, invert, and remove the pan. Cover with a rack and invert again so that the cake is right side up. Let cool completely and then refrigerate briefly — the cake cuts best if it is cold.

Transfer the cake to a cutting board. Use a long, thin, sharp knife or a finely serrated one to cut the cake into squares or fingers.

If you like, top the bars with confectioners' sugar. Press it through a fine strainer held over the bars to cover the tops generously.

CHARLESTON CHEESECAKE BARS

16 small bars **When we visited Charleston, South Carolina, I found a wonderful cookie recipe in the *Post and Courier.* When we returned home I made these cookies before unpacking the suitcases. They have a crunchy, nutty oatmeal base, a lemon-cream cheese filling, and a layer of the crunchy oats sprinkled over the top. They are unusual and wonderful, fancy enough for a party, but easy to make. These should be stored in the refrigerator.**

OATMEAL BASE

- 1 cup *sifted* all-purpose flour
- ¼ teaspoon salt
- ½ teaspoon ground cinnamon
- 4 ounces (1 stick) unsalted butter
- ½ cup firmly packed dark brown sugar
- 2 ounces (½ cup) pecans, toasted and chopped fine
- 1 cup quick-cooking (not instant) rolled oats

CREAM CHEESE LAYER

- Finely grated zest of 1 lemon
- 1 tablespoon lemon juice
- 8 ounces Philadelphia-brand cream cheese
- ½ cup granulated sugar
- 1 large egg
- 2 tablespoons sour cream

FOR THE OATMEAL BASE

Adjust a rack one-third up from the bottom of the oven and preheat oven to 350 degrees. Line an 8-inch square cake pan with foil as follows: Turn the pan over, place a 12-inch square of foil shiny side down over the pan, and press down on the sides and corners to shape the foil. Remove the foil, turn the pan over again, place the foil in the pan, and press it gently into place. To butter the foil, place a piece of butter in the pan and place it in the oven to melt; then spread it with a pastry brush or crumpled wax paper over the bottom and sides of the pan. Set the pan aside.

Sift together the flour, salt, and cinnamon and set aside.

In the small bowl of an electric mixer, beat the butter until soft, then beat in the brown sugar. On low speed, add the sifted dry ingredients, the nuts, and the rolled oats. When well mixed, remove and reserve 1 cup of the mixture.

Turn the remaining mixture into the prepared pan. With your fingertips, spread it evenly over the bottom of the pan and then press firmly to make a compact layer.

Bake for 15 minutes.

FOR THE CREAM CHEESE LAYER

Combine the zest and juice and set aside.

In the small bowl of an electric mixer, beat the cheese until it is soft. Beat in the

continues ↘

granulated sugar and then the egg and sour cream. When smooth, remove from the mixer and stir in the zest and juice.

Pour the mixture over the baked bottom crust (which may still be hot). Smooth the top. Now, with your fingertips, sprinkle the reserved oat mixture as evenly as you can to cover the cheese mixture completely (or almost completely). Then, with your fingertips, press the oat mixture slightly into the cheese mixture so that none of it remains loose and also to smooth the top. Bake for 25 minutes.

Set aside to cool completely.

Place the cooled cake in the freezer for about an hour. Then cover the top of the pan with a piece of foil and fold down the sides. Cover the foil with a board or a cookie sheet, turn the pan and the board or cookie sheet over, and remove the pan. Peel off the foil lining, cover the cake with a board or cookie sheet, and turn over again. Remove the remaining foil (it was put there only to catch any loose bits of topping that might fly around when the pan is turned over).

Now, to cut the cake: Use a strong, sharp knife. If the cheese mixture sticks to the blade, hold the blade under very hot running water before making each cut (cut with the hot, wet blade). If the cheese mixture squashes out even a bit, place the cake in the freezer again for 10 to 20 minutes (or as necessary) until it is firm enough.

Cut into quarters and then cut each quarter into 4 pieces. Cover and refrigerate until serving time. These may be frozen; if so, thaw in the refrigerator for an hour or two, or longer.

CHOCOLATE MINT STICKS

32 small bars **These are similar to brownies, but are covered with a layer of mint-flavored icing and a thin bitter-chocolate glaze.**

- **2 ounces unsweetened chocolate**
- **4 ounces (1 stick) unsalted butter**
- **2 large eggs**
- **Pinch of salt**
- **½ teaspoon vanilla extract**
- **1 cup granulated sugar**
- **½ cup *sifted* all-purpose flour**
- **2 ounces (generous ½ cup) walnuts, cut into medium-size pieces**

MINT ICING

- **2 tablespoons unsalted butter, at room temperature**
- **1 cup strained or *sifted* confectioners' sugar**
- **1 tablespoon (or a few drops more) heavy cream**
- **½ teaspoon peppermint extract**

BITTER-CHOCOLATE GLAZE

- **1 ounce unsweetened chocolate**
- **1 tablespoon unsalted butter**

Adjust a rack one-third up from the bottom of the oven and preheat oven to 350 degrees. Butter a 9-inch square cake pan and dust it all over with fine, dry bread crumbs; invert the pan to shake out excess. (This cake has a tendency to stick to the pan; using the crumbs will prevent that.)

Melt the chocolate and the butter in the top of a small double boiler over hot water on moderate heat. Stir until smooth. Remove the top of the double boiler and set aside to cool slightly.

In the small bowl of an electric mixer, beat the eggs until they are foamy. Beat in the salt, vanilla, and granulated sugar. Add the chocolate mixture (which may still be warm) and beat to mix. On low speed, add the flour, scraping the bowl with a rubber spatula and beating only until mixed. Stir in the nuts. Pour the mixture into the prepared pan and spread it to make a smooth layer.

Bake for 28 minutes, or until a toothpick inserted in the center of the cake comes out clean. Remove the cake from the oven and let it stand, in the pan, at room temperature until completely cool.

FOR THE ICING

Place all of the icing ingredients in the small bowl of an electric mixer and beat until smooth. It might be necessary to add a few drops more of the cream, but it should be a thick mixture, not runny.

Spread the icing evenly over the cake still in the pan. It will be a very thin layer. Place the cake in the refrigerator for 5 minutes, no longer.

continues ↘

FOR THE GLAZE

Melt the chocolate and the butter in the top of a small double boiler over hot water on moderate heat. Stir until completely smooth.

Pour the hot glaze onto the chilled icing and quickly tilt the pan in all directions to cover the icing completely with the glaze. It will be a very, very thin layer of glaze, just barely enough to cover all of the icing. (But if the icing does show through in a few small spots, don't worry.) Refrigerate the cake for about half an hour, or until the glaze starts to look dull.

With a small, sharp knife, cut around the sides of the cake to release it. Wipe the knife blade as necessary to keep it clean, and cut the cake into quarters.

With a wide metal spatula, transfer the quarters to a cutting board. With a long, sharp knife, cut each quarter in half and then cut each half into 4 small bars, wiping the knife blade as necessary. Transfer the bars to a tray or cake plate and let stand at room temperature for at least several hours before serving to allow the glaze to dry.

These may be frozen and are very good when served directly from the freezer.

CREAM CHEESE BROWNIES

24 brownies **Part brownie, part cheesecake—layered and marbled together. The bars must be stored in the refrigerator or frozen. And they may be eaten directly from the freezer or thawed.**

CHOCOLATE MIXTURE

- 1 cup *unsifted* all-purpose flour
- ½ teaspoon baking powder
- ¼ teaspoon salt
- 4 ounces semisweet chocolate
- 3 tablespoons unsalted butter
- 2 large eggs
- ¾ cup sugar
- 1 teaspoon vanilla extract
- 2½ ounces (¾ cup) walnuts, cut into medium-size pieces

CREAM CHEESE MIXTURE

- 4 ounces cream cheese
- 2 tablespoons unsalted butter
- ½ teaspoon vanilla extract
- ¼ cup sugar
- 1 large egg

Adjust a rack one-third up from the bottom of the oven and preheat oven to 350 degrees. Prepare a 9-inch square pan as follows: Turn it upside down and place a 12-inch square of aluminum foil shiny side down over the inverted pan. Turn down the sides and corners of the foil just to shape it. Remove the foil, turn the pan right side up, and place the foil in the pan. In order not to tear the foil, place a folded towel or a pot holder in the pan and, pressing against the towel or pot holder, press the foil gently into place. Coat the foil with soft or melted butter, spreading it thinly with a pastry brush or crumpled wax paper.

FOR THE CHOCOLATE MIXTURE

Sift together the flour, baking powder, and salt and set aside.

Melt the chocolate and butter in the top of a small double boiler over hot water on moderate heat. Stir until smooth, remove from heat, and set aside to cool slightly.

In the small bowl of an electric mixer, beat the eggs until foamy. Add the sugar and vanilla and beat at high speed for 3 to 4 minutes, until the mixture is slightly lemon-colored and forms a ribbon when the beaters are lifted. On low speed, beat in the melted chocolate and butter and then the sifted dry ingredients, scraping the bowl with a rubber spatula and beating only until the dry ingredients are incorporated.

Remove and set aside ¾ cup of the chocolate mixture. To the remaining batter, add ½ cup of the nuts (reserve ¼ cup for topping) and stir to mix. Spread the chocolate mixture evenly in the pan; it will be a very thin layer.

continues

FOR THE CREAM CHEESE MIXTURE

In the small bowl of an electric mixer, beat the cream cheese with the butter until soft and smooth. Add the vanilla and sugar and beat well. Then add the egg and beat again until very smooth.

To cover the chocolate mixture with a thin layer of the cheese mixture, slowly pour the cheese mixture over the chocolate layer, then smooth with the back of a spoon to the edges of the pan. Place the reserved ¾ cup of the chocolate mixture by heaping large spoonfuls onto the cheese layer, letting the cheese show through between mounds—you should have 8 or 9 chocolate mounds. With a small metal spatula or a table knife, cut through the chocolate mounds and the cheese layer. It is best if you don't cut down into the bottom layer. Zigzag the knife to marbleize the batters slightly; don't overdo it. Sprinkle with reserved ¼ cup nuts. Bake for 35 minutes.

Let stand at room temperature for a few hours. Then cover the pan with a sheet or board. Turn upside down and remove the pan and foil. Cover with another sheet or board and turn upside down again. Cut the cake into quarters and then each quarter into 6 bars.

Transfer the bars to a serving plate, cover airtight with plastic wrap, and refrigerate. Or pack them in a freezer box and freeze. Or they may be wrapped individually in clear cellophane or wax paper and placed in the refrigerator or freezer.

PALM BEACH BROWNIES WITH CHOCOLATE-COVERED MINTS

NOTE

When you remove the cake from the pan you might see burned and caramelized edges. (You might not—it depends on the pan.) If you do, you can leave them or cut them off. I have friends who say that this is the best part. I cut them off, but then I can't resist eating them.

32 brownies **This recipe is one of the two or three most popular recipes in all of my books. These are the thickest, gooiest, chewiest, darkest, sweetest, mostest-of-the-most chocolate bars with an almost wet center and a crisp, crunchy top. A layer of chocolate-covered mints in the middle stays whole (the mints don't melt), and they look and taste gorgeous.**

The baked cake should be refrigerated for at least a few hours or overnight, or frozen for an hour or two before it is cut into bars.

- **8 ounces unsweetened chocolate**
- **8 ounces (2 sticks) unsalted butter**
- **8 ounces (generous 2 cups) walnut halves or pieces**
- **5 large eggs (1 cup)**
- **2 teaspoons vanilla extract**
- **½ teaspoon almond extract**
- **¼ teaspoon salt**
- **1 tablespoon plus 1 teaspoon instant espresso or coffee powder**
- **3¾ cups sugar**
- **1⅔ cups *sifted* all-purpose flour**
- **2½ (12-ounce) bags York chocolate-covered Peppermint Patties (Miniature Classics), unwrapped**

Adjust an oven rack one-third up from the bottom and preheat oven to 425 degrees. Line a 13 x 9 x 2-inch pan as follows: Invert the pan and center a 17-inch length of nonstick aluminum foil, shiny side down, over the pan. With your hands, press down the sides and corners of the foil on the pan. Then remove the foil, turn the pan right side up, and place the foil in the pan. Very carefully press it into place in the pan. Now, to butter the foil, place a piece of butter (additional to that in ingredients) in the pan, and put the pan in the oven. When the butter is melted, use a pastry brush or a piece of crumpled wax paper to spread the butter all over the foil. Set the prepared pan aside.

Place the chocolate and butter in the top of a large double boiler over hot water on moderate heat, or in a 4- to 6-cup heavy saucepan over low heat. Stir occasionally until the chocolate and butter are melted. Stir to mix. Remove from the heat and set aside. (Or you may wish to zap this in a microwave

continues

one minute at a time at 50 percent power until melted.)

Break any walnut halves into large pieces; set aside.

In the large bowl of an electric mixer, beat the eggs with the vanilla and almond extracts, salt, espresso, and sugar at high speed for 10 minutes. On low speed, add the chocolate mixture (which may still be warm) and beat only until mixed. Then add the flour and again beat on low speed only until mixed. Remove the bowl from the mixer.

Stir in the nuts.

Spoon half the mixture (about 3½ cups) into the prepared pan and smooth the top.

Place a layer of the mints, touching each other and the edges of the pan, all over the chocolate layer. (You will not use all the mints; there will be some left over.)

Spoon the remaining chocolate mixture all over the mints and smooth the top.

Bake for 35 minutes (but begin checking the brownies after 25 minutes to prevent burning, as individual ovens vary), reversing the pan front to back once to ensure even baking. At the end of 35 minutes the cake will have a firm crust on top, but if you insert a toothpick in the middle it will come out wet and covered with chocolate. Nevertheless, it is done. *Do not bake any longer.*

Remove the pan from the oven; let stand until cool. Cover the pan with a cookie sheet and invert the pan and the sheet. Remove the pan and foil lining. Cover the cake with a length of wax paper and another cookie sheet and invert again, leaving the cake right side up.

Now the cake must be refrigerated for a few hours or overnight before it is cut into bars.

When you are ready to cut the cake, use a long, heavy knife with a sharp blade, either serrated or straight—try both. Cut the cake into quarters. Cut each quarter in half, cutting through the long sides. Finally, cut each piece into 4 bars, cutting through the long sides. (I think these are better in narrow bar shapes than in squares.)

Pack in an airtight box, or wrap individually in clear cellophane, wax paper, or foil.

These freeze perfectly and can be served very cold or at room temperature.

BROWNIES

24 or 32 brownies **These are the Brownies with which I started my reputation as a pastry chef when I was about ten years old. People who barely knew me, knew my Brownies. Since I always wrapped them individually I usually carried a few to give out. I occasionally run into people I never knew well and haven't seen in many years, and the first thing they say is, "I remember your Brownies." Sometimes they have forgotten my name—but they always remember my Brownies. I have continually revised the recipe over the years.**

- **5 ounces unsweetened chocolate**
- **6 ounces (1½ sticks) unsalted butter**
- **1 tablespoon instant espresso or coffee powder**
- **4 large eggs**
- **½ teaspoon salt**
- **2 cups sugar**
- **1 teaspoon vanilla extract**
- **¼ teaspoon almond extract**
- **1 cup *sifted* all-purpose flour**
- **10 ounces (generous 2½ cups) walnut halves or large pieces**

Adjust rack one-third up from the bottom of the oven and preheat oven to 450 degrees. Butter a 10½ x 15½ x 1-inch rimmed baking sheet, and then line it with aluminum foil as follows: Turn the pan upside down. Center a piece of foil 18 to 19 inches long (12 inches wide) over the pan, shiny side down. Fold down the sides and corners to shape the foil. Remove the foil, turn the pan right side up, place the shaped foil in the pan, and press it carefully into place. Brush the foil all over with melted butter.

Melt the chocolate and butter in a heavy saucepan over low heat or in the top of a large double boiler over hot water on moderate heat. Stir with a small wire whisk to blend. When melted and smooth, add the instant coffee and stir to dissolve. Remove from the heat and set aside to cool.

Meanwhile, in the small bowl of an electric mixer, beat the eggs and salt until slightly fluffy. Gradually add the sugar and continue to beat at medium-high speed for 15 minutes, until the mixture forms a ribbon when the beaters are raised. Transfer to large mixer bowl.

Add the vanilla and almond extracts to the cooled chocolate mixture. On lowest speed, add the chocolate mixture to the egg mixture, scraping the bowl with a rubber spatula and beating *only enough to blend*. Still using lowest speed and with a rubber spatula, add the flour, again beating *only enough to blend*. Fold in the nuts, handling the mixture as little as possible.

Pour into prepared pan and spread smooth. Place in oven. *Immediately* reduce oven temperature to 400 degrees. Bake for 21 to 22 minutes. Test with a toothpick. It should come out just barely dry. Do not

continues ↘

overbake. Brownies should be slightly moist inside.

Remove from oven. Immediately cover with a large rack or cookie sheet and invert. Remove the pan and foil. Cover with a large rack and invert again. After 10 or 15 minutes, invert once again only for a moment to make sure that the Brownies are not sticking to the rack.

Cool completely and then chill for about 30 minutes or a bit longer in the freezer, or overnight in the refrigerator. Transfer to a large cutting board.

To mark portions evenly, measure with a ruler and mark with toothpicks to get the number and size you desire. Use a long, thin, very sharp knife, or one with serrated edge. Cut with a sawing motion into squares. I wrap these individually in clear cellophane, but you may package them in any way that is airtight — do not let them stand around to dry out.

FUDGE BROWNIES

24 brownies **On the theory that there can't be too much of a good thing, here is still another brownie—another fudgy, moist, candylike, dark-chocolate bar cookie.**

NOTE

If you overbeat the eggs or the eggs and sugar, it will make the brownies cakey, spongy, and dry, instead of moist.

- **4 ounces unsweetened chocolate**
- **4 ounces (1 stick) unsalted butter, cut into large pieces**
- **3 large eggs**
- **1½ cups sugar**
- **1 teaspoon vanilla extract**
- **Pinch of salt**
- **¾ cup *sifted* all-purpose flour**
- OPTIONAL: **2½ ounces (¾ cup) walnuts, cut or broken into medium-size pieces (these are equally good with or without the nuts)**

Adjust a rack one-third up from the bottom of the oven and preheat oven to 350 degrees. Prepare a 9-inch square pan as follows: Turn it upside down and place a 12-inch square of aluminum foil shiny side down over the inverted pan. Turn down the sides and corners of the foil just to shape it. Remove the foil, turn the pan right side up, and place the foil in the pan. In order not to tear the foil, place a folded towel or a pot holder in the pan and, pressing against the towel or pot holder, press the foil gently into place. Coat the foil with soft or melted butter, spreading it thinly with a pastry brush or crumpled wax paper.

Place the chocolate and butter in the top of a small double boiler over hot water on moderate heat. Cover and cook until almost melted. Remove the cover and stir until completely melted and smooth. Then remove the top of the double boiler and set it aside to cool slightly.

In the small bowl of an electric mixer, beat the eggs at high speed for only about half a minute, until foamy and slightly increased in volume. On low speed, gradually add the sugar and beat for only a few seconds to mix. Add the vanilla, salt, and chocolate mixture, scraping the bowl with a rubber spatula and beating only until barely mixed. Do not overbeat (see Note). Now add the flour, still scraping the bowl and beating only until mixed.

Remove the bowl from the mixer and, if you are using the walnuts, fold them in.

Turn the mixture into the prepared pan and smooth the top.

Bake for 35 minutes or a few minutes longer, until a toothpick inserted in the center of the cake comes out barely clean. The inside should still be soft. Do not overbake.

Remove the pan from the oven, place it on a rack, and let it stand for 45 minutes to

continues ↘

1 hour, until the bottom of the pan is only slightly warm. Cover the cake with a rack, invert, and remove the cake pan and foil. Cover the cake again with a rack or a small cookie sheet and invert again.

In order to cut the cake neatly, it is best to chill it first in the freezer or refrigerator. If you partially freeze it, it will cut perfectly.

Slide the chilled cake onto a cutting board and, with a long, sharp knife or a finely serrated one, cut it into bars. The bars may be placed on a tray and covered airtight with plastic wrap or stored airtight in a plastic freezer box — or, preferably, wrap each bar in clear cellophane or wax paper.

TEXAS COWBOY BARS

24 bars **Rich, he-man oatmeal bars with a baked-in soft date filling.**

FILLING

- **8 ounces (1 cup) pitted dates**
- **1 cup water**
- **1 cup granulated sugar**
- **Finely grated zest of 1 large lemon**

CRUST

- **1½ cups *sifted* all-purpose flour**
- **½ teaspoon salt**
- **1 cup firmly packed dark brown sugar**
- **1½ cups old-fashioned or quick-cooking (not instant) rolled oats**
- **2 ounces (generous ½ cup) walnuts or pecans, cut medium fine**
- **8 ounces (2 sticks) unsalted butter, melted**

FOR THE FILLING

Cut the dates into medium-size pieces. Place the dates, water, and granulated sugar in a heavy 2-quart saucepan over moderate heat and bring to a boil, stirring occasionally. Continue to boil, stirring occasionally, for 10 to 12 minutes, until the mixture is thick. Watch it carefully toward the end: As it begins to thicken, it will bubble and splash; reduce the heat as necessary. Stir in the grated lemon zest and set aside to cool to lukewarm.

FOR THE CRUST

Adjust a rack one-third up from the bottom of the oven and preheat oven to 350 degrees. Prepare a 9-inch square cake pan as follows: Turn the pan upside down and place a 12-inch square of aluminum foil over it. Turn down the sides and corners of the foil just to shape. Lift off the foil, turn the pan right side up, and place the foil in the pan. In order not to tear the foil, place a folded towel or a pot holder in the pan and, pressing against the towel or pot holder, press the foil gently into place. Butter the foil; this is most easily done with melted butter and a pastry brush.

Place the flour, salt, and brown sugar in a mixing bowl and stir to mix. Mix in the oats and nuts. Add the melted butter and stir well until completely mixed.

Remove 1 generous cup of the mixture and set it aside for the topping. Place the remaining crust mixture over the bottom of the prepared pan and press it firmly with your fingertips to make a smooth, even layer.

Cover the crust with the filling and spread evenly. Sprinkle the reserved crust mixture evenly over the filling. Press gently with your fingertips to make a smooth, even layer.

Bake for 45 minutes.

Cool in the pan for 45 minutes. Cover with a rack or a cookie sheet and invert. Remove the pan and the aluminum foil. Cover with a rack and very gently invert again — handle with care.

Cool completely and then chill briefly in the freezer or refrigerator until the cake is firm enough to be cut.

Use a long, thin, sharp knife to cut the cake into squares or bars.

CALIFORNIA FRUIT BARS

About 32 bars **We were living in La Jolla in a house right on the beach. It was a spectacular location with a picture-postcard view. But the thing I looked forward to the most each day was food shopping: The fruits and vegetables bowled me over. Even when we didn't need anything, I went just to look. In my favorite market, located in what had been a private home and staffed by a crew of friendly young people, they sold these fruit bars to customers who arrived early enough; the bars sold out quickly. When I brought them some brownies, they offered me this recipe.**

These are butterless, wonderfully chewy, chock-full of nuts and dried fruits, brown-sugar-caramelly, and delicious. They keep well, they travel well, they are good for mailing. As a matter of fact, they are good for everything.

- **1 cup firmly packed assorted dried fruits (in La Jolla they use dates, figs, apricots, and raisins — or see Variations)**
- **4 large eggs**
- **1 (1-pound) box light brown sugar (2¼ firmly packed cups)**
- **¼ teaspoon salt**
- **1 teaspoon vanilla extract**
- **2 cups *sifted* all-purpose flour**
- **7 ounces (2 cups) walnut halves or large pieces**

Adjust a rack one-third up from the bottom of the oven and preheat oven to 400 degrees. Line a 10½ x 15½ x 1-inch rimmed baking sheet with foil as follows: Turn the pan over. Center a length of foil about 18 inches long, shiny side down, over the pan. With your hands, fold down the sides and corners to shape the foil. Remove the foil and turn the pan over again. Put the foil in the pan and press it firmly into place. To butter the foil, place a piece of butter in the pan and put it in the oven to melt. Then, with a pastry brush or crumpled wax paper, spread the melted butter over the foil; set the pan aside.

With scissors, cut the dried fruit (except the raisins) into small pieces.

Steam all the fruit: Place in a vegetable steamer over shallow water (not touching the fruit) in a saucepan, cover, and place on high heat. When the water comes to a boil, reduce the heat and let simmer for 15 minutes. Uncover and set aside. The fruit should be very soft and moist.

In a 2½- to 3-quart saucepan, beat the eggs with a beater or a whisk to mix well. Add the sugar and stir with a rubber spatula to mix. Place over medium-low heat, stir, and scrape the bottom and sides with the rubber spatula for 10 to 15 minutes, until the sugar is dissolved; taste to test. Remove from the heat.

Add the salt, vanilla, and then the flour 1 cup at a time. Beat briskly with a heavy whisk to incorporate the flour smoothly. Stir in the fruit and mix well to be sure that the fruit is not lumped together. Now stir in the nuts.

Turn into the prepared pan and spread to distribute the fruit and nuts all over. Smooth the top. It will be a thin layer; be sure it is the same thickness all over (watch the corners).

Bake for 15 to 20 minutes, until the top is a rich golden color and shiny. If the cake is not browning evenly after 10 to 12 minutes, reverse the pan front to back.

Let stand until cool. Cover with a cookie sheet, turn the pan and the sheet over, remove the pan, and very gradually peel off the foil. Cover with wax paper and another cookie sheet and turn over again.

Slide the cake and the wax paper onto a cutting board. With a ruler and toothpicks, mark the cake into even sections. Use a long, sharp knife to cut the bars. These are chewy and they might want to stick to the knife (they will stick if you cut them too soon, but not if you wait a while); if you have any trouble, spray the blade lightly with cooking spray.

I recommend that you wrap these individually in clear cellophane, wax paper, or foil; plastic wrap is too hard to handle.

VARIATIONS

The 1 cup "assorted dried fruits" called for is a variable ingredient. I recently made these with 1 cup (8 ounces) dried apricots and 1 cup (8 ounces) dried figs. I cut both the apricots and the figs, with scissors, into slices—some rather coarse. The bars were yummy. (Because of this larger amount of fruit the cake was thicker and took a little longer to bake.)

California Pecan Bars: Omit the dried fruits and use 3 cups pecans, toasted, in place of the 2 cups walnuts.

BRITTLE PEANUT BARS

32 bars **These are hard, chewy, and crunchy like brittle candy.**

- **8 ounces (2 sticks) unsalted butter**
- **1 cup sugar**
- **2 cups *sifted* all-purpose flour**
- **4 ounces (1 cup) salted peanuts, chopped into medium-size pieces**

Adjust a rack to the center of the oven and preheat oven to 375 degrees.

In the large bowl of an electric mixer, cream the butter. Add the sugar and beat to mix well. On low speed, gradually add the flour, scraping the bowl with a rubber spatula and beating only until the dough holds together. Mix in one-half of the nuts (reserve the remaining nuts for topping).

Turn the dough into an unbuttered 15½ x 10½ x 1-inch rimmed baking sheet. Dip your fingertips in flour and use them to press the dough into a thin layer. Don't worry about smoothing the layer now; that will come soon. Sprinkle the reserved nuts evenly over the dough.

Place a large piece of wax paper over the nuts. With a small rolling pin or a straight-sided glass, roll over the paper to press the nuts firmly into the top of the dough and to smooth the dough at the same time.

Bake for 23 to 25 minutes, until golden brown. Reverse the pan once during baking to ensure even browning. The cake will puff up during baking and then sink, leaving the edges higher and the surface slightly wrinkled.

Cool in the pan for about 5 minutes and then, while the cake is still warm, cut into bars. (When cool, it will become too hard and brittle to cut.)

With a wide metal spatula, remove the bars from the pan and finish cooling them on racks.

LEBKUCHEN

28 large cookies **Lebkuchen are traditional German cookies baked at Christmastime. They are usually the first cookies baked for the holiday season because they not only keep well for weeks, but they get better as they age. There are many varieties, although most contain honey, spices, and candied fruits. And most, like these, stand overnight after they are shaped and before they are baked. These are rolled out with a rolling pin and cut with a knife into oblongs. As soon as they are baked they are brushed with a white sugar glaze. They are very firm and chewy, mildly spiced, and just as delicious in the summer as in the winter.**

These take longer to prepare than most cookies do, but they are worth it.

NOTE

When I bake these, I double the recipe. But it takes hours, and it spreads out of the kitchen into the living room and dining room.

- **6 ounces (scant 1¼ cups) blanched almonds**
- **2 large eggs**
- **½ teaspoon baking powder**
- **¼ teaspoon salt**
- **½ teaspoon ground cinnamon**
- **½ teaspoon ground cloves**
- **1 cup granulated sugar**
- **1 tablespoon plus 1½ teaspoons brandy**
- **⅓ cup honey**
- **¾ cup (generous 4 ounces) mixed candied citron, candied lemon peel, and candied orange peel, finely diced**
- **About 3½ cups *sifted* cake flour (use a triple sifter, or sift the flour three times before measuring)**

GLAZE

- **1½ cups strained or *sifted* confectioners' sugar**
- **Scant 1 tablespoon fresh lemon juice**
- **Scant 1 tablespoon boiling water**

The almonds must be ground to a fine powder; this can be done in a food processor or a nut grinder (see page 19). Set the ground almonds aside.

In the small bowl of an electric mixer, beat the eggs for several minutes, until they are slightly thickened. While beating, add the baking powder, salt, cinnamon, and cloves, and then gradually add the granulated sugar. Continue to beat for a few minutes, until the mixture is pale and forms a ribbon when the beaters are raised.

Transfer to the large bowl of the mixer. On low speed, add the ground almonds, brandy, honey, and then the diced candied fruit. Gradually add about 3 cups of the flour, scraping the bowl with a rubber spatula and beating only until incorporated. Remove from the mixer. With a large wooden spoon, stir in the remaining flour—it will be a very stiff dough.

(However, if the dough is too wet or too sticky to be rolled out, add a bit more flour, but not unless you are sure you need it. It is best to first flour a pastry cloth and rolling pin and try to roll about one-third of the dough. If it needs more flour, return it to the bowl and work in as much as you need.) Let the dough stand while you prepare the cookie sheets.

These cookies will stick to plain aluminum foil. Therefore it is necessary either to butter and flour the foil, or to use baking parchment. Nonstick cookie sheets will work too, but since these stand overnight on the paper or cookie sheets, you might not have enough nonstick sheets. Prepare the foil or paper (cut the foil or paper to fit the sheets; butter and then flour the foil), or have the nonstick sheets ready.

Turn the dough out onto a well-floured pastry cloth, flour your hands, and form the dough into a heavy cylinder. Cut it into thirds. Working with one piece at a time, form the dough into a rectangle and flour it on all sides. Roll on the floured pastry cloth with a floured rolling pin into a ¼-inch-thick rectangle. Turn it over as necessary to keep both the top and bottom floured.

It is easiest to cut the cookies with a large, heavy knife. The blade will become sticky after almost every cut unless you keep it wet. Either wipe it with a damp cloth, or hold it under running water, or dip it in a deep pitcher of water. Cut the dough into 2 x 4-inch rectangles.

To transfer the cookies, use a wide metal spatula. (If the cookies lose their shape slightly while being transferred, just straighten them with the edge of the spatula.) Place the cookies, as you cut them, on the foil, paper, or nonstick sheets, about ½ inch apart.

Press the scraps together, reroll, cut out more cookies, and transfer to foil, paper, or sheets.

Cover the cookies loosely with plastic wrap and let stand overnight.

To bake, adjust two racks to divide the oven into thirds and preheat oven to 325 degrees.

Place one sheet of cookies in the oven, and wait 5 minutes before starting the second sheet, so they do not all finish baking at once. Bake for 20 minutes, until the cookies are lightly colored all over, reversing the sheets top to bottom and front to back once during baking to ensure even baking.

While the cookies are baking, prepare the glaze.

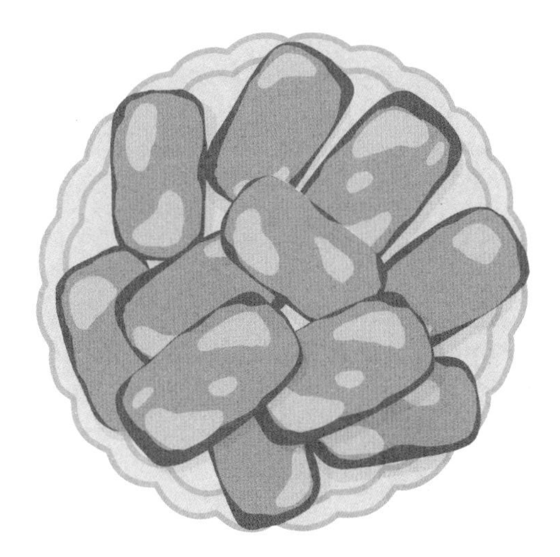

continues ↘

FOR THE GLAZE

Stir the glaze ingredients together in a small bowl. The mixture should be thick but fluid, as thick as molasses. If necessary, adjust with more sugar or liquid.

When the cookies are baked, with a wide metal spatula, transfer them to racks set over foil, wax paper, or a brown paper bag. Immediately, with a pastry brush, brush the glaze on the hot cookies. The heat will melt the glaze and make it almost transparent. Let stand to dry.

Store airtight. I wrap these individually in clear cellophane. They will be very crisp, but they will soften, as they should, after a few days.

PALM BEACH PINEAPPLE SQUARES

24 to 36 bars **These have a soft cakey chocolate bottom and a pineapple topping.**

- **1½ cups *sifted* all-purpose flour**
- **1½ teaspoons baking powder**
- **¼ teaspoon salt**
- **2 ounces unsweetened chocolate**
- **1 (8-ounce) can (1 cup) crushed pineapple**
- **6 ounces (1½ sticks) unsalted butter**
- **1 teaspoon vanilla extract**
- **1½ cups sugar**
- **3 large eggs**
- **Finely grated zest of 1 lemon**
- **4 ounces (generous 1 cup) walnuts, cut into medium-size pieces**

Adjust a rack one-third up from the bottom of the oven and preheat oven to 375 degrees. Butter a 13 x 9 x 2-inch pan and then dust it all over lightly with fine dry bread crumbs; invert the pan to shake out excess.

Sift together the flour, baking powder, and salt and set aside.

Melt the chocolate in the top of a small double boiler over hot water on moderate heat and then set aside to cool.

Place the pineapple in a strainer set over a bowl and let stand to drain.

In the large bowl of an electric mixer, cream the butter. Add the vanilla and sugar and beat well. Add the eggs one at a time, beating well after each addition. On low speed, add the sifted dry ingredients, scraping the bowl with a rubber spatula and beating only until thoroughly mixed.

Remove 1 cup of the mixture and place it in a medium-size bowl. Stir the lemon zest and the drained pineapple into this cup of batter. Set aside.

Add the melted chocolate to the mixture remaining in the large bowl and beat until thoroughly mixed. Stir in the nuts.

Spread the chocolate mixture in an even layer in the prepared pan. Place the pineapple mixture by small spoonfuls evenly over the chocolate layer. With the back of a small spoon, spread the pineapple mixture to make a smooth thin layer — it is all right if a bit of the chocolate shows through in places.

Bake for 40 to 45 minutes, reversing the position of the pan once to ensure even

continues ↘

browning. The cake is done when the top springs back if lightly pressed with a fingertip and the cake begins to come away from the sides of the pan.

Let the cake cool in the pan for about 15 minutes. Then cover it with a cookie sheet and invert. Remove the pan and cover the cake with a large rack. Invert again to cool completely right side up.

When completely cool, transfer the cake to a cutting board. With a long, thin, sharp knife, cut into squares or bars.

GEORGIA PECAN BARS

32 bars **The taste and texture of these will remind you of pecan pie.**

CRUST

- **1½ cups *sifted* all-purpose flour**
- **½ teaspoon baking powder**
- **½ cup firmly packed dark brown sugar**
- **4 ounces (1 stick) unsalted butter, cut into ½- to 1-inch slices**

TOPPING

- **2 large eggs**
- **1 teaspoon vanilla extract**
- **¼ cup firmly packed dark brown sugar**
- **¾ cup dark corn syrup**
- **3 tablespoons *sifted* all-purpose flour**
- **7 ounces (2 cups) pecan halves or large pieces**

Adjust a rack one-third up from the bottom of the oven and preheat oven to 350 degrees. Butter a 13 x 9 x 2-inch square cake pan as follows: Turn it upside down and place a 17-inch length of aluminum foil shiny side down over the inverted pan. Turn down the sides and corners of the foil just to shape it. Remove the foil, turn the pan right side up, and place the foil in the pan. In order not to tear the foil, place a folded towel or a pot holder in the pan and, pressing against the towel or pot holder, press the foil gently into place. Coat the foil with soft or melted butter, spreading it thinly with a pastry brush or crumpled wax paper.

FOR THE CRUST

Sift the flour and baking powder together into a bowl. Stir in the sugar. Add the pieces of butter to the bowl with the dry ingredients. With a pastry blender, cut in the butter until the mixture resembles fine meal.

Turn the crust mixture into the buttered pan. With your fingertips and the palm of your hand, press down on the crust to make a smooth, firm layer. Set aside and prepare the topping.

FOR THE TOPPING

In a bowl, beat the eggs lightly just to mix. Add the vanilla, sugar, corn syrup, and flour and beat until smooth.

Pour the topping over the crust and tilt the pan gently to form an even layer. If the pecan halves are large they may be placed evenly, rounded side up, to cover the topping completely. But if the halves are small or if you use pieces, sprinkle them over the topping.

Bake for 35 to 40 minutes, until the top is golden, reversing the position of the pan once during baking to ensure even browning. If the cake puffs up during baking, pierce it gently with a cake tester or a small, sharp knife to release the trapped air.

Do not overbake; the bars should remain slightly soft in the center.

Cool the cake in the pan for 15 to 20 minutes. Then cover the cake pan with a cookie sheet and invert. Remove the pan and foil. Cover the cake with a rack and invert again to finish cooling right side up.

When the cake is completely cool, transfer to the freezer for about 20 minutes or to the refrigerator for about an hour, until firm enough to cut.

If the cookies are cut with a plain, straight knife they will squash and look messy. Use a serrated bread knife and cut with a back-and-forth, sawing motion—they will cut perfectly. Cut into bars.

They may be placed on a serving tray and covered with plastic wrap or they may be wrapped individually in clear cellophane or wax paper. Or go ahead and freeze them.

VIENNESE MARZIPAN BARS

24 small bars **These fancy little cakes are really petits fours. They have a tender, buttery base, a thin layer of apricot preserves, a ground-almond filling, and a thin, dark-chocolate glaze.**

CRUST

- 1 cup *sifted* all-purpose flour
- ½ teaspoon baking powder
- 5⅓ tablespoons unsalted butter
- ½ cup granulated sugar
- 1 large egg yolk (reserve the white for the filling)
- 1 tablespoon milk

ALMOND FILLING

- ¼ cup apricot preserves
- 4 ounces (generous ¾ cup) blanched almonds
- ⅔ cup granulated sugar
- ¼ teaspoon salt
- 1 large egg plus 1 egg white
- ½ teaspoon vanilla extract
- Few drops of green food coloring

CHOCOLATE GLAZE

- ½ cup confectioners' sugar
- ½ ounce unsweetened chocolate
- 1 tablespoon unsalted butter
- ½ teaspoon vanilla extract
- 1 tablespoon boiling water

FOR THE CRUST

Adjust a rack one-third up from the bottom of the oven and preheat oven to 375 degrees. Butter the bottom and sides of an 8-inch square cake pan.

Sift together the flour and baking powder and set aside.

In the small bowl of an electric mixer, cream the butter. Add the granulated sugar and beat to mix well. Beat in the egg yolk and the milk. On low speed, gradually add the sifted dry ingredients, scraping the bowl with a rubber spatula and beating only until the mixture holds together.

Place the dough in the prepared pan. Press it firmly with floured fingertips to make a smooth layer. Bake for 12 to 15 minutes, or until barely colored around the edges. The crust will sink slightly when it is removed from the oven.

MEANWHILE, FOR THE FILLING

In a small bowl, stir the preserves just to soften and set aside.

Grind the almonds to a fine powder in a processor or nut grinder (see page 19) and place in a bowl. Add the granulated sugar and salt and stir with a rubber spatula to mix. Add the egg and egg white, the vanilla extract, and 2 or 3 drops of food coloring. (Add another drop or two of food coloring if necessary to make a pale pea-green.) Stir to mix thoroughly.

Spread the preserves over the hot crust, leaving a ½-inch border—it will be a thin layer of preserves. Top with the almond filling and spread to make an even layer.

Bake at 375 degrees for 25 minutes, or until the top of the cake barely

continues ↘

springs back when lightly pressed with a fingertip.

Cool completely.

FOR THE GLAZE

Strain the confectioners' sugar by pressing it with your fingertips through a strainer set over a bowl. Set aside.

Place the chocolate and butter in the top of a small double boiler over hot water on moderate heat. Cover until it is melted and then stir until smooth. Stir in the confectioners' sugar, vanilla, and water and stir again until completely smooth.

Pour the glaze over the cooled cake and spread evenly. It will be a thin layer.

Let the cake stand in the pan for an hour or longer. Then, with a small, sharp knife, cut around the sides to release. Cut the cake into quarters. With a wide metal spatula, transfer the quarters to a cutting board. If it is difficult to move the first quarter, cut it into individual portions—bars or slices. Use a fork to ease out the first few portions and then, with a wide metal spatula, transfer the remaining pieces to a cutting board and cut them into portions.

These little cakes are best after they stand for a few hours. Place them on a serving dish, cover with plastic wrap, and let stand at room temperature.

"I've had a few problems in life, but what to do with cookies has never been one of them. I give them away, and it is magic."

ICEBOX COOKIES

Somehow the word "refrigerator" just doesn't sound right for icebox cookies. The dough is shaped, wrapped, and chilled until firm enough to be sliced. Most of these recipes may be prepared ahead of time and then sliced whenever you want to bake the cookies.

MAXINES

24 cookies **Chewy, fudgy, chocolate-almond slices edged with a buttery brown-sugar layer.**

CHOCOLATE DOUGH

- **6 ounces (1 cup) semisweet chocolate morsels**
- **1 tablespoon vegetable shortening (such as Crisco)**
- **⅓ cup sweetened condensed milk**
- **½ teaspoon vanilla extract**
- **¼ teaspoon almond extract**
- **5 ounces (1 cup) blanched almonds, coarsely cut (each almond should be cut into 3 or 4 pieces)**

BROWN-SUGAR DOUGH

- **1 cup *sifted* all-purpose flour**
- **¼ teaspoon baking powder**
- **¼ teaspoon salt**
- **2 ounces (½ stick) unsalted butter**
- **½ teaspoon vanilla extract**
- **½ cup firmly packed light brown sugar**
- **1 large egg yolk**

FOR THE CHOCOLATE DOUGH

Place the chocolate and shortening in the top of a medium-size double boiler over hot water on medium heat, cover, and cook until partially melted. Uncover and stir until completely melted. Remove from heat. Stir in the condensed milk and the vanilla and almond extracts, then the almonds.

Tear off a piece of wax paper about 15 inches long. Place the dough by large spoonfuls the long way down the middle of the paper, forming a heavy strip about 10 inches long. Fold the sides of the paper up against the chocolate mixture. With your hands, press against the paper and shape the mixture into an even round or square roll 12 inches long and 1½ inches in diameter. Wrap in the paper. Slide a cookie sheet under the paper and transfer to the freezer or refrigerator until firm.

MEANWHILE, FOR THE BROWN-SUGAR DOUGH

Sift together the flour, baking powder, and salt and set aside.

In the small bowl of an electric mixer, cream the butter. Add the vanilla and sugar and beat well. Beat in the egg yolk and then, gradually, on low speed, add the sifted dry ingredients. Beat only until thoroughly mixed. The mixture will be crumbly; remove it from the mixer and press it together with your hands until it forms a ball.

Place the ball of dough on a piece of wax paper a little more than 12 inches long. With your hands, shape it into a flattened oblong. Cover with another long piece of wax paper. Roll a rolling pin over the top piece of paper to form the dough into an oblong 12 inches long and 8 inches wide. While rolling, occasionally remove and then

continues ↘

replace the top wax paper; then invert and do the same with the bottom wax paper, in order to keep both pieces of paper smooth and unwrinkled.

Remove the top piece of wax paper. Unwrap the chocolate roll and center it on the brown-sugar dough. Using the wax paper, lift one long side of the brown-sugar dough and press it firmly against the chocolate. Then lift the other side so that the sides of dough overlap slightly. (If the dough does not fit perfectly, the excess may be cut off and pressed into place where needed.)

Enclose the roll in the wax paper, then run your hands firmly over the roll to remove any air trapped between the brown-sugar dough and the chocolate mixture.

Rechill the roll only until it is firm enough to slice. (If the dough is frozen firm it will crack when sliced. If this happens, let it stand briefly at room temperature.)

Before baking, adjust two racks to divide the oven into thirds and preheat oven to 375 degrees.

Unwrap the roll of dough and place it on a cutting board. With a sharp knife, cut slices ½ inch thick—no thinner! Place the slices flat, 1 inch apart, on unbuttered cookie sheets. Bake for about 12 minutes, until the cookies are lightly colored. Reverse sheets top to bottom and front to back once during baking to ensure even browning.

Let the cookies stand on sheets for a minute or so until firm enough to transfer, then, with a wide metal spatula, transfer cookies to racks to cool.

NEW MEXICAN CHOCOLATE ICEBOX COOKIES

66 cookies **These are not solid chocolate but are filled with chopped chocolate chips.**

NOTE

Other nuts may be substituted — walnuts, pecans, cashews, or hazelnuts — cut into medium-size pieces. Or you can leave out the nuts if you prefer.

- **3½ cups *sifted* all-purpose flour**
- **1 teaspoon baking soda**
- **½ teaspoon salt**
- **½ teaspoon ground nutmeg**
- **6 ounces (1 cup) semisweet chocolate morsels**
- **5⅓ tablespoons unsalted butter**
- **⅓ cup vegetable shortening (such as Crisco)**
- **2 cups firmly packed dark brown sugar**
- **1 tablespoon vanilla extract**
- **1 large egg**
- **½ cup sour cream**
- **3 ounces (generous ½ cup) pignoli (pine nuts) (see Note)**

Prepare a 10 x 5 x 3-inch loaf pan as follows: Cut two long strips of wax paper or aluminum foil, one for the length and one for the width. The pieces should be long enough to fold over the top of the pan and cover the surface completely. Fit them carefully in the pan. Set aside.

Sift together the flour, baking soda, salt, and nutmeg and set aside.

Grind the chocolate in a blender, or chop it fine with a long, heavy knife on a cutting board; it must be fine — any large chunks would make it difficult to slice the cookies. Set aside.

In the large bowl of an electric mixer, cream together the butter and shortening. Beat in the sugar and mix well, then beat in the vanilla and egg and then the sour cream. On low speed, add the sifted dry ingredients, scraping the bowl with a rubber spatula and beating only until thoroughly incorporated. Finally, mix in the ground or chopped chocolate and the nuts.

Pack the dough firmly into the prepared pan. Fold the paper or foil over the top and press down firmly to smooth the dough.

Freeze for 6 to 8 hours (or longer if you wish), until the dough is firm all the way through.

Before baking, adjust two racks to divide the oven into thirds and preheat oven to 400 degrees. Cut aluminum foil to fit cookie sheets.

Remove the block of dough from the pan. Remove the paper and place the dough on a cutting board. With a long, heavy knife, slice the block of dough in half the long

continues ↘

way. Rewrap one piece and return it to the freezer. With a sharp knife, cut the frozen dough into slices a generous ¼ inch thick. Place them 1½ to 2 inches apart on the cut foil. (The reserved half of the dough may be sliced now or later, as you wish.)

Slide cookie sheets under the foil and bake the cookies for about 10 minutes, until they are semi-firm to the touch. During baking, reverse the sheets top to bottom and front to back to ensure even browning.

Slide the foil off the sheets and, with a wide metal spatula, transfer the cookies to racks to cool.

CARDAMOM COOKIES FROM COPENHAGEN

40 cookies **This is a classic Danish butter cookie—plain, light, crisp, and dry, with a definite cardamom flavor.**

- **2 cups *sifted* all-purpose flour**
- **¼ teaspoon baking soda**
- **1½ teaspoons ground cardamom**
- **4 ounces (1 stick) unsalted butter**
- **½ teaspoon vanilla extract**
- **½ cup firmly packed light brown sugar**
- **⅓ cup light cream**
- **2½ ounces (generous ½ cup) slivered almonds (julienne-shaped pieces)**

Sift together the flour, baking soda, and cardamom and set aside.

In the large bowl of an electric mixer, cream the butter. Beat in the vanilla and then add the sugar and beat well.
On low speed, alternately add the sifted dry ingredients in three additions, alternating with the cream in two additions, scraping the bowl with a rubber spatula and beating only until thoroughly mixed. Remove from the mixer and, with a rubber or wooden spatula, stir in the almonds.

Turn the dough out onto a smooth work surface or piece of wax paper. Knead it slightly and then, with your hands, form it into a smooth roll or oblong about 2 inches wide and 10 inches long.

Wrap the dough in plastic wrap or wax paper and place in the freezer for several hours, or as much longer as you wish—this dough slices best when it is frozen solid.

Before baking, adjust two racks to divide the oven into thirds and preheat oven to 350 degrees.

Unwrap the dough and place it on a cutting board. With a long, heavy, sharp knife, cut the dough into ¼-inch slices and place them 1 inch apart on unbuttered cookie sheets—these do not spread or change shape during baking.

Bake for about 15 minutes, until the cookies are only slightly sandy-colored on the edges—these barely color, if at all, on the tops. Reverse the position of the sheets top to bottom and front to back as necessary during baking to ensure even browning.

With a metal spatula, transfer the cookies to racks to cool.

NEAPOLITANS

80 cookies **Dramatic and unusual, these Italian cookies present an interesting way of making icebox cookies. You will make two entirely separate recipes for the dough—and the two doughs must chill together overnight.**

DARK DOUGH

- 3 cups *sifted* all-purpose flour
- ¼ teaspoon salt
- 1 teaspoon baking soda
- ½ teaspoon ground cloves
- ½ teaspoon ground cinnamon
- 6 ounces (1 cup) semisweet chocolate morsels
- 8 ounces (2 sticks) unsalted butter
- 2 teaspoons instant coffee powder
- 1½ cups firmly packed dark brown sugar
- 2 large eggs
- 5 ounces (1 cup) nuts, either whole pignoli (pine nuts) or green pistachios, or walnuts or pecans, cut into medium-size pieces

LIGHT DOUGH

- 2 cups *sifted* all-purpose flour
- ¼ teaspoon salt
- ¼ teaspoon baking soda
- 4 ounces (1 stick) unsalted butter
- 1 teaspoon vanilla extract
- ½ teaspoon almond extract
- ¾ cup granulated sugar
- 2 tablespoons water
- 1 large egg
- 3½ ounces (¾ cup) currants, unchopped, or raisins, coarsely chopped
- Finely grated zest of 1 large lemon
- 12 candied red cherries, cut into quarters
- 12 candied green cherries, cut into quarters

NOTES

If you use wax paper instead of foil to line the loaf pan, each piece should be folded so that it is two or three thicknesses. Wax paper is weaker than foil and a single layer would tear.

When slicing the cookies, if the dough crumbles and is difficult to slice, it has not chilled enough. It should be wrapped and placed in the freezer for about an hour.

You will need an 11 x 5 x 3-inch loaf pan, or any other loaf pan with an 8- to 9-cup capacity. To prepare the pan: Cut two pieces of aluminum foil or two pieces of wax paper (see Notes), one for the length and one for the width; they should be long enough so that they can be folded over the top of the pan when it is filled and cover the whole surface. Place them in the pan and set aside.

FOR THE DARK DOUGH

Sift together the flour, salt, baking soda, cloves, and cinnamon and set aside.

continues ↘

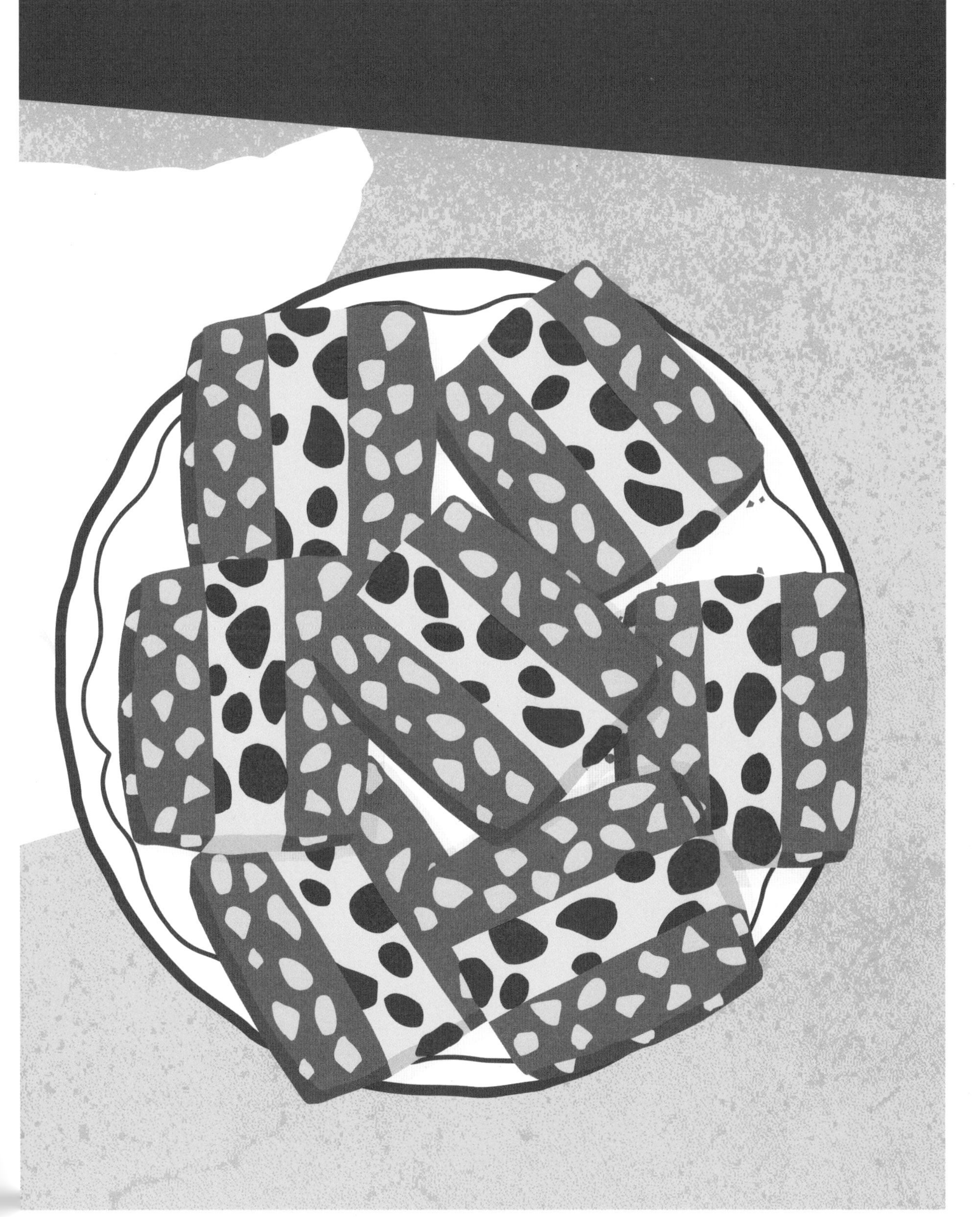

Grind the chocolate morsels in a blender, or chop them fine with a long, heavy knife on a cutting board (the chocolate must be fine, or it will be difficult to slice the cookies); set aside.

In the large bowl of an electric mixer, cream the butter. Add the coffee and brown sugar and beat well. Add the eggs and beat to mix. Beat in the ground chocolate. On low speed, gradually add the sifted dry ingredients, scraping the bowl with a rubber spatula and beating only until blended. Beat in the nuts.

Transfer the dough to another bowl, unless you have another large bowl for the electric mixer. Set the dough aside at room temperature.

FOR THE LIGHT DOUGH

Sift together the flour, salt, and baking soda and set aside.

In a clean large bowl of the electric mixer, with clean beaters, cream the butter. Add the vanilla and almond extracts, the granulated sugar, and water and beat well. Beat in the egg. On low speed, gradually add the dry ingredients, scraping the bowl with a spatula and beating only until blended. Mix in the currants or raisins, lemon zest, and both kinds of cherries.

To layer the doughs in the prepared pan: Use half (about 2¾ cups) of the dark dough and place it by spoonfuls over the bottom of the pan. Pack the dough firmly into the corners of the pan and spread it as level as possible. With another spoon, spread all of the light dough in a layer over the dark dough—again, as level as possible. Form an even top layer with the remaining dark dough. Cover the top with the foil or wax paper and, with your fingers, press down firmly to make a smooth, compact loaf.

Chill the dough overnight in its pan in the freezer or refrigerator.

Before baking, adjust two racks to divide the oven into thirds and preheat oven to 400 degrees. The cookies may be baked on unbuttered cookie sheets or on sheets lined with foil—either is OK.

To remove the dough from the pan: Use a small, narrow metal spatula or a table knife to release the dough from the corners of the pan. Fold back the foil or wax paper from the top, invert the pan onto a cutting board, and remove the pan and the foil or paper.

With a long, *heavy,* sharp knife, cut the dough in half the long way. Wrap one half and return it to the freezer or refrigerator while working with the other half.

With a very sharp knife, cut the dough into slices about ¼ inch thick. Place the slices 1 to 1½ inches apart on the cookie sheets. (If you are using foil you can cut several pieces of foil to fit the cookie sheets, place the cookies on them, and then, later, slide the cookie sheets under the foil.) The second half of the dough may be sliced and baked now or it may be frozen for future use.

Bake for about 10 minutes, reversing the cookie sheets top to bottom and front to back as necessary during baking to ensure even browning. Bake until the light dough is lightly colored, but watch them carefully—the dark dough has a tendency to burn.

Transfer the cookies to racks to cool.

PECAN BUTTERSCOTCH ICEBOX COOKIES

NOTE

These may also be baked without the foil on unbuttered cookie sheets. Without foil, the cookies will brown faster.

70 to 80 cookies **An Early American recipe from Massachusetts, these originated before baking powder was available. Instead, early recipes used baking soda plus cream of tartar. These are thin and crisp.**

- **2 cups *sifted* all-purpose flour**
- **½ teaspoon baking soda**
- **½ teaspoon cream of tartar**
- **¼ teaspoon salt**
- **4 ounces (1 stick) unsalted butter**
- **½ teaspoon vanilla extract**
- **1 cup firmly packed light brown sugar**
- **1 large egg**
- **4 ounces (generous 1 cup) pecan halves or pieces**

Sift together the flour, baking soda, cream of tartar, and salt and set aside.

In the large bowl of an electric mixer, cream the butter. Add the vanilla and sugar and beat well. Add the egg and beat until smooth. Gradually, on low speed, add the sifted dry ingredients and beat until the mixture holds together. Mix in the nuts.

Turn the dough out onto a board, smooth work surface, or piece of wax paper. The dough will be firm enough to handle and not sticky. With your hands, shape it into a long rectangle.

Place it lengthwise on a piece of wax paper about 18 inches long. Fold the paper up on the sides and, with your hands, press and smooth over the paper to form a 12- to 14-inch roll about 2 inches in diameter.

Wrap the dough in the wax paper, slide a cookie sheet under it, and transfer to the freezer or refrigerator for several hours or overnight. The dough must be very firm, preferably frozen solid, in order to slice thin enough.

Before baking, adjust two racks to divide oven into thirds and preheat oven to 375 degrees. Cut aluminum foil to fit cookie sheets (see Note).

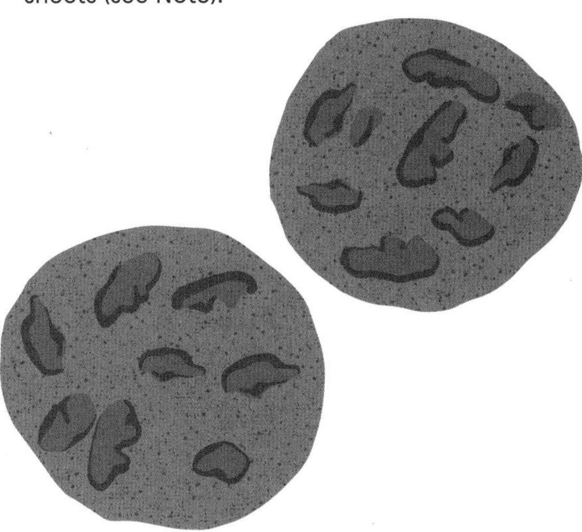

continues ↘

Unwrap the dough and place it on a cutting board. With a thin, sharp knife, cut into very thin slices — ⅛ to ¼ inch thick, or about 6 slices to an inch.

Place the slices 1 inch apart on the foil. Slide cookie sheets under the foil.

Bake for 8 to 10 minutes, until the cookies are golden brown all over, reversing the sheets top to bottom and front to back as necessary to ensure even browning.

With a wide metal spatula, transfer to racks to cool.

OATMEAL ICEBOX COOKIES

80 cookies **These are thin, crisp, and crunchy.**

- **1½ cups *sifted* all-purpose flour**
- **½ teaspoon salt**
- **1 teaspoon baking soda**
- **1 teaspoon ground ginger**
- **8 ounces (2 sticks) unsalted butter**
- **1 teaspoon vanilla extract**
- **1 cup granulated sugar**
- **1 cup firmly packed dark brown sugar**
- **2 large eggs**
- **3 cups old-fashioned or quick-cooking (not instant) rolled oats**
- **4 ounces (generous 1 cup) walnuts, cut medium fine**

Sift together the flour, salt, baking soda, and ginger and set aside.

In the large bowl of an electric mixer, cream the butter. Add the vanilla and both sugars and beat well. Add the eggs one at a time and beat to incorporate after each addition. On low speed, gradually add the sifted dry ingredients and then the oats, scraping the bowl as necessary with a rubber spatula and beating only until thoroughly mixed. Stir in the nuts.

Spread out two pieces of wax paper, each 13 to 15 inches long. Place spoonfuls of the dough lengthwise on each piece of paper to make strips 9 to 10 inches long. Fold the long sides of the papers up against the dough and, pressing against the papers with your hands, shape the dough into rectangles about 10 inches long, 3 inches wide, and 1 to 1½ inches thick. Wrap the dough in the wax paper.

Slide a cookie sheet under the two rectangles of dough and place in the freezer for an hour or two, or in the refrigerator overnight, until the dough is firm enough to slice (or longer if you wish).

Before baking, adjust two racks to divide the oven into thirds and preheat oven to 350 degrees. Cut aluminum foil to fit cookie sheets.

Working with one piece of dough at a time, unwrap and place on a cutting board. With a thin, sharp knife, cut the dough into ¼-inch slices and place them on the cut foil 2 inches apart (these will spread). Slide cookie sheets under the foil.

Bake for 12 to 14 minutes, until the cookies are well browned. Reverse the sheets top to bottom and front to back as necessary to ensure even browning.

Slide the foil off the cookie sheet and let stand for a few minutes until the foil can be easily peeled away from the backs of the cookies. Place the cookies on racks to finish cooling.

These must be stored airtight.

PEANUT BUTTER PILLOWS

16 to 20 filled cookies **Peanut butter is sandwiched between two peanut butter icebox cookies and then the cookies are baked. They are crisp; the filling is soft.**

- **1½ cups *sifted* all-purpose flour**
- **½ teaspoon baking soda**
- **¼ teaspoon salt**
- **4 ounces (1 stick) unsalted butter**
- **½ cup smooth (not chunky) peanut butter, plus more (a scant ½ cup) for the filling**
- **½ cup sugar**
- **¼ cup light corn syrup (e.g., Karo)**
- **1 tablespoon milk**

NOTE

This dough may be mixed without a mixer. Simply place the *sifted* dry ingredients and the sugar in a mixing bowl. With a pastry blender, cut in the butter and the peanut butter until the mixture resembles coarse meal. Stir in the syrup and milk. Then, on a board or a smooth work surface, knead the dough briefly with the heel of your hand until it is smooth.

Sift together the flour, baking soda, and salt and set aside.

In the small bowl of an electric mixer (or see Note), cream the butter. Add the peanut butter and sugar and beat until thoroughly mixed. Beat in the corn syrup and milk. On low speed, add the sifted dry ingredients, scraping the bowl as necessary with a rubber spatula and beating only until smooth.

Turn the dough out onto a large board or a smooth work surface. Knead it briefly and then, with your hands, form it into an even roll about 6 inches long and 2¼ to 2½ inches in diameter. Wrap the dough in wax paper. Slide cookie sheet under the paper and transfer the dough to the refrigerator and chill for several hours, or longer if you wish.

Before baking, adjust two racks to divide the oven into thirds and preheat oven to 350 degrees. Line cookie sheets with baking parchment.

With a sharp knife, cut half of the roll of dough into slices ⅛ to ¼ inch thick and, as you cut the slices, place them 2 inches apart on the cookie sheets.

Place 1 level measuring teaspoon of the additional peanut butter in the center of each cookie. Then spread the peanut butter only slightly to flatten it, leaving a ½- to ¾-inch border.

Slice the remaining half of the roll of dough (same thickness) and, as you cut each slice, place it over one of the peanut butter–topped cookies. Let the cookies stand for 2 to 3 minutes for the dough to soften slightly. Then seal the edges by pressing them lightly with the back of the tines of a fork, dipping the fork in flour as necessary to keep it from sticking. (Don't worry about slight cracks in the tops.)

Bake for 12 to 15 minutes, until the cookies are lightly colored, reversing the position of the cookie sheets top to bottom and front to back to ensure even browning. (If you bake only one sheet at a time, bake it high in the oven.)

Let the cookies stand on the sheets for about a minute. Then, with a wide metal spatula, transfer them to racks to cool.

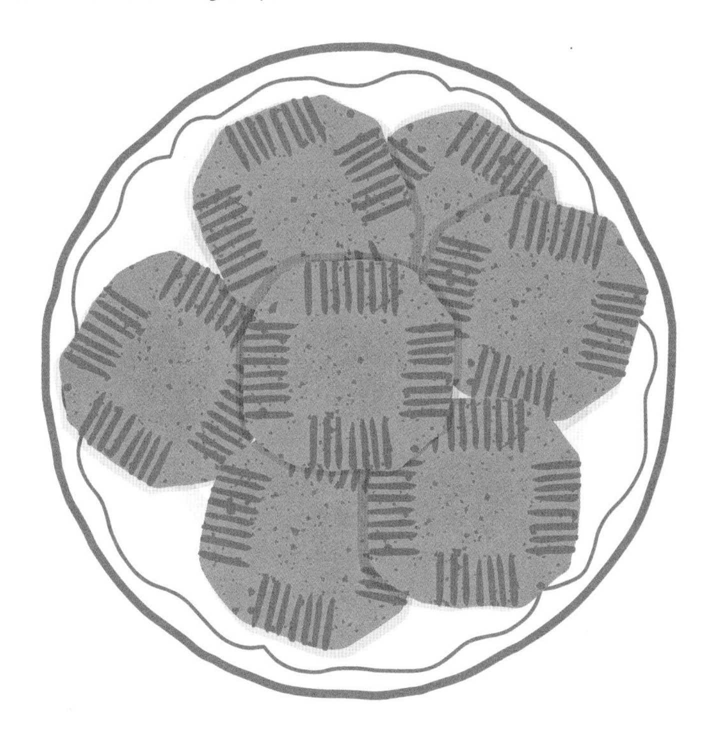

SESAME FINGERS

NOTE

Sesame seeds vary in color from so-called white (hulled) to grayish-tan (unhulled). I use the white.

48 cookies **There is an old saying in the South that sesame seeds, also known as benne seeds, bring good luck. These cookies from Charleston, South Carolina, are hard and dry and full of toasted sesame seeds. The dough should be chilled overnight in the freezer.**

- **4 ounces (¾ cup) sesame seeds (see Note)**
- **4 ounces (1 stick) unsalted butter**
- **¾ teaspoon vanilla extract**
- **¼ teaspoon salt**
- **1 cup sugar**
- **1 large egg**
- **2 cups *sifted* all-purpose flour**
- **¼ cup milk**

Place the sesame seeds in a large, heavy frying pan over medium-low heat. Stir and shake the pan constantly until the seeds are toasted to a golden-brown color. (Toasting brings out the sweet, nutty flavor of the seeds.) Be careful not to let them burn. Transfer the toasted seeds to a plate and set aside to cool.

In the large bowl of an electric mixer, cream the butter. Add the vanilla, salt, and sugar and beat to mix well. Add the egg and beat to mix. On low speed, gradually add half of the flour, then all of the milk, and finally the remaining flour, scraping the bowl with a rubber spatula and beating only until smooth after each addition. Mix in the cooled toasted sesame seeds.

If the dough is too soft at this point to form it into a block for icebox cookies, chill it in the mixing bowl, stirring occasionally, until it is slightly firm.

Tear off a piece of wax paper about 18 inches long. Place the dough by large spoonfuls lengthwise down the center of the paper to form a strip about 10 inches long. Fold up the two long sides of the paper. Press against the paper to mold the dough into a rectangle 12 inches long, 3 to 4 inches wide, and 1 inch thick.

Slide a cookie sheet under the paper and transfer the dough to the freezer. Let chill overnight.

Before baking, adjust two racks to divide the oven into thirds and preheat oven to 375 degrees. Cut aluminum foil to fit cookie sheets.

Lightly flour a section of a cutting board a little larger than the rectangle of dough. Unwrap the dough and place it on the floured board.

With a sharp, heavy knife, quickly cut the dough into ¼-inch slices and place them 1 inch apart on the cut foil. Slide cookie sheets under the foil.

Bake for about 15 minutes, reversing the position of the sheets top to bottom and front to back as necessary to ensure even browning. (If you bake only one sheet at a time, use the higher rack.) When done, the cookies will be slightly brown on the edges but still pale on the tops.

Transfer the cookies to racks to cool.

COCONUT COOKIES

About 36 cookies **These are plain, old-fashioned, thin, extra-crisp, perfectly wonderful refrigerator cookies. They are a homemade version of a famous coconut cookie that used to be sold in Havana. My Cuban friends tell me these are better. Note that the dough must be refrigerated overnight or longer before baking.**

- **3½ ounces (1 to 1⅓ cups) sweetened shredded coconut**
- **2 cups *sifted* all-purpose flour**
- **½ teaspoon baking powder**
- **¼ teaspoon salt**
- **6 ounces (1½ sticks) unsalted butter**
- **1 teaspoon vanilla extract**
- **¼ teaspoon almond extract**
- **1 cup firmly packed light or dark brown sugar**
- **1 large egg**

Place the coconut in a shallow baking pan in the center of a preheated 350-degree oven. Stir it occasionally until it is toasted to a golden color. Set aside.

Sift together the flour, baking powder, and salt and set aside.

In the large bowl of an electric mixer, cream the butter. Add the vanilla and almond extracts, then the sugar, and beat to mix. Add the egg and beat to mix. On low speed, gradually add the sifted dry ingredients, beating only to mix. Remove from the mixer and stir in the coconut.

Place the dough in the refrigerator for 20 to 30 minutes to chill a bit. Then flour your hands and a work surface. Turn the

continues ↘

dough out onto the floured surface, press it together, and shape it into a cylinder about 6 inches long and 2 to 2½ inches in diameter. Wrap in plastic wrap. Refrigerate overnight. (If this is frozen it becomes difficult to slice thin enough without cracking, but it can be refrigerated for a few days if you wish.)

Before baking, adjust two racks high in the oven, or adjust them to divide the oven into thirds. If your oven has enough adjustments, higher is better. Preheat the oven to 325 degrees.

With a very sharp knife, cut extra-thin cookies; they should be less than ¼ inch thick. Place the cookies 1 inch apart on unbuttered cookie sheets.

Bake for about 16 minutes, reversing the sheets top to bottom and front to back once during baking to ensure even baking. Watch carefully; if the cookies appear to be browning too much on the bottom, be prepared to slide an additional cookie sheet under them. Do not underbake. Bake until the cookies are lightly browned. You won't believe how wonderfully crisp these are, but only if they are baked enough. (And then they will only stay that way if they are stored airtight.)

With a wide offset metal spatula, gently transfer the cookies to a rack to cool. As soon as they are cool, package them airtight.

ALMOND SP-ICEBOX COOKIES

90 cookies **These lovely icebox cookies have almonds and spice, hence their name. They are crunchy and loaded with nuts, cinnamon, and brown sugar. They make a large batch, so they are perfect for sharing or sending as a gift.**

- **4 cups *sifted* all-purpose flour**
- **1 tablespoon ground cinnamon**
- **1 teaspoon ground ginger**
- **½ teaspoon salt**
- **1 teaspoon baking soda**
- **8 ounces (2 sticks) unsalted butter**
- **2 teaspoons instant coffee powder**
- **½ teaspoon almond extract**
- **1 cup granulated sugar**
- **1 cup firmly packed dark brown sugar**
- **3 extra-large or jumbo eggs**
- **8 to 10 ounces (2½ to 3 cups) blanched and thinly sliced almonds**

Sift together the flour, cinnamon, ginger, salt, and baking soda and set aside.

In the large bowl of an electric mixer, cream the butter. Add the coffee, almond extract, and both sugars and beat well. Add the eggs one at a time, beating until smooth after each addition. On low speed, gradually add the sifted dry ingredients, scraping the bowl with a rubber spatula and beating only until the mixture is smooth. (When most of the dry ingredients have been added the mixture might start to crawl up on the beaters; if so, finish stirring it by hand with a wooden spatula; the dough will be stiff.) With a wooden spatula and/or your bare hands, mix in the almonds.

Spread out two pieces of wax paper, each about 16 inches long. Place large spoonfuls of the dough lengthwise on each piece of paper to form heavy strips 10 to 11 inches long. Fold the long sides of the paper up against the dough and, pressing against the paper with your hands, shape each strip of dough into a smooth rectangle 12 inches long, 3 inches wide, and about 1 inch thick. Wrap the dough in the wax paper.

Slide a cookie sheet under both packages of dough and transfer them to the freezer or refrigerator for several hours or overnight (or longer if you wish). This dough slices best when it is frozen solid.

Before baking, adjust two racks to divide the oven into thirds and preheat oven to 375 degrees.

Working with one roll of dough at a time, unwrap and place on a cutting board. With a very sharp knife, cut the dough into ¼-inch slices and place 1 to 1½ inches apart on unbuttered cookie sheets.

continues ↘

Bake the cookies for about 12 minutes, reversing the position of the sheets top to bottom and front to back as necessary to ensure even browning. The cookies are done when they are slightly colored and spring back if lightly pressed with a fingertip.

With a wide metal spatula, transfer the cookies to racks to cool.

PENNIES FROM HEAVEN

About 70 small cookie sandwiches **Tiny cookie sandwiches, delicate and dainty, with a dough that is a delicious classic shortbread. It is baked in rounds not much larger than quarters, and they are sandwiched together with just a bit of buttercream. Make these for a tea party. Or serve them alongside a fruit or ice cream dessert.**

The recipe is from Chris Gargone, the executive pastry chef at Remi, which Gael Greene called the best Italian restaurant in New York City. At Remi they served these on a plate of assorted cookies. However I serve them, I don't have enough. They are too good.

NOTE

I want to thank my good friends Nick Malgieri and the late Richard Sax. Without their help, I couldn't have gotten this recipe.

- ½ cup old-fashioned rolled oats (to use when shaping the dough into long, thin rolls)
- 1 cup plus 1 tablespoon *sifted* all-purpose flour
- 1 cup plus 1 tablespoon strained cornstarch
- 1 cup plus 1 tablespoon confectioners' sugar
- 8 ounces (2 sticks) unsalted butter
- Pinch of salt
- 1 teaspoon vanilla extract

FILLING

- 3 ounces (¾ stick) unsalted butter
- ¼ teaspoon vanilla extract
- ¼ teaspoon dark rum
- 2 teaspoons heavy cream
- ½ cup confectioners' sugar

Place the oats in the bowl of a food processor fitted with the metal chopping blade. Pulse the machine several times, until the oats are powdery. Remove from the processor and set aside.

It is not necessary to wash and dry the processor bowl and blade now.

Place the flour, cornstarch, and sugar in the bowl of the food processor fitted with the metal chopping blade. Pulse once or twice to mix. Cut the butter into ½-inch pieces and add to the flour mixture, along with the salt and vanilla. Process only until the ingredients form a ball and hold together.

Work with half the dough at a time.

Spread the processed oats on a large board or work surface. Place the dough on the oats. With your hands, form the dough into a cylinder. Roll gently, back and forth, using both hands. Start at the center and work your hands outward—as you roll—to the ends. Roll until the dough is 11 inches long, about 1½ inches in diameter, and evenly shaped. Set aside. Roll the remaining half of the dough to the same size and shape.

continues

Place the rolls on a cookie sheet (you can just roll them onto it) and refrigerate for about an hour (or longer if you wish).

Before baking, adjust a rack in the center of the oven and preheat oven to 325 degrees. Line cookie sheets with baking parchment or aluminum foil, shiny side up.

Use a knife with a very sharp and very thin blade. Cut the dough into slices about ⅛ inch thick or a little thicker. Place the slices 1 inch apart on the lined sheets.

Bake one sheet at a time for 14 to 16 minutes, until the cookies are sandy-colored around the edges (they can still be pale in the centers). Reverse the sheet front to back once during baking to ensure even browning. (If some are done before others, remove them individually.)

Transfer the cookies to a rack to cool or slide the paper or foil off the sheet and let stand until the cookies are cool. You can slice and bake both rolls now or, if you wish, you can wrap and freeze one to bake at some other time.

FOR THE FILLING

In the small bowl of an electric mixer, beat the butter until soft. Beat in the vanilla, rum, and cream. Then beat in the sugar.

When well mixed, transfer to a small bowl for ease in handling. Place a small dab (a scant teaspoon) of the filling on the bottom of one cookie. Place another cookie over it, bottoms together, and press gently all around to spread out the filling. There should not be enough to show; it should really be just enough filling to hold the two cookies together. Continue sandwiching all the cookies.

Place them in the refrigerator briefly, only long enough to harden the filling.

You will probably have leftover filling. It can be saved in the freezer for the next time you make these.

Store the cookie sandwiches in an airtight container.

PINWHEELS

56 cookies **This is an attractive crisp, black-and-white cookie (the two doughs are rolled together like a jelly roll). They are fancy cookies but not difficult to make.**

- **1¾ cups *sifted* all-purpose flour**
- **½ teaspoon baking powder**
- **¼ teaspoon salt**
- **1 ounce unsweetened chocolate**
- **4 ounces (1 stick) unsalted butter**
- **½ teaspoon vanilla extract**
- **¾ cup sugar**
- **1 large egg**
- **1 teaspoon instant coffee powder (see Notes)**
- **¼ teaspoon almond extract**
- **⅓ cup pecans, finely chopped**

Sift together the flour, baking powder, and salt and set aside.

Melt the chocolate in the top of a small double boiler over hot water on moderate heat. Set aside to cool.

In the large bowl of an electric mixer, cream the butter. Add the vanilla and then the sugar and beat to mix well. Add the egg and beat well. On low speed, gradually add the sifted dry ingredients, scraping the bowl with a rubber spatula and beating only until thoroughly mixed.

Place half of the dough (scant 1 cup) in another mixing bowl. To that one-half, add the melted chocolate and the coffee powder, mix thoroughly, and set aside.

To the other half of the dough, add the almond extract and the pecans, mix thoroughly, and set aside.

Tear off four pieces of wax paper, each about 17 inches long. On one piece, place one of the doughs. Cover with another piece of paper. Flatten the dough well with your hands. With a rolling pin, roll over the paper to roll the dough into an oblong 14 x 9 inches. (During rolling, check both pieces of wax paper — if the paper wrinkles, peel it off and then replace it to remove the wrinkles.) When the dough is almost the right size, remove the top piece of paper, cut away excess dough (from the sides), and place it where needed (in the corners). Be careful not to have the edges thinner than the center or there will be an air space in each end of the roll. Replace wax paper and roll the dough again to

NOTES

Powdered coffee is better than granules for this recipe. If you do not have powdered coffee, any other instant type may be powdered in a blender. Or the coffee may be left out.

A wonderful trick that makes it easy to place one dough exactly over the other: slide a cookie sheet beneath each piece of waxed paper under the rolled-out dough. Transfer both doughs to the freezer and leave until they are firm. Then invert the chocolate dough over the white as directed. (Because the dough is firm, if you haven't placed the chocolate layer evenly it will be easy to correct.) Remove the top piece of waxed paper, then let the doughs stand at room temperature until they are completely thawed before rolling them up together.

continues

smooth it, check the size, then set it aside. Repeat with the remaining piece of dough.

Remove the top piece of wax paper from both of the rolled doughs. Place the white dough in front of you. Now, the chocolate dough must be inverted over the white dough, but you must be careful because you will not be able to move it if it is not placed correctly; the two doughs will stick together. So invert it cautiously over the white dough, lining up the edges as evenly as possible (see Notes). Then remove the piece of wax paper from the top of the chocolate dough. There will still be one piece of paper under the white dough; use that to help roll up the doughs, jelly-roll fashion, starting with a long side.

Wrap the roll in the wax paper. Slide a cookie sheet under the roll in order to transfer it to the freezer or refrigerator to chill until firm. (This should be very firm, and may be sliced when frozen.)

Before baking, adjust two racks to divide the oven into thirds and preheat oven to 350 degrees.

Unwrap the dough and place it on a cutting board. Cut into ¼-inch slices. (If the dough softens while you are slicing it, rewrap and rechill it until firm.) Place the slices 1 inch apart on unbuttered cookie sheets.

Bake for about 12 minutes, until the cookies are slightly colored on the edges. Reverse the position of the sheets top to bottom and front to back as necessary to ensure even browning. (If you bake only one sheet at a time, bake it on the higher rack.) Do not overbake. With a wide metal spatula, transfer the cookies to racks to cool.

ROLLED COOKIES

These cookies are all rolled with a rolling pin and then cut into shapes with cookie cutters, a knife, or a pastry wheel. Cookie cutters come in a variety of shapes and sizes. In each recipe I have specified the shape and size that I use—it is generally a plain round shape. I like to see a neat row of plain round cookies, all exactly alike, arranged overlapping each other on a long narrow tray. Cookies, more than cakes or puddings, express your own personality, your taste, and your temperament. Me, I'm a Virgo—neat and orderly. But if variety or even chaos suits you better, it's up to you.

However, some cookie doughs do not lend themselves to fancy shapes with intricate cutouts. They might not hold their forms when removed from the cutter. Or some doughs will run slightly in baking—if they were cut with a scalloped cutter they might lose their scalloped edge. Since there is such a variety of cutters, I suggest that if a recipe calls for a plain round cutter, and you want to use a fancy one, please try a sample first to see how it works.

SWEDISH RYE WAFERS

50 cookies **These are thin, crisp, buttery, and exotic, with caraway seeds. They may easily be made without a mixer; simply use a wooden spatula or your bare hands for creaming and mixing.**

- 8 ounces (2 sticks) unsalted butter
- ½ cup sugar
- 1¼ cups strained rye flour (see Notes)
- 1¼ cups *sifted* all-purpose white flour
- Milk
- Caraway seeds

Adjust two racks to divide the oven into thirds and preheat oven to 350 degrees.

In the large bowl of an electric mixer, cream the butter. Beat in the sugar and then, on low speed, gradually mix in both of the flours, scraping the bowl as necessary with a rubber spatula and beating only until thoroughly mixed.

Dust a pastry cloth and a rolling pin with either white or rye flour or with untoasted wheat germ (see Notes). Do not use any more flour or wheat germ than is necessary to keep the dough from sticking.

Roll out half of the dough at a time into an ⅛-inch thickness. If the dough is too sticky to roll, form it into a ball, flatten slightly, and let stand on the floured pastry cloth for 30 minutes to 1 hour before rolling out. Cut out cookies with a plain round 2½-inch cookie cutter. Then, with a very small round cutter, about ½ inch in diameter, cut a hole out of each cookie. The hole should not be in the center of the cookie; it should be about ¾ inch from the edge (see Notes). Or use either the wide end of a pastry-bag decorating tube or a thimble. Reserve the scraps and roll and cut them all at one time in order not to use any more flour than necessary.

With a metal spatula, transfer the cookies to unbuttered cookie sheets, placing them about ½ inch apart.

Using a soft pastry brush, brush milk all over the top of each cookie and then sprinkle with a moderate number of caraway seeds.

Bake for 12 to 14 minutes, until cookies are lightly colored, reversing the sheets top to bottom and front to back to ensure even browning.

Transfer cookies to racks to cool.

NOTES

Rye flour is available at health-food stores.

Since rye flour is too coarse to be sifted, it must be strained to aerate it. With your fingertips, press it through a large strainer set over a large bowl. The part that doesn't go through the strainer should then be stirred into the strained part.

Traditionally the hole in these cookies is off center. You *could* cut them out with a doughnut cutter, and have the hole in the middle, but then the cookies would not have their classic and charming look.

CHECKERBOARDS

48 cookies **A checkerboard cookie must be neat and precise; therefore it is often thought of as a petit four to be ordered from a fancy patisserie, or possibly as a nibble served with the compliments of the chef in a fancy restaurant—not something that the average home cook would play around with. But believe me, you can make them—they are not difficult. Neat and precise, yes—but not difficult. Gorgeous is what they are.**

- **8 ounces (2 sticks) unsalted butter**
- **½ teaspoon vanilla extract**
- **¼ teaspoon almond extract**
- **½ cup sugar**
- **¼ teaspoon salt**
- **2¾ cups *sifted* all-purpose flour**
- **2 tablespoons unsweetened cocoa powder (preferably Dutch-process)**
- **1 large egg, lightly beaten and strained**

In the large bowl of an electric mixer, cream the butter. Add the vanilla and almond extracts and then the sugar and salt and beat to mix well. On low speed, gradually add the flour and beat, scraping the bowl with a rubber spatula, for a few minutes. The mixture will be crumbly.

Turn it out onto a large board or smooth work surface, squeeze it between your hands, and knead it until it holds together and is smooth. Extra kneading is good—work it well.

Now the dough has to be divided into two exactly equal halves. You have scant 2½ cups of dough; carefully measure 1¼ cups minus 1 tablespoon of the dough, pressing it down in the cup (use the metal measuring cups that are made for measuring dry ingredients) and set it aside.

Add the cocoa to the remaining dough. Knead to incorporate the cocoa thoroughly. The mixture must be smooth. With the heel of your hand, push off small amounts of the dough, pushing on the board and away from you; re-form the dough and push it off again. Repeat until the mixture is evenly colored. Now, with your hands, shape each piece of dough into a flat square.

Place one square on a lightly floured pastry cloth and, with a lightly floured rolling pin, roll it into a square shape that is ½ inch thick and 6 inches square (no smaller); keep the edges straight and the corners as square as you can. The edges may be pressed into a straight line by pushing a ruler or a long, heavy knife against them, or they may be trimmed with a long, heavy knife. Use your fingers to square off the corners. Roll out the remaining square.

Hold a ruler facing you against the farthest edge of one of the squares and, with the tip of a small, sharp knife, mark the dough

continues ↘

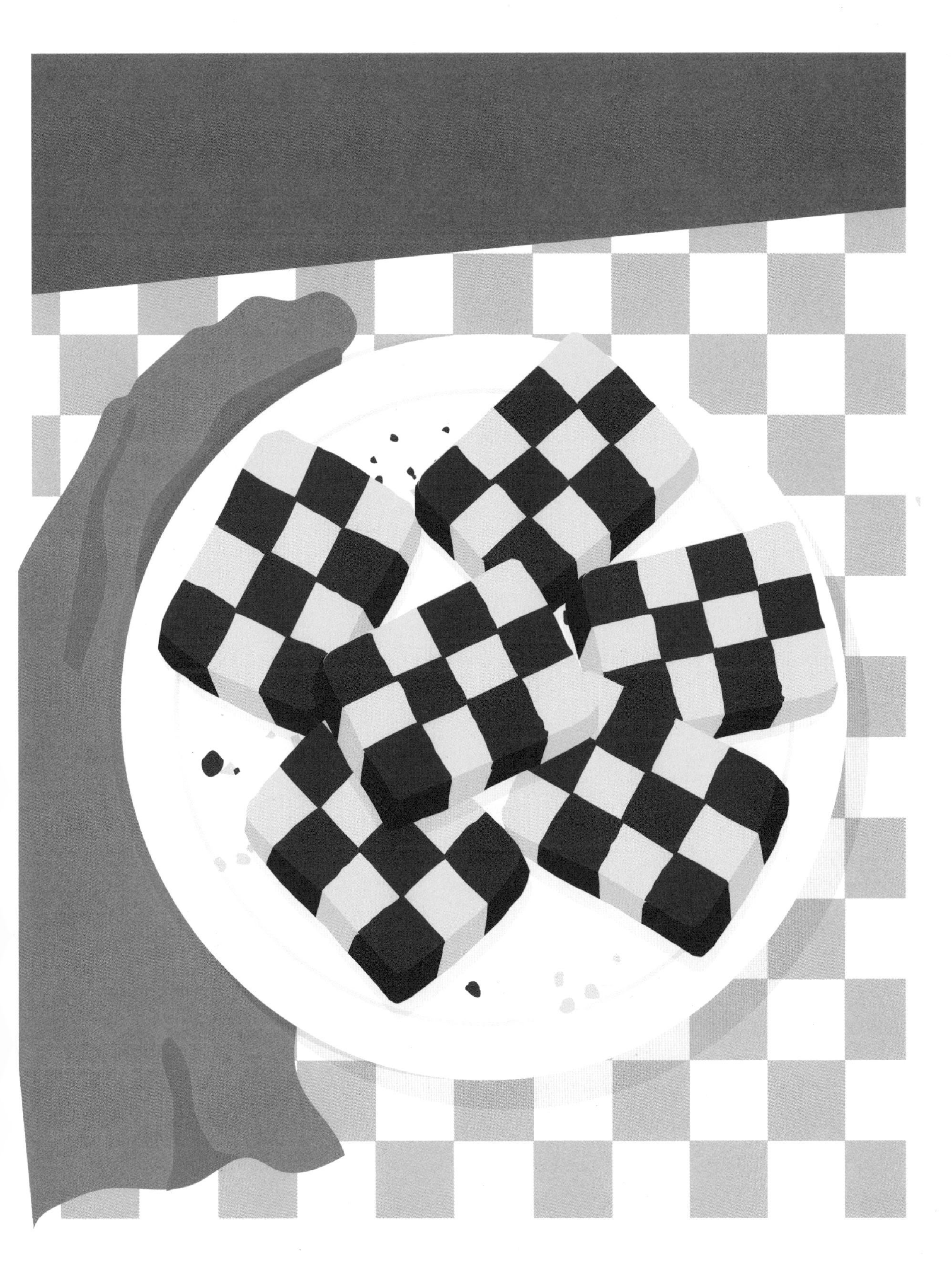

into ½-inch lengths. (The strips must be cut straight; for extra insurance, mark the opposite side of the square also.) With a long, heavy, sharp knife, cut the square into ½-inch strips. You will need 12 perfect strips.

Repeat with the remaining square of dough.

(There might be some leftover scraps of dough; if so, set them aside until later.)

Tear off a piece of plastic wrap or wax paper (I think plastic wrap is better for this) about 10 inches long and place it near the strips of dough.

To form the cookies: Place one strip of dark dough the long way on the paper or plastic. With a soft pastry brush, lightly brush one long edge of the strip with the beaten egg. Place a strip of light dough touching the egg-brushed edge. Brush the free long edge of the light dough with egg. Another dark strip, beaten egg, and then another light one. (You now have 4 strips of alternate colors touching each other, held together with a bit of beaten egg where they meet.)

Brush the top of the 4 strips lightly with the beaten egg. Place 4 more strips on top, placing dark over light and vice versa, and brushing a bit of egg between each strip as on the bottom layer. Be careful as you handle the strips and as you place them — they will not be easy to move because of the egg wash.

Brush the second layer with egg and then form a third layer, again dark over light, etc.

Now you have a three-layered bar, each layer made up of 4 narrow strips.

Wrap in the paper and refrigerate.

On a second piece of paper, form another three-layered bar. (Most of the egg will be left over — you will not need it for the cookies.)

Wrap the second bar in the paper and refrigerate. The bars must be refrigerated for at least half an hour, or until they are firm enough to slice, but they may be refrigerated for several days or they may be frozen — if they are frozen they must be thawed before they are sliced.

Before baking, adjust two racks to divide the oven into thirds and preheat oven to 350 degrees. Line cookie sheets with aluminum foil.

Unwrap one bar of dough. Cut a thin slice off one narrow end to make it perfectly straight.

With the ruler and the tip of a small, sharp knife, mark the bar into ¼-inch lengths. With a sharp knife, cut the cookies along the marks to ¼ inch thick. If the squares separate a bit as the cookies are cut, put them back in place where they belong — they will go together in baking. Place the cookies ½ inch to 1 inch apart on the lined cookie sheets.

(Leftover scraps of dough may be shaped now or later. Press them together lightly to form a marbleized dough. Roll it out ¼ inch thick on the pastry cloth and cut into shapes with a cookie cutter or cut into squares with a knife. Or roll pieces between your hands into little sausage shapes with tapered ends; place on cookie sheet and form into crescents.)

Bake for 18 to 20 minutes, until lightly colored, reversing the sheets top to bottom and front to back during baking to ensure even browning.

With a wide metal spatula, transfer cookies to racks to cool.

Repeat with second bar, or reserve it to bake at some other time.

CHOCOLATE SCOTCH SHORTBREAD COOKIES

35 to 40 cookies **Traditionally, shortbread is not chocolate. Untraditionally, this is very chocolaty. These are thick, dry, crisp cookies that are buttery and plain. They keep well, mail well, and are lovely to package as a gift.**

NOTE

If you make this in a food processor, the butter should be firm and cold, right out of the refrigerator. If you make it in an electric mixer, the butter should be removed from the refrigerator 20 or 30 minutes before using.

- **2 cups *sifted* all-purpose flour**
- **½ cup strained unsweetened cocoa powder (preferably Dutch-process)**
- **1 cup confectioners' sugar**
- **¼ teaspoon salt**
- **8 ounces (2 sticks) unsalted butter (see Note)**
- **1 teaspoon vanilla extract**

Adjust two racks to divide the oven into thirds and preheat oven to 300 degrees.

This may be prepared in a food processor (it's a breeze) or in an electric mixer. (I have also made it without either by just mixing all the ingredients together on a board with my bare hands.)

To use a processor: Fit it with a steel blade and place the dry ingredients in the bowl. Cut the cold butter into ½-inch slices over the dry ingredients. Add the vanilla. Cover and process until the ingredients hold together.

To use an electric mixer: Cream the butter in the large mixer bowl. Add the vanilla, sugar, and salt and beat to mix. On low speed, add the flour and cocoa, scraping the bowl with a rubber spatula and beating only until the mixture holds together.

If the dough is not perfectly smooth, place it on a board or smooth work surface and knead it briefly with the heel of your hand.

Form the dough into a ball and flatten it slightly.

Flour a pastry cloth, rubbing the flour in well, and a rolling pin. Place the dough on the cloth and turn it over to flour both sides. With the floured rolling pin (reflour it as necessary), roll the dough until it is ½ inch thick (no thinner). It is important to make it the same thickness all over.

Use a plain round cookie cutter 1½ inches in diameter. Before cutting each cookie,

continues ↘

dip the cutter in flour and tap it to shake off excess. Cut the cookies as close to each other as possible. Place the cookies 1 inch apart on unbuttered cookie sheets.

Press together leftover scraps of dough, reflour the cloth lightly if necessary, and reroll the dough. Cut out more cookies and place on cookie sheets, discarding any leftover scraps of dough.

Now each cookie should be pierced three times in a vertical row in the middle with the tines of a four-pronged fork, piercing all the way through the cookie each time. If the dough sticks to the fork, or if removing the fork causes the cookies to lose their shape, transfer the sheets of cookies to the refrigerator or freezer and chill only until the dough becomes slightly firm — do not let it freeze or become too firm or the fork will crack the cookies.

Bake for 25 to 30 minutes, until the cookies are firm to the touch, reversing the sheets top to bottom and front to back once during baking to ensure even baking. (If you bake only one sheet, bake it on the higher rack; one sheet will bake in less time.) Watch these carefully — they could burn and become bitter before you know it unless you check them often.

With a wide metal spatula, transfer the cookies to racks to cool.

VARIATIONS

While working on this recipe I tried many variations and they were all good. Many of our friends like it better with the addition of 1 teaspoon of instant espresso powder or any other powdered (not granular) instant coffee. And it may be made without salt and/or vanilla. Some authorities claim that the chocolate flavor is stronger without vanilla.

Stamped Shortbread: If you have a ceramic or wooden cookie stamp, or a little wooden form for stamping butter, use it to make stamped shortbread cookies. Follow the recipe above up to the direction for piercing the cookies with a fork. Do not pierce these. Instead, press the stamp onto each cookie firmly enough to imprint the design and, at the same time, flatten the cookie slightly. Bake as above.

RUM-RAISIN SHORTBREAD

15 large cookies **These are large and thick, with rum-soaked raisins all through them. The dough is very short; the cookies are rather delicate and quite unusual. The raisins must be prepared several hours ahead of time or the day before.**

- **5 ounces (1 cup) raisins**
- **½ cup dark rum**
- **2 cups *sifted* all-purpose flour**
- **¼ teaspoon baking powder**
- **¼ teaspoon salt**
- **8 ounces (2 sticks) unsalted butter**
- **½ cup confectioners' sugar**

Bring the raisins and the rum to a boil in a small saucepan over moderate heat. Remove from the heat, cover, and let stand for several hours or overnight. When ready to bake the cookies, drain the raisins in a strainer set over a small bowl; use any leftover rum for something else.

Sift together the flour, baking powder, and salt and set aside.

In the large bowl of an electric mixer, cream the butter until it is very soft. Add the sugar and beat well until completely smooth. On low speed, gradually add the sifted dry ingredients, scraping the bowl with a rubber spatula and beating until smooth. Stir in the soaked raisins.

Transfer the dough to a large piece of wax paper or aluminum foil, wrap, flatten slightly, and refrigerate for 1½ to 2 hours. Do not freeze the dough or it will become too firm to roll.

Before baking, adjust two racks to divide the oven into thirds and preheat oven to 375 degrees.

Place the dough on a lightly floured pastry cloth and turn it over to flour all sides lightly. With a floured rolling pin, roll the dough gently only until it is ½ inch thick, no thinner! Use a plain round cookie cutter about 2½ inches in diameter. Dip the cutter in flour before cutting each cookie and cut them as close to each other as possible. When cutting a cookie, press the cutter very firmly into the dough and rotate it slightly in order to cut through the raisins. Press the scraps together, chill them, and reroll.

Place the cookies 1 to 2 inches apart on unbuttered cookie sheets.

Bake the cookies for 20 minutes, or until golden brown. Reverse the sheets top to bottom and front to back to ensure even browning.

With a wide metal spatula, transfer the cookies to racks to cool.

Since these are fragile I like to wrap them individually in clear cellophane. However you store them — handle with care.

RUGELACH (WALNUT HORNS)

About 48 cookies **This is a traditional Jewish recipe that my grandmother used to make. Like all pastry, Rugelach are best when very fresh, but they freeze perfectly. The dough must be refrigerated overnight. This is one of the most popular recipes I ever wrote.**

CREAM CHEESE PASTRY

- **8 ounces (2 sticks) unsalted butter**
- **8 ounces Philadelphia-brand cream cheese**
- **½ teaspoon salt**
- **2 cups *sifted* all-purpose flour**

FILLING

- **½ cup plus 2 tablespoons sugar**
- **1 tablespoon ground cinnamon**
- **3 tablespoons unsalted butter, melted**
- **¾ cup currants**
- **5 ounces (1¼ cups) walnuts, finely chopped**

GLAZE

- **1 large egg yolk**
- **1 teaspoon water**
- OPTIONAL: **coarse or sanding sugar**

FOR THE PASTRY

In the large bowl of an electric mixer, cream the butter and cream cheese together until completely blended and smooth. Beat in the salt and, on low speed, gradually add the flour. While beating in the flour, the dough might start to run up on the beaters toward the end. If so, the last of it may be stirred in by hand. When the dough is smooth, flour your hands lightly and, with your hands, form it into a short, fat roll. Cut the roll into three equal pieces. Form each piece into a round ball, flatten slightly, and wrap each individually in plastic wrap or wax paper. Refrigerate the balls of dough overnight or for at least 5 to 6 hours.

Before baking, adjust two racks to divide the oven into thirds. Preheat the oven to 350 degrees. Line cookie sheets with baking parchment.

TO FILL THE PASTRY

Stir the sugar and cinnamon together and set aside. (Do not mix the remaining ingredients.)

Place one ball of dough on a floured pastry cloth. With a floured rolling pin, pound the dough firmly to soften it slightly. On the floured cloth with the floured rolling pin, roll out the dough (turn it over occasionally) into a 12-inch circle—don't worry about slightly uneven edges.

With a pastry brush, brush the dough with 1 tablespoon of the melted butter and,

continues ↘

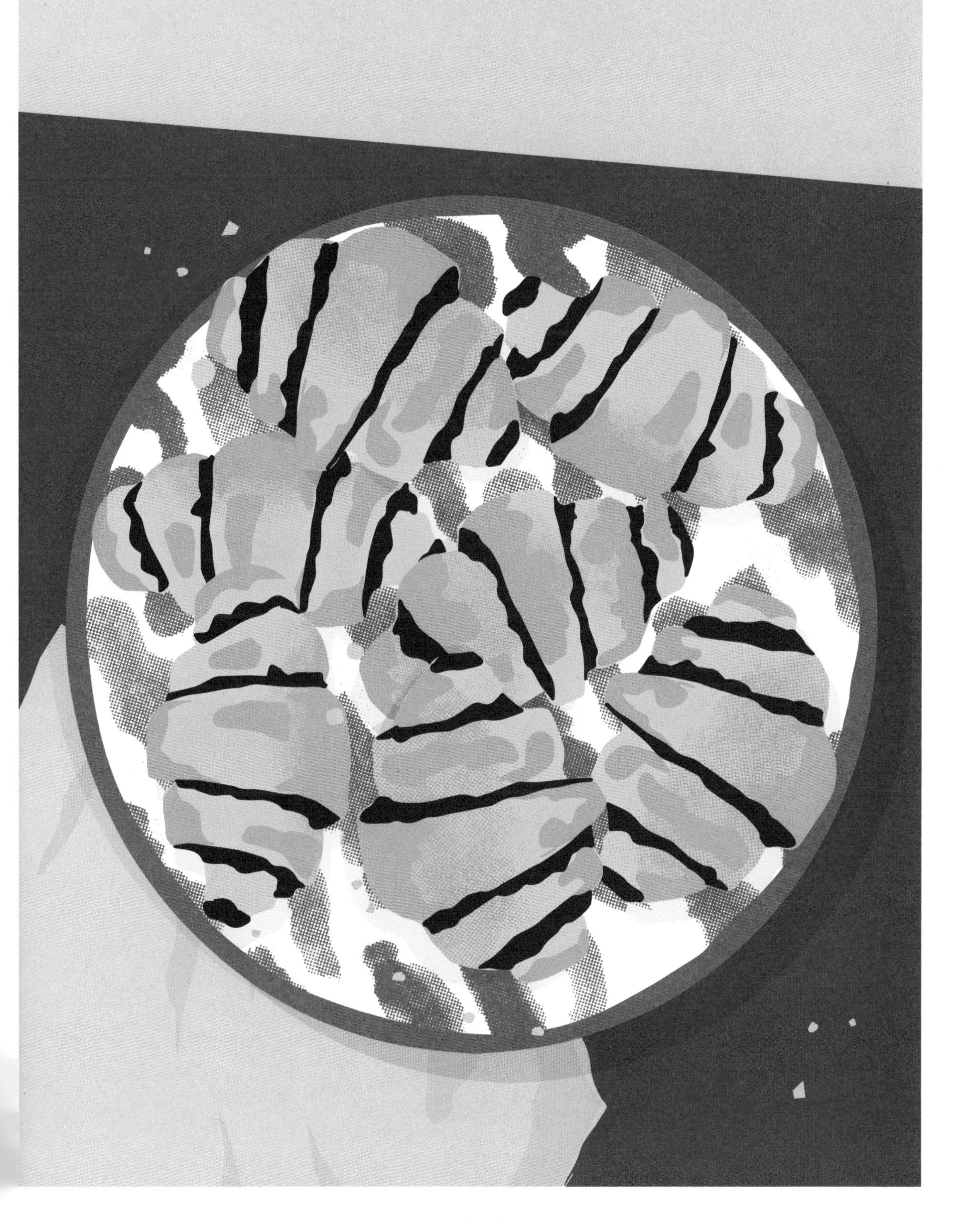

quickly before the cold dough hardens the butter, sprinkle with one-third of the sugar-cinnamon mixture. Then sprinkle with one-third of the currants and one-third of the nuts. With the rolling pin, roll over the filling to press the topping slightly into the dough.

With a long, sharp knife, cut the dough into roughly 16 pie-shaped wedges. Roll each wedge jelly-roll fashion, rolling from the outside toward the point. Then place the little rolls, with the point down, 1 inch apart on a lined sheet.

Repeat with the remaining dough and filling. Since some of the filling will fall out while you are rolling up the horns, after preparing each third of the dough it will be necessary to clean the pastry cloth; either shake it out or scrape it with a dough scraper or a wide metal spatula and then reflour it.

FOR THE GLAZE

In a small cup with a fork, stir the yolk and water just to mix. With a pastry brush, brush the glaze over the tops of the horns. If you like, sprinkle generously with coarse or sanding sugar.

Bake two sheets at a time for about 30 minutes, until the horns are golden brown. (If you bake one sheet at a time, use the higher rack.) Reverse the sheets top to bottom and front to back once to ensure even browning.

With a wide metal spatula, immediately transfer the horns to racks to cool.

Store in an airtight container.

VIENNESE ALMOND WAFERS

9 large squares or 24 small rectangles These are rich and buttery, simple but elegant. The recipe makes a small amount; if you double it, roll only half at a time.

NOTE

"Sliced" almonds are those that have been cut into very thin slices—they are the ones to use for this recipe. The fatter, oblong, julienne-shaped pieces are called "slivered" and are too thick for these cookies.

- **3¾ ounces (¾ cup) sliced blanched almonds (see Note), frozen**
- **4 ounces (1 stick) unsalted butter**
- **Scant ⅛ teaspoon salt**
- **¼ teaspoon almond extract**
- **⅓ cup sugar**
- **¾ cup plus 1 tablespoon *sifted* all-purpose flour**
- **1 large egg white**

Adjust two racks to divide the oven into thirds and preheat oven to 350 degrees.

The almonds should be coarsely crushed; this is most easily done if they are frozen. Place them in a plastic bag and press with your fingers to break into coarse pieces. Set aside.

In the small bowl of an electric mixer, cream the butter with the salt and almond extract. Beat in the sugar and then the flour, beating only until mixed.

If the dough is too soft to be rolled, chill it briefly. It may be chilled in the mixing bowl and should be stirred occasionally.

Transfer the dough to a well-floured pastry cloth, turn it over to flour all sides, and form it into a square or an oblong. With a well-floured rolling pin (continue to flour the pin as necessary to keep it from sticking), roll the dough into an even square with straight edges; the square will be 9 to 10 inches across and the dough will be a scant ⅛ inch thick.

Trim the edges of the dough with a pastry wheel, or use a long, thin, sharp knife and wipe the blade after each cut to keep the dough from sticking. Cut the dough into even squares or rectangles.

continues

Beat the egg white until foamy, but not at all stiff. With a pastry brush, brush some of the white generously over each cookie. Sprinkle the almonds evenly over the egg white. Press down gently with the palms of both hands to press the nuts slightly into the dough. Carefully brush the remaining egg white over the almonds – it will help to keep them from falling off after the cookies have been baked.

With a wide metal spatula, transfer the cookies to unbuttered cookie sheets, placing them ½ to 1 inch apart.

Bake about 20 minutes, reversing the position of the cookie sheets top to bottom and front to back to ensure even browning. (If you bake only one sheet at a time, use the higher rack.) Bake until the cookies are lightly browned; do not underbake.

With a wide metal spatula, transfer the cookies to racks to cool.

BIG NEWTONS

30 large cookies **A thick, juicy version of the Fig Newtons you buy at the store.**

PASTRY

- **1 cup *sifted* all-purpose white flour**
- **1 teaspoon baking powder**
- **½ teaspoon baking soda**
- **½ teaspoon salt**
- **2 cups *unsifted* all-purpose whole-wheat flour**
- **4 ounces (1 stick) unsalted butter**
- **½ cup firmly packed light brown sugar**
- **½ cup honey**
- **1 large egg**

FILLING

- **1½ pounds dried brown figs (although technically they are "dried," they should be soft and moist; do not use them if they are dry and hard)**
- **¾ cup honey**
- **3 tablespoons water**
- **2 tablespoons lemon juice**
- **2 tablespoons orange juice**

FOR THE PASTRY

Into a bowl, sift together the white flour, baking powder, baking soda, and salt. Add the whole-wheat flour and stir to mix well. Set aside.

In the large bowl of an electric mixer, cream the butter. Add the sugar and beat well. Beat in the honey and then the egg. On low speed, gradually add the dry ingredients, scraping the bowl with a rubber spatula and beating until completely mixed.

Turn out onto a large piece of wax paper, flatten slightly, and wrap airtight. Refrigerate for several hours or overnight, or freeze for an hour or two, until the dough is firm enough to be rolled.

Meanwhile, prepare the filling. Or the filling may be made days ahead and refrigerated.

FOR THE FILLING

Remove the tough stems from the figs. On a large board with a long, heavy chef's knife, chop the figs very fine to make 3 cups of finely chopped figs. Or if you have some way of grinding them – in a food processor or a meat grinder – do.

In a large, heavy saucepan, mix the figs with the honey, water, lemon juice, and orange juice. Place over moderate heat and cook, stirring almost constantly, for about 10 minutes, until very hot but not boiling. Transfer to a dinner plate or a shallow tray to cool. When cool, refrigerate. The filling must be cold when it is used.

Before baking, adjust a rack to the highest position in the oven and preheat oven to 400 degrees. Cut two pieces of aluminum foil the size of your largest cookie sheet.

continues ↘

Work with half of the dough at a time; reserve the other half in the refrigerator. Work on a floured pastry cloth with a floured rolling pin. If the dough is too hard to roll, place it on the cloth and pound it with the rolling pin until it softens slightly. Roll the dough into an even rectangle 15 inches long, 6 inches wide, and ¼ inch thick. Use a ruler as a guide and trim the edges evenly. If necessary, excess cut-off dough may be used to fill in where needed. *Work quickly before the dough becomes sticky.*

With two spoons, one for picking up and one for pushing off, spoon half of the filling evenly down the middle of the dough, lengthwise, forming a band of filling 1 inch deep and 2 inches wide. Stop it ½ inch away from the narrow ends. Smooth it with the back of a spoon but do not flatten it.

Use the pastry cloth to help fold the two long sides of the pastry over the filling. They should overlap each other by ¼ to ½ inch. Press lightly to seal. Use the pastry cloth again to help turn the roll over so that it is now seam side down. Do not worry about any shallow surface cracks.

With both hands, one on each long side of the roll, quickly and carefully transfer the roll to a piece of the cut foil, placing the roll either lengthwise down the middle, or on an angle from one corner to the opposite corner. With your hands, perfect the shape of the roll so that it is smooth and even. Press down gently on the two narrow open ends to seal the dough.

If your cookie sheet is big enough (14 x 17 inches) to fit both rolls, by all means bake them together. Otherwise, prepare the second roll while the first is baking.

Slide a cookie sheet under the foil and bake for 15 minutes, until golden brown all over, reversing the position of the sheet during baking to ensure even browning. Slide the aluminum foil off the cookie sheet and let the roll stand for about 10 minutes, until it is firm enough to be removed from the foil. Transfer the roll to a rack to finish cooling.

When cool, refrigerate the rolls briefly—the strips are easier to cut when cold.

Use a very sharp knife or a finely serrated one to cut the rolls crossways into 1-inch slices. If necessary, wipe the blade occasionally with a damp cloth.

SWEDISH GINGER COOKIES

Although these do not have to be hung on a Christmas tree, this is a good recipe for making cookies to hang. I am including directions for hanging, but the cookies may be cut with a plain or fancy cookie cutter, and not hung. I have also used this recipe for Christmas-card cookies; using a long knife, cut the dough into rectangles, bake, and then write the greeting on the baked cookies with the following Royal Icing. Once I tripled the recipe and made one huge cookie, as large as my oven would hold. It was made of many different layers that were pasted together with melted chocolate. Although it could have been eaten, it was strictly for show—it won first prize in a professional baking competition. The design was a large flower. I pasted petals on top of petals and decorated the whole thing with thin, wiggly lines of Royal Icing. If you're artistic and creative and want to design things, use this recipe. Or if you simply want to make plain round or square ginger cookies that are wonderfully good, use this recipe.

NOTE

To measure ¾ tablespoon baking soda, first measure 1 level tablespoon and then, with a table knife or small metal spatula, mark it into quarters and return one quarter to the box.

- **⅔ cup dark or light molasses**
- **⅔ cup sugar**
- **1 tablespoon ground ginger**
- **1 tablespoon ground cinnamon**
- **5⅓ ounces (10⅔ tablespoons) unsalted butter, at room temperature**
- **¾ tablespoon baking soda (see Note)**
- **1 large egg**
- **5 cups *sifted* all-purpose flour**

If you are making small cookies, adjust two racks to divide the oven into thirds and preheat oven to 325 degrees. If you are making something very large and thick on one cookie sheet, adjust a rack to the center of the oven and preheat oven to 300 degrees. Cut aluminum foil to fit cookie sheets.

In a heavy 2-quart saucepan over moderate heat, bring the molasses, sugar, ginger, and cinnamon just to a low boil, stirring occasionally.

Meanwhile, cut the butter into 1-inch pieces and place them in a large mixing bowl.

When the molasses mixture comes to a boil, add the baking soda and stir until the mixture foams up to the top of the saucepan. Then pour it over the butter and stir to melt the butter.

With a fork, stir the egg lightly just to mix and then stir it into the molasses mixture. Gradually stir in the flour with a rubber or wooden spatula.

Turn the dough out onto a large board or smooth work surface and knead lightly until it is mixed thoroughly.

If you are making thin cookies, work with half of the dough at a time, but for thick cookies work with it all.

Place the dough on a lightly floured pastry cloth, turn it to flour all sides, and form it into a ball. With a lightly floured rolling pin, roll the dough to the desired thickness. If the dough is rolled thick, and if the cookies are not baked until thoroughly dry, they will be similar to gingerbread. But if they are rolled thin and baked dry, they will be like crisp gingersnaps. (I have used this recipe for cookies ranging from a scant ⅛-inch to a generous ½-inch thickness.) Cut the shapes as you wish—with cookie cutters (which should be floured as necessary if the dough sticks to them); with a long knife, cutting squares or rectangles; or with a small knife, either cutting freehand or tracing around your own pattern. Place the cookies on the cut aluminum foil. Slide a cookie sheet under the foil. Reserve all scraps. Try not to incorporate any more flour (from the cloth) than necessary. Press scraps together, knead well until smooth, and then reroll them.

If you bake two sheets at a time, reverse them once top to bottom and front to back to ensure even browning. Bake until cookies feel firm to the touch. A rough guide is if the cookies are rolled ⅛ inch thick and baked 13 to 15 minutes they will be very crisp. If the cookies are ¼ inch thick and baked 15 minutes they will be slightly soft. If they are ⅜ inch thick and baked 15 minutes, the cookies will be semisoft like gingerbread. This timing will vary depending on the diameter of the cookies—small shapes will take a bit less time, large shapes a bit more. If you make something extremely large and thick, the baking time should be longer. It might take 45 minutes or more at 300 degrees. You will be able to judge by the feel of the cookie.

With a wide metal spatula, transfer the cookies to racks to cool. If you are making a very large shape, as large as the cookie sheet, let it cool briefly on the foil and then use a cookie sheet as a spatula to transfer the cookie to the rack to cool.

VARIATION

Ginger Cookie Ornaments: Before baking, sew a length of heavy cotton or linen thread through each cookie, sewing from the front of the cookie to the back, about ¼ to ½ inch in from the edge, depending on the size of the cookie. Place the cookies on the foil, carefully arranging the threads so that they do not touch other cookies. After baking and cooling the cookies, tie the threads for hanging.

Another way is to use a small pastry tube (the kind that fits into a decorating bag) to cut a small hole near the edge of the cookie. But if you do, bake one sample first to make sure that the hole is not so small that it closes during baking. After baking and cooling the cookies, thread string or ribbon through the holes.

continues ↘

A third method is to place a small piece of spaghetti upright, inserting it from the front to the back near the edge of the cookie (do this after the cookies are placed on the foil). After baking, while the cookies are still warm, push the spaghetti out through the back of the cookie and thread a thin string through the hole.

Royal Icing for Decorating

Generous amount

1 pound (packed 3½ cups) confectioners' sugar

⅓ cup egg whites (2 to 3 large eggs), at room temperature

¼ teaspoon cream of tartar

Strain the sugar by pressing it with your fingertips through a large strainer set over a large bowl. In the small bowl of an electric mixer, beat the egg whites with about half of the sugar at high speed for 5 minutes. Beat in the cream of tartar. Continue to beat while gradually adding more of the sugar, about ½ cup at a time, until the icing reaches the desired consistency. The icing should be thick enough to hold its shape without running or flattening when it is pressed through a pastry bag, but not so thick that it is difficult to press it through the bag. Also, if it is too stiff it will not stick to the cookies. It will probably not be necessary to add all of the sugar. If the icing is too stiff, add a bit more egg white or a few drops of water, very little at a time. If it is too soft, add a little more sugar. Keep the icing covered with a damp cloth to prevent a crust from forming.

For fine line decorating or lettering: Use a pastry bag fitted with a tube that has a small round opening. Or use a cone made of a triangle of baking parchment. Traditionally the triangle is made by cutting a 15-inch square in half diagonally, but it may be a little smaller than that if you wish. Cut a very small opening in the tip of the cone and try it with some icing. You can always cut away more if necessary.

Practice first on a piece of paper to be sure that the icing is the correct consistency.

If you wish, the icing may be dyed with food coloring—you may divide the icing and make several different colors—but the cookies will be dark and I prefer white icing.

Just a suggestion: It is fun to use silver dragées. I spread them out on a piece of wax paper, and place them with tweezers where I want on the icing before it dries.

MY MOTHER'S GINGERSNAPS

35 cookies **These are the cookies that my mother and I made together probably more often than any other. They may seem like Christmas cookies, but we had jars and boxes of them around the house all year. For three decades my father did his radio news broadcasts from home; that meant that people were coming and going all day and often late into the night. With plenty of these gingersnaps, we were always prepared, and many famous people left the house carrying a box or a bag.**

Crisp, chewy, large and thin, spicy and peppery but mellow. The dough should be refrigerated overnight before rolling, cutting, and baking.

NOTE

It is best to pour some vinegar into a cup and spoon out the amount you need. If you pour it into a spoon held over the mixing bowl, there is a very good chance you might pour more than you need.

- 3½ ounces (½ cup loosely packed) candied ginger
- 2 cups *unsifted* all-purpose white flour
- 1½ teaspoons baking soda
- ¾ teaspoon salt
- ¾ teaspoon finely ground black pepper (preferably fresh ground)
- 1½ teaspoons ground ginger
- 8 ounces (2 sticks) unsalted butter
- 1 cup sugar
- ¾ cup dark molasses
- 1 large egg
- 1¼ teaspoons cider vinegar (see Note)
- 1 cup *unsifted* all-purpose whole-wheat flour

Cut the candied ginger into pieces ¼ inch or less and set aside.

Sift together the white flour, baking soda, salt, pepper, and ground ginger and set aside.

In the large bowl of an electric mixer, beat the butter until it is soft. Add the sugar and beat to mix. Beat in the molasses, egg, and vinegar (it might look curdled; it is OK). Then beat in the cut-up candied ginger. Add the sifted dry ingredients and the whole-wheat flour and beat on low speed until incorporated.

Spread out three lengths of wax paper or foil. Place one-third of the dough on each paper. Wrap and refrigerate overnight. (If you can't wait, freeze the packages for about an hour.)

Before baking, adjust two racks to divide the oven into thirds and preheat oven to 350 degrees. Line cookie sheets with baking parchment.

To roll the dough, generously flour a pastry cloth and rolling pin. Place one piece of the chilled dough on the cloth and press down on it a few times with the rolling pin. Turn the dough over to flour both sides; roll out the dough until it is ¼ inch thick. Work quickly. Do not leave the dough unattended; it becomes sticky and gooey if it is allowed to reach room temperature (which seems to happen quickly). Reflour the cloth and the pin as necessary.

With a round cookie cutter measuring 3⅛ inches in diameter (or any other size), cut out the cookies; start cutting at the outside edge of the dough and cut the cookies just barely touching each other. Reserve the scraps and press them together (the dough will be too sticky for you to press the scraps together with your hands – it is best to put the scraps in a bowl and mix them together with a spatula), wrap, and rechill.

With a wide metal spatula, quickly transfer the cookies to the parchment-lined sheets, placing them 2 inches apart (if the cookies are 3⅛ inches wide, I place only 5 cookies on a 15½ x 12-inch sheet – they spread).

Bake two sheets at a time, reversing the sheets top to bottom and front to back once during baking to ensure even baking. As they bake, the cookies will rise and then settle down into thin wafer-like cookies. They will take about 15 minutes to bake. (If you bake only one sheet, use a rack in the middle of the oven – one sheet might bake in slightly less time.)

When the cookies are done, remove the sheets from the oven and let stand until they are just barely cool. Then transfer the cookies with a wide metal spatula. (If the bottoms of the cookies stick to the parchment, the cookies were not baked long enough – return them to the oven.)

Place on racks to finish cooling or just turn them over to allow the bottoms to dry. Store airtight.

ISCHLER COOKIES

24 sandwich cookies **This is a classic and elegant Viennese cookie made of two rich and fragile almond cookies sandwiched together with preserves and partially covered with chocolate glaze. They are made without a mixer and should be stored in the refrigerator and served cold.**

- 8 ounces (1⅔ cups) blanched almonds
- 2¼ cups *sifted* all-purpose flour
- ⅔ cup sugar
- 10 ounces (2½ sticks) cold unsalted butter, cut into ½-inch slices
- ½ to ¾ cup smooth, thick apricot preserves

CHOCOLATE GLAZE

- 12 ounces (2 cups) semisweet chocolate morsels
- 2 tablespoons vegetable shortening (such as Crisco)

NOTES

These directions make rather large cookies, which is traditional for this recipe. However, they may be rolled thinner and/or cut smaller if you wish.

If there is any glaze left over it may be saved for some other time, some other cookies. Line a small bowl with aluminum foil, pour in the glaze, and let stand (or chill) until the glaze is firm. Then remove it—with the foil—from the bowl. Place it in a freezer bag or wrap it in enough foil to protect it. It may stand at room temperature for a few days, or for longer storage it may be refrigerated or frozen. When ready to use, remove it from the foil, chop it coarsely, and melt slowly over hot water.

In a nut grinder, blender, or food processor, grind the almonds to a fine powder (see page 19); place them in a large mixing bowl. Add the flour and sugar and stir to mix. With a pastry blender, cut the butter into the dry ingredients until the mixture resembles a coarse meal.

Turn the dough out onto a large board or smooth work surface, then squeeze it between your hands until it holds together. Form the dough into a ball, flatten slightly, and then "break" it as follows: Using the heel of your hand, start at the farther end of the dough and push off small pieces (about 2 tablespoons), smearing it against the work surface and away from you. Continue until all the dough has been pushed off. Re-form the dough and then push it off or "break" it again.

Working with half of the dough, form it into a ball and place on a large piece of wax paper. Cover with another large piece of wax paper. With your hand, flatten the dough slightly, and then, with a rolling pin, roll over the paper to roll the dough until it is ¼ inch thick. If the wax paper wrinkles, peel it off and then replace it in order to remove the wrinkles. (During rolling, check both pieces of wax paper for wrinkles.)

Slide a cookie sheet under the dough (still between the two pieces of wax paper) and transfer to the freezer or refrigerator until

continues ↘

the dough is firm and the paper may be pulled off easily.

Repeat with the second half of the dough.

While the dough is chilling, adjust two racks to divide the oven into thirds and preheat oven to 350 degrees.

When the dough is firm, peel off one piece of the wax paper from each piece of dough just to release it, then replace it. Turn each piece of dough over, then peel off but do not replace the second piece of paper.

With a plain round cookie cutter measuring 2¼ to 2½ inches in diameter, cut out cookies and place them (with the help of a metal spatula if necessary) 1 inch apart on unbuttered cookie sheets. The dough must be firm enough for the rounds to hold their shape when they are transferred. Reserve scraps and roll, chill, and cut them. You should have about 48 cookies. (For thinner or smaller cookies, see Notes.)

Bake for 15 to 18 minutes, reversing the sheets top to bottom and front to back as necessary to ensure even baking. When done, the cookies should be sandy-colored or lightly golden but not brown.

Let stand for a few seconds and then, with a wide metal spatula, transfer the cookies to racks to cool.

If the cookies are different sizes (because the dough was not all rolled to the same thickness), match them up into pairs of equal size. Place one cookie from each pair upside down. Then, holding the cookie in your hand (carefully because these are fragile), spread the underside with a thin layer of the apricot preserves, keeping it a bit away from the edges. Cover this with another cookie and press them together very gently.

FOR THE GLAZE

Place the chocolate and shortening in the top of a small double boiler over warm water on low heat. Cover until partially melted. Then uncover and stir until completely melted and smooth. Transfer the glaze to a small narrow bowl for ease in handling. A soup cup is good.

Line cookie sheets with wax paper. Hold a cookie sandwich between your fingers so that you are touching the two cookies, not the open ends. Dip it, edge down, into the glaze. Dip it deeply enough so that the glaze covers about half of the sandwich, both top and bottom. Gently wipe the edge of the sandwich against the top of the bowl to remove excess glaze. Place the cookie on the wax paper–lined cookie sheet, laying it on either of the glazed sides.

Glaze the remaining cookies.

When the cookie sheet is covered with glazed cookies, transfer it to the freezer or refrigerator to chill until the glaze is set and the cookies may be lifted from the paper easily and don't stick.

Then place the cookies on a tray or in a freezer box with plastic wrap over each layer to make them airtight. Refrigerate until serving time and serve cold.

TROPICAL SOUR-CREAM COOKIES

20 large cookies **St. Augustine, Florida, is the oldest city in the United States. This recipe is adapted from one of the first cookbooks published in St. Augustine. The cookies are large, plain, and semisoft, with a tropical orange and lemon flavor. Plan to chill the dough overnight before baking.**

NOTE

If the brown sugar has any hard lumps, it must be strained; place it in a large strainer set over a large bowl and, with your fingertips, press the sugar through the strainer.

- **2 cups *sifted* all-purpose flour**
- **½ teaspoon baking soda**
- **⅛ teaspoon salt**
- **Finely grated zest of 1 large, deep-colored orange**
- **Finely grated zest of 1 large lemon**
- **1 tablespoon lemon juice**
- **4 ounces (1 stick) unsalted butter**
- **1 cup firmly packed light brown sugar (see Note)**
- **1 large egg**
- **½ cup sour cream**
- **Granulated sugar (for topping)**

Sift together the flour, baking soda, and salt and set aside.

In a small cup, mix the orange zest, lemon zest, and lemon juice and set aside.

In the large bowl of an electric mixer, cream the butter. Add the brown sugar and beat well. Add the egg and beat to mix well. On low speed, gradually beat in half of the sifted dry ingredients, then all of the sour cream, and finally the remaining dry ingredients, scraping the bowl with a rubber spatula and beating only until blended. Remove the bowl from the mixer and stir in the zests and juice.

The dough will be soft. Turn it out onto a large piece of aluminum foil, wrap in the foil, and place in the freezer or refrigerator overnight.

Before baking, adjust two racks to divide the oven into thirds and preheat oven to 375 degrees. Cut aluminum foil to fit cookie sheets.

The dough will soften quickly and become sticky at room temperature, so work quickly and with half of the dough at a time, keeping the remainder chilled.

Generously flour a pastry cloth and a rolling pin. Turn the dough over on the floured cloth to flour all sides and then form it into a ball and flatten slightly. With the rolling pin, roll the dough to a generous ¼-inch thickness, turning the dough over occasionally while rolling and adding additional flour to the cloth or pin if necessary to keep the dough from sticking.

continues ↘

Quickly cut the cookies with a plain round 3- to 3½-inch cookie cutter. And then, quickly, transfer the cookies with a wide metal spatula to the cut aluminum foil, placing them about 1 inch apart—these spread only slightly in baking.

Reserve the scraps of dough, press them together, rechill, and roll them all out together in order not to incorporate any more flour than necessary.

Sprinkle the tops of the cookies with granulated sugar. Slide cookie sheets under the foil.

Bake for about 15 minutes, until the cookies are lightly colored. Reverse the cookie sheets top to bottom and front to back as necessary to ensure even browning.

With a wide metal spatula, transfer the cookies to racks to cool.

HOT BUTTER WAFERS

60 wafers **An early Colonial recipe reportedly used by Dolley Madison and served at the White House. These are very plain, thin, crisp, and buttery. They may be served as a plain cookie, or as a cracker with soup or salad. The absence of salt, flavoring, and leavening is typical of Early American cookies.**

NOTE

After the dough has been rolled twice, it becomes rubbery and difficult to roll thin enough. So try to end up with as few scraps as possible. The first time the dough is rolled you might cut it into rounds and then, the second time, cut into squares, thereby eliminating scraps. In any event, roll it thin, thin, thin.

- **4 cups *sifted* all-purpose flour**
- **8 ounces (2 sticks) unsalted butter**
- **½ cup sugar**
- **3 large eggs**

Place the flour in the large bowl of an electric mixer. Cut the butter into 1-inch pieces and melt it in a small, heavy saucepan over moderate heat. Pour the hot butter all at once into the flour. Beat at low speed to mix—the mixture will be crumbly. Beat in the sugar and then the eggs, one at a time. Beat only until the last egg is incorporated.

Turn the dough out onto a large floured board or a smooth work surface and knead briefly only until completely smooth.

Wrap the dough in wax paper or aluminum foil and chill in the freezer for 15 minutes—no longer!

Adjust two racks to divide the oven into thirds and preheat oven to 350 degrees.

Cut the dough into quarters. Work with one piece at a time, keeping the remainder covered at room temperature.

Turn the dough over several times on a floured pastry cloth to flour all sides lightly. Roll the dough with a floured rolling pin, turning it over frequently to keep both sides floured. Reflour the cloth and pin as necessary but don't use any more flour than you really need. Roll the dough until it is paper thin. (Each quarter of the dough should be rolled until it is 15 inches or more in diameter.)

Cut the cookies with a plain round 4-inch cookie cutter. Or use a long knife or a pastry wheel, and trim the edges of the dough, then cut it into 4-inch squares. Prick the cookies all over with a fork at ½-inch intervals.

With a wide metal spatula, transfer the cookies to unbuttered cookie sheets. These may be placed on the sheets actually touching each other since, instead of spreading, they shrink slightly when baked.

continues ↘

Reserve scraps of dough, knead them together briefly, and roll them all together in order not to incorporate any more flour than necessary (see Note).

Bake the cookies for 13 to 18 minutes, reversing the cookie sheets top to bottom and front to back as necessary to ensure even browning. Bake until the cookies are golden brown all over with no white spots remaining.

With a wide metal spatula, remove the cookies individually as they are done and place them on racks to cool.

DIONE LUCAS'S SABLÉS

36 cookies **These French almond cookies are similar to shortbread. *Sablé* is French for "sandy," which describes the cookies' texture. Dione Lucas, one of the greatest cooks of her time, once served them for dessert along with a cold soufflé at a memorable formal dinner party.**

- **2½ ounces (½ cup) blanched almonds**
- **6 ounces (1½ sticks) unsalted butter**
- **Pinch of salt**
- **½ cup confectioners' sugar**
- **2 tablespoons rum (I use Myers's dark rum)**
- **2 cups *sifted* all-purpose flour**
- **1 large egg yolk**
- **1 teaspoon water**
- **36 whole blanched almonds**

Adjust a rack to the top position in the oven and preheat oven to 350 degrees.

Grind the ½ cup blanched almonds either in a nut grinder or a blender — they must be ground to a powder (see page 19). Set aside.

In the large bowl of an electric mixer, cream the butter well. Add the salt and sugar and beat until smooth. Beat in the rum and then the ground almonds. On lowest speed, gradually add the flour, scraping the bowl with a rubber spatula and beating only until smooth.

Turn the dough out onto a large board or a smooth work surface. Work the dough with your hands, first squeezing it between your fingers, and then pushing it away from you, a bit at a time, with the heel of your hand, until very smooth.

Form the dough into a ball and flatten it slightly. Place on a large piece of wax paper and cover with another large piece of wax paper. With a rolling pin, roll over the top of the paper until the dough is a scant ⅜ inch thick (don't make these too thin) and perfectly level. If the wax paper wrinkles during the rolling, remove and then replace the paper to remove the wrinkles.

Slide a cookie sheet under the bottom wax paper and transfer the dough to the freezer for about 10 minutes, or a little longer in the refrigerator, until the dough is almost firm.

Remove the top piece of wax paper just to release it, then replace it. Turn the dough over, still between the two pieces of paper. Remove the second piece of wax paper and do not replace it.

Cut the cookies with a round 1¾-inch cookie cutter. Place them ½ inch apart on an unbuttered cookie sheet; these barely spread at all in baking and may be placed quite close to each other. Press the scraps together. Reroll and chill before cutting.

In a small cup, mix the egg yolk with the water. With a soft brush, brush the egg wash over the tops of the cookies. Place a whole blanched almond on top of each cookie and press gently until the almond is

continues ↘

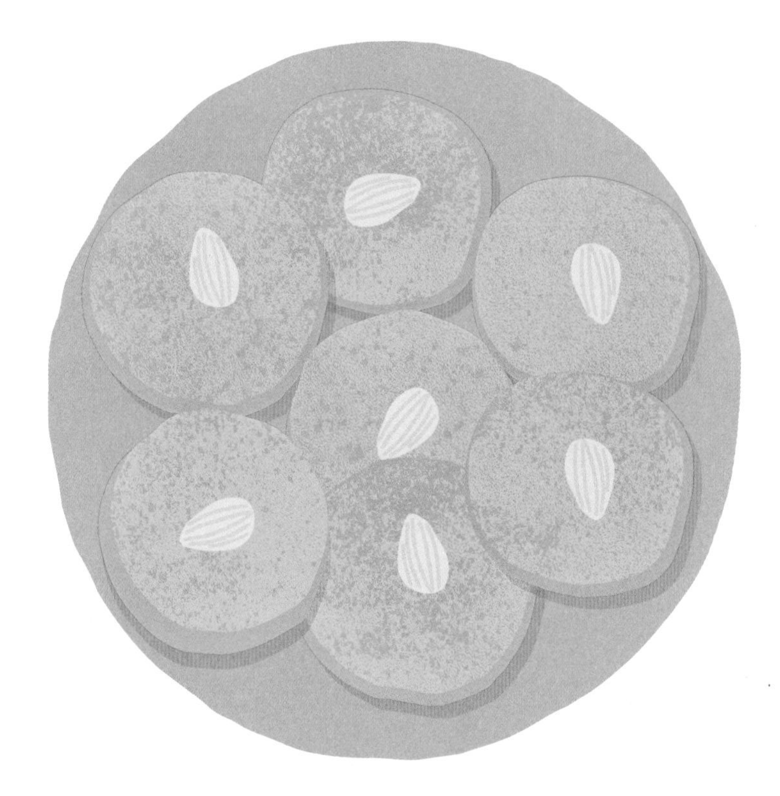

slightly embedded—if the cookies are too firm, let them stand for a few minutes to soften slightly.

Now brush the egg wash over each cookie again, generously covering the top of the cookie and the almond.

Bake for 15 to 17 minutes, reversing the position of the cookie sheet front to back to ensure even browning. Bake only until the cookies are slightly colored; do not overbake.

With a wide metal spatula, transfer the cookies to racks to cool.

PLAIN OLD-FASHIONED SUGAR COOKIES

20 extra-large cookies **These cookies are traditionally made very large, almost saucer size, but you can make any size or shape you want.**

- 3¼ cups *sifted* all-purpose flour
- 2½ teaspoons baking powder
- Scant ½ teaspoon salt
- 6 ounces (1½ sticks) unsalted butter
- 1½ teaspoons vanilla extract
- 1½ cups sugar
- 2 large eggs
- 1 tablespoon milk
- Additional sugar (for topping)

Sift together the flour, baking powder, and salt and set aside.

In the large bowl of an electric mixer, cream the butter. Add the vanilla and sugar and beat well. Beat in the eggs one at a time and then add the milk. On low speed, gradually add the sifted dry ingredients, scraping the bowl as necessary with a rubber spatula and beating only until thoroughly mixed.

Divide the dough in two and wrap each half separately in wax paper or aluminum foil. Chill the dough in the refrigerator for 3 hours or longer if you wish. (Chilling the dough in the freezer makes it too hard to roll.)

Before baking, adjust two racks to divide the oven into thirds and preheat oven to 400 degrees.

Place one piece of the dough on a lightly floured pastry cloth. Turn it over to flour all sides and then form into a ball. With a floured rolling pin, roll the dough to the desired thickness: For very large cookies, roll to a generous ¼ inch. Cut the cookies as you wish. If you want very large cookies, cut with a plain round 4-inch cookie cutter.

With a wide metal spatula, transfer the cookies to unbuttered cookie sheets. If the cookies are large and thick, place them 1½ to 2 inches apart. They may be closer if they are small and thin.

Sprinkle the tops of the cookies generously with granulated sugar.

Bake until the cookies are lightly browned, reversing the position of the sheets top to bottom and front to back as necessary during baking to ensure even browning. Large, thick cookies will need to bake for 10 to 12 minutes.

With a wide metal spatula, transfer the cookies to racks to cool.

GRANNY'S OLD-FASHIONED SUGAR COOKIES

18 to 24 large cookies **These are crisp, large, thin, plain cookies with a divine lemon-and-cinnamon flavor. Everyone raves about them and asks for the recipe.**

It is best to refrigerate this dough overnight before rolling it out and cutting it with a cookie cutter.

- 1¾ cups *unsifted* all-purpose flour
- 2 teaspoons baking powder
- ¼ teaspoon salt
- 4 ounces (1 stick) unsalted butter
- Finely grated zest of 2 lemons
- 1 tablespoon lemon juice
- 1 cup sugar
- 1 large egg
- 2 tablespoons whipping cream

CINNAMON SUGAR

- 1 tablespoon sugar
- ⅓ teaspoon ground cinnamon
- Pinch of ground nutmeg

Sift together the flour, baking powder, and salt and set aside.

In the large bowl of an electric mixer, beat the butter until it is soft. Beat in the lemon zest and juice and then add the sugar. Beat in the egg and cream. Then, on low speed, gradually add the sifted dry ingredients and beat until smoothly mixed. Remove from the mixer.

Turn the dough out onto a length of wax paper or plastic wrap, wrap it, and refrigerate overnight. (In a hurry, I have used the freezer instead of the refrigerator — only until the dough was cold and firm but not frozen.)

When you are ready to bake, adjust two racks to divide the oven into thirds and preheat oven to 375 degrees. Line cookie sheets with baking parchment or with foil shiny side up. Set aside.

Spread out a pastry cloth, flour it well, and flour a rolling pin. Unwrap the dough, cut it into thirds, and place one piece on the floured cloth. If it was refrigerated overnight, it will be too stiff to roll out; pound it firmly with the floured rolling pin, turning the dough over occasionally until it is soft enough to be rolled. Roll it out until it is quite thin, about ⅛ to 3⁄16 inch thick.

Use a large round cookie cutter about 3½ inches in diameter (more or less). Start to cut the cookies at the outside edge of the dough and cut them so close to each other that they are touching. With a wide metal spatula, transfer the rounds to the lined sheets, placing them ½ inch apart.

It is best not to reroll the scraps if possible because they would absorb additional flour and would become a bit tougher than otherwise. **Here's a hint:** Do not press the scraps together but, with smaller cutters, cut out as many smaller cookies as you can. Or use a knife and cut squares or triangles. There will still be some leftover scraps, but much less than otherwise. Reserve the scraps. Roll and cut the remaining dough. Then press all the scraps together, refrigerate if necessary (it will not be), roll it out, and cut with a knife or with cutters.

FOR THE CINNAMON SUGAR

Mix the sugar, cinnamon, and nutmeg. With your fingertips, sprinkle over the cookies.

Bake for 10 to 13 minutes, reversing the sheets top to bottom and front to back as necessary to ensure even browning. When done, the cookies will be only sandy-colored, slightly darker on the rims.

With a wide metal spatula, transfer the cookies to racks to cool. Store airtight. These last well if you stay away from them.

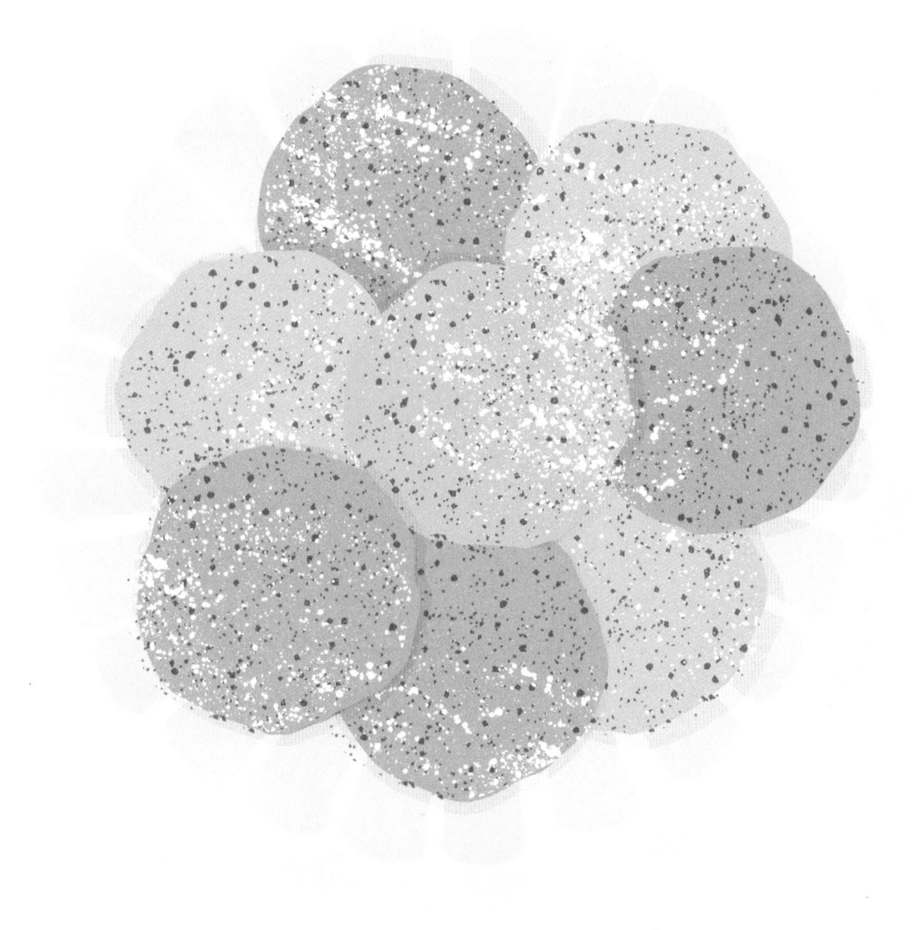

CHOCOLATE CHIP PILLOWS

NOTE

You may use mini morsels if you wish. Just use as many as you can easily sandwich between the two cookies.

18 cookies **Chocolate chips are sandwiched between two thin, buttery, brown-sugar cookies and baked together.**

1⅓ cups *sifted* all-purpose flour

½ teaspoon salt

¼ teaspoon baking soda

4 ounces (1 stick) unsalted butter

½ teaspoon vanilla extract

2 tablespoons granulated sugar

¼ cup firmly packed dark brown sugar

1 large egg yolk

2 ounces (⅓ cup) semisweet chocolate morsels (see Note)

Adjust two racks to divide the oven into thirds and preheat oven to 425 degrees.

Sift together the flour, salt, and baking soda and set aside.

In the small bowl of an electric mixer, cream the butter. Add the vanilla and both sugars and beat well. Beat in the egg yolk and then, on low speed, gradually add the sifted dry ingredients, scraping the bowl with a rubber spatula and beating until the dough holds together.

Tear off two pieces of wax paper, each 16 to 18 inches long. Place the dough on one piece of the paper and flatten it slightly. Cover with the other piece of paper and, with a rolling pin, roll over the wax paper until the dough is ⅛ inch thick—it will be about 14 inches long and almost as wide as the paper.

Slide a cookie sheet under the dough and papers and transfer to the freezer or refrigerator very briefly, only until the dough is firm enough to cut and handle. (It will take only a few minutes in the freezer.)

Pull off the top piece of wax paper just to loosen it and then replace it. Turn the dough, still between both papers, over. Pull off the second piece of paper and do not replace it.

Now work quickly before the dough softens. Cut about half of the rolled dough with a plain round 2-inch cookie cutter. Place the cookies 1½ to 2 inches apart on unbuttered cookie sheets, using a small metal spatula if necessary to transfer the cookies.

Replace the remaining rolled dough in the freezer or refrigerator to keep it firm until you are ready to use it.

Place 6 chocolate morsels in the center of each round of dough on the cookie sheets.

Then remove the reserved chilled dough and, following the above directions, cut it into rounds. Place a round of dough over each cookie.

Reroll and form the scraps of dough the same way, chilling the dough as necessary.

Seal the edges of the sandwiched cookies by pressing them with the back of the tines of a fork.

Bake for about 10 minutes, until lightly browned, reversing the sheets top to bottom and front to back once to ensure even browning.

With a wide metal spatula, transfer the cookies to a rack to cool.

JOE FROGGERS

16 to 18 (5-inch) cookies Once upon a time—actually, it was over one hundred years ago, in Marblehead, Massachusetts—there was an old man who was called Uncle Joe. The details of the story are murky, but one version has it that Joe lived alongside a frog pond that was known as Uncle Joe's Frog Pond.

Uncle Joe made the biggest and the best molasses cookies for miles around. The local fishermen would swap a jug of rum for a batch of the cookies, which came to be known as Joe Froggers, because they were as big and as dark as the frogs in the pond. The fishermen liked them because they never got hard when they took them to sea.

Uncle Joe said the secret of keeping them soft was that he used rum and seawater. But that was all he said. He would not part with the recipe. When he died, people said, "That's the end of Joe Froggers."

However, there was a woman named Aunt Cressy, who was Uncle Joe's wife. She gave the recipe to a fisherman's wife. And soon most of the women in Marblehead were making Joe Froggers. And they were sold at a local bakery. And the recipe traveled. The last I heard about them, years ago, was that they were still being served with a pitcher of cold milk on Sunday nights at the Publick House in the Colonial village in Sturbridge, Massachusetts.

With their background, it is obvious that these would be a good choice for mailing or traveling.

The original Joe Froggers were 6 inches in diameter. I use a plain, round cookie cutter that is 5 inches in diameter (that's my largest one). They can be smaller, but they are wonderful large.

The dough should be refrigerated overnight before the cookies are rolled, cut, and baked. Allow plenty of time for baking since they are baked only four at a time.

4⅓ cups *sifted* all-purpose flour

1 teaspoon baking soda

¾ teaspoon salt

2 teaspoons ground ginger

¾ teaspoon ground cloves

¾ teaspoon ground nutmeg

¼ teaspoon ground mace

¼ teaspoon ground allspice

OPTIONAL: 1 teaspoon finely ground black pepper (Uncle Joe did not use the pepper, but I do)

6 ounces (1½ sticks) unsalted butter

¾ cup sugar

1 cup dark or light molasses

⅓ cup water (it needn't be seawater), coffee, and dark rum, mixed (amounts can vary according to your taste; use all of any one, or try 1 tablespoon instant coffee powder dissolved in 3 tablespoons water, and the rest rum)

Sift together the flour, baking soda, salt, ginger, cloves, nutmeg, mace, allspice, and optional black pepper. Set aside.

In the large bowl of an electric mixer, beat the butter until it softens. Add the sugar and beat to mix. Beat in the molasses. Then, on low speed, add about half of the sifted dry ingredients, scraping the bowl as necessary with a rubber spatula and beating until mixed. Beat in the water, coffee, and rum, and then the remaining dry ingredients.

Cover the bowl with plastic wrap or foil and refrigerate until it is firm enough to be handled. Then divide it in thirds and wrap each piece in plastic wrap. Refrigerate overnight.

Before baking, adjust a rack to the center of the oven and preheat oven to 375 degrees. Line cookie sheets with baking parchment or foil.

Flour a pastry cloth and a rolling pin, using more rather than less flour. Unwrap one of the packages of dough and place it on the cloth. Pound it a bit with the rolling pin to soften it slightly. Turn it over to flour both sides. Work very quickly because the dough will become sticky and unmanageable if it softens too much. Roll out in all directions until the dough is ¼ inch thick.

Quickly cut with a floured 5-inch round cutter (or what have you). Use a wide metal spatula to transfer the cookies to the sheets, quickly and carefully placing them about 1 inch apart. (I place 4 on a 12 x 15½-inch sheet.)

Press the scraps together and rechill (the freezer is OK), then reroll and cut.

Bake one sheet at a time for 13 to 15 minutes, reversing the sheet front to back once during baking to ensure even

continues

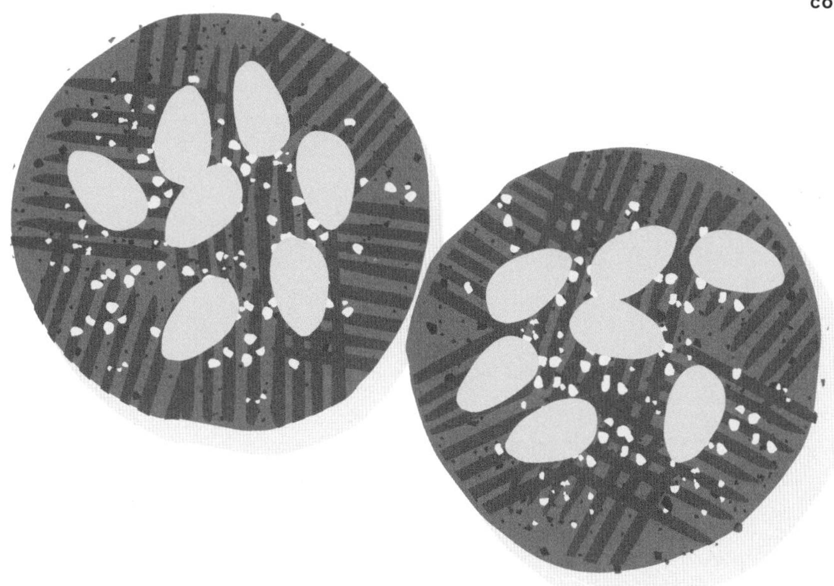

baking. Watch these very carefully. They must not burn even a bit on the bottoms or it will spoil the taste. If they seem to be browning too much on the bottoms, be prepared to slide an extra cookie sheet under the one that is baking. Or raise the rack slightly higher in the oven. (But I have found that if I bake these high in the oven, they crack. It is only minor, but it does not happen when they are baked on the middle rack. That is why I bake these only one sheet at a time.)

Be very careful not to overbake these cookies. They will become firmer as they cool, and they should remain a bit soft and chewy in the middle. If you use a smaller cutter, the cookies will probably bake in slightly less time.

Remove from the oven and let stand for a few minutes. Use a wide metal spatula to transfer the cookies to racks to cool. Since these are so large, if the rack is not raised enough (at least ½ inch or more), place the rack on any right-side-up bowl or pan to make more room for air to circulate underneath.

When completely cool, store these airtight. I wrap them, two to a package, bottoms together, in clear cellophane.

LES PETITES

46 small sandwich cookies **These are dainty, delicate, delicious, fancy little French cookies sandwiched together with chocolate between them; the top cookie has a hole cut out in the middle for the chocolate to show through. They are nicknamed Black-Eyed Susans.**

Make these for a wedding reception (there is an old saying that a ring-shaped cookie symbolizes eternal happiness because it has no end), a bridal shower, a tea party, or anything fancy and special.

- **5 ounces (1 cup) blanched hazelnuts or almonds, or a combination of both**
- **6 ounces (1½ sticks) unsalted butter**
- **½ teaspoon vanilla extract**
- **½ cup sugar**
- **Pinch of salt**
- **1½ cups *sifted* all-purpose flour**
- **5 ounces semisweet chocolate (to be used for sandwiching the cookies)**

Adjust two racks to divide the oven into thirds and preheat oven to 350 degrees. Line two cookie sheets with baking parchment, or with foil shiny side up.

The nuts must be ground fine. This can be done in a food processor or nut grinder (see page 19).

The dough can be put together in a mixer or a processor.

In a mixer: Cream the butter, mix in the vanilla, sugar, and salt, then the flour, and finally the ground nuts, beating until mixed.

In a food processor: After grinding the nuts, do not remove them from the bowl; add the butter, which should be cut into small pieces, and all the other ingredients except the chocolate and process until the dough holds together.

Do not chill the dough before rolling it; chilling makes it crack when it is rolled.

Flour a pastry cloth and a rolling pin. Use only half of the dough at a time. Form a piece into a ball and flour lightly. Flatten it slightly between your hands. Then roll out carefully (flouring the top, the bottom, and the rolling pin as necessary) until it is a scant ¼ inch or a generous ⅛ inch thick.

You will need a round (preferably scalloped) cookie cutter that measures 1½ inches in diameter. Starting at the outside edge of the rolled-out dough, cut rounds and place them about ½ inch apart on the lined sheets. Then, with a round cutter that measures ¾ inch in diameter, cut holes out of the middle of half of the cookies. (Save the cutout holes and the leftovers and roll them out again to make more cookies.)

Bake for 10 to 15 minutes or a bit longer (depending on the thickness of the cookies), reversing the sheets top to

continues

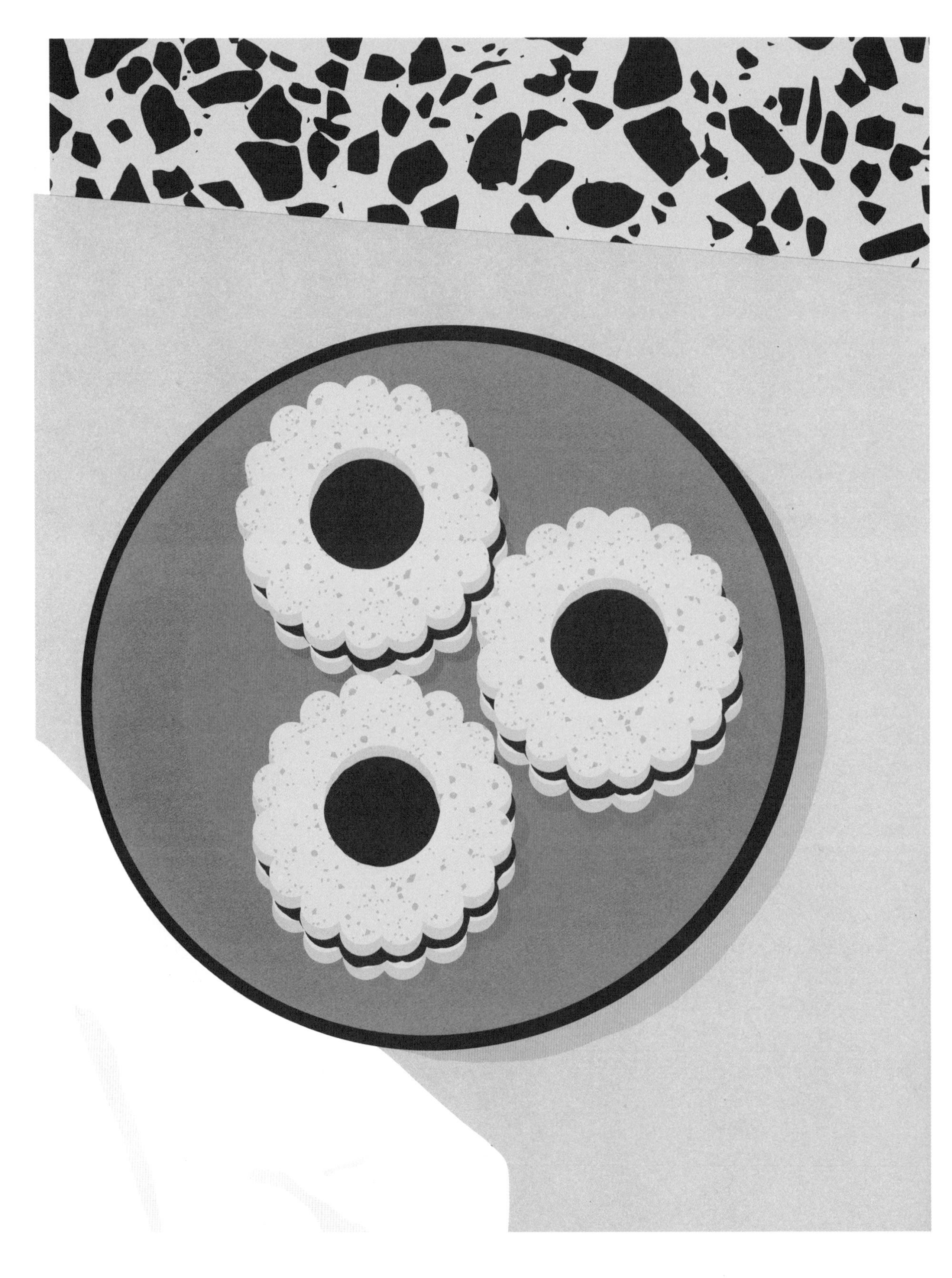

LES PETITES

46 small sandwich cookies **These are dainty, delicate, delicious, fancy little French cookies sandwiched together with chocolate between them; the top cookie has a hole cut out in the middle for the chocolate to show through. They are nicknamed Black-Eyed Susans.**

Make these for a wedding reception (there is an old saying that a ring-shaped cookie symbolizes eternal happiness because it has no end), a bridal shower, a tea party, or anything fancy and special.

- **5 ounces (1 cup) blanched hazelnuts or almonds, or a combination of both**
- **6 ounces (1½ sticks) unsalted butter**
- **½ teaspoon vanilla extract**
- **½ cup sugar**
- **Pinch of salt**
- **1½ cups *sifted* all-purpose flour**
- **5 ounces semisweet chocolate (to be used for sandwiching the cookies)**

Adjust two racks to divide the oven into thirds and preheat oven to 350 degrees. Line two cookie sheets with baking parchment, or with foil shiny side up.

The nuts must be ground fine. This can be done in a food processor or nut grinder (see page 19).

The dough can be put together in a mixer or a processor.

In a mixer: Cream the butter, mix in the vanilla, sugar, and salt, then the flour, and finally the ground nuts, beating until mixed.

In a food processor: After grinding the nuts, do not remove them from the bowl; add the butter, which should be cut into small pieces, and all the other ingredients except the chocolate and process until the dough holds together.

Do not chill the dough before rolling it; chilling makes it crack when it is rolled.

Flour a pastry cloth and a rolling pin. Use only half of the dough at a time. Form a piece into a ball and flour lightly. Flatten it slightly between your hands. Then roll out carefully (flouring the top, the bottom, and the rolling pin as necessary) until it is a scant ¼ inch or a generous ⅛ inch thick.

You will need a round (preferably scalloped) cookie cutter that measures 1½ inches in diameter. Starting at the outside edge of the rolled-out dough, cut rounds and place them about ½ inch apart on the lined sheets. Then, with a round cutter that measures ¾ inch in diameter, cut holes out of the middle of half of the cookies. (Save the cutout holes and the leftovers and roll them out again to make more cookies.)

Bake for 10 to 15 minutes or a bit longer (depending on the thickness of the cookies), reversing the sheets top to

continues ↘

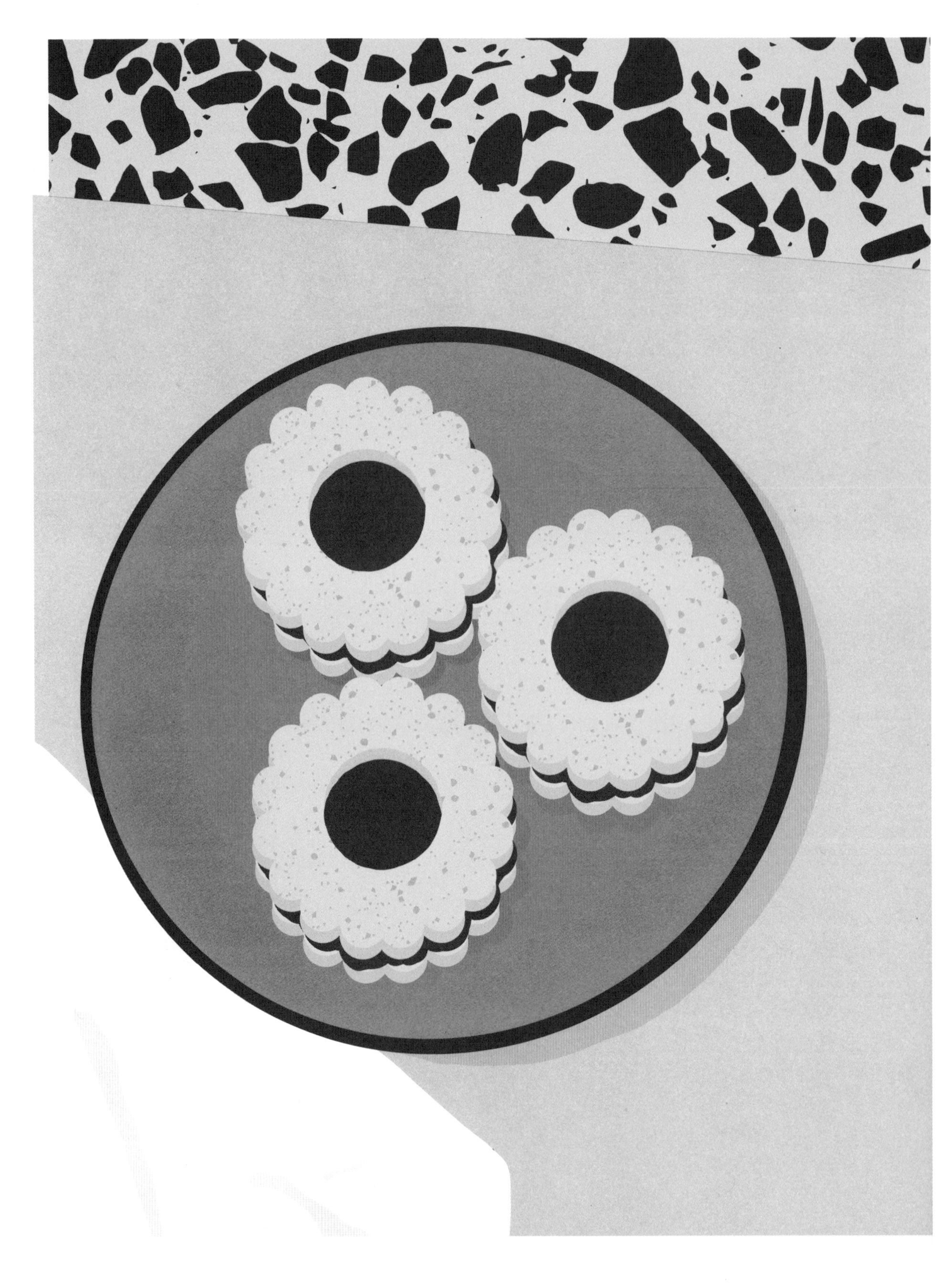

bottom and front to back as necessary to ensure even browning. Bake until the cookies are sandy-colored. Do not underbake.

With a wide metal spatula, transfer the cookies to racks to cool.

Coarsely chop the chocolate and place in the top of a small double boiler over hot water on low heat. Cover until partly melted, then uncover and stir until completely melted. Transfer to a small shallow cup for easy handling.

Turn the cookies that do not have holes in them upside down. With the tip of a small spoon, place a bit (about ¼ teaspoon) of melted chocolate in a mound in the center of each cookie. Do not spread it out. Then place one of the cookies that has a hole in it over the chocolate with the two undersides together. Press together lightly. The chocolate should not extend out to the edges. Repeat, sandwiching all the cookies.

Let stand until the chocolate is firm. (A few minutes in the refrigerator or freezer will save time, if you wish.)

Store airtight.

HAND-FORMED COOKIES

Rolling the dough between your hands to shape these cookies might take a little time, but it is creative, expressive, and gratifying.

KANSAS COOKIES

40 cookies **Margie McGlachlin of Sedgwick, Kansas, won first place in a Kansas State Fair with these very unusual and wonderfully delicious cookies. They are soft, moist, and chewy, and they stay that way.**

This recipe, an adaptation of the original, has a lemon filling similar to lemon cheese (an English spread) mixed with a generous amount of shredded coconut. The cookie dough has molasses and cinnamon; it is all a luscious combination. You will find making these a bit of a challenge but a lot of fun. The dough and the filling can both be made a day ahead if you wish.

COOKIE DOUGH

- 2¼ cups *sifted* all-purpose flour
- ½ teaspoon baking soda
- ¼ teaspoon salt
- 1 teaspoon ground cinnamon
- 4 ounces (1 stick) unsalted butter
- 1 cup sugar
- 1 large egg
- ¼ cup light molasses

LEMON COCONUT FILLING

- 2 large eggs
- ½ cup sugar
- ¼ teaspoon salt
- Finely grated zest of 2 lemons
- ¼ cup lemon juice
- 3½ ounces (1 packed cup) shredded coconut (may be sweetened or unsweetened)

FOR THE DOUGH

Sift together the flour, baking soda, salt, and cinnamon and set aside.

In the large bowl of an electric mixer, beat the butter until soft. Add the sugar and beat until mixed. Beat in the egg and then the molasses. (The mixture will appear curdled—it is OK.) On low speed, gradually add the sifted dry ingredients and beat, scraping the bowl with a rubber spatula, until the mixture holds together and is smooth. Remove the bowl from the mixer.

Turn the dough out onto a piece of wax paper about 15 inches long. Fold up the long sides of the paper and with your hands form the dough into a fat sausage shape about 12 inches long and the same thickness all over.

Bring up the sides of the paper to wrap the dough and carefully transfer it to the refrigerator to chill for at least 2 hours or longer. To save time, it may be placed in the freezer for about 15 minutes and then transferred to the refrigerator for an hour. The dough will be much easier to work with if it is thoroughly chilled (but not frozen); at room temperature it is too soft.

continues ↘

MEANWHILE, FOR THE FILLING

Place the eggs in the top of a small double boiler off the heat and beat them with a small wire whisk until thoroughly mixed. Gradually beat in the sugar and then the salt, lemon zest, and lemon juice.

Place over shallow hot water on moderate heat and stir and scrape the sides constantly with a rubber spatula for 7 to 8 minutes, until the mixture thickens to the consistency of soft mayonnaise.

Remove the top of the double boiler and mix in the coconut. Set aside to cool. (The dough must be cold when you use it, but the filling can be cold or at room temperature.)

To shape and bake the cookies: Adjust a rack to the middle of the oven and preheat oven to 350 degrees. Have ready several unbuttered cookie sheets.

Cut the dough crossways into equal quarters.

Lightly flour a large work surface and transfer one piece of the cold dough to the floured surface. Return the remaining pieces of dough to the refrigerator. With your hands, elongate the cold dough's sausage shape. Then roll it back and forth under your fingers on the floured surface into a very thin sausage shape, 15 inches long. Roll it toward you a few inches in order to reflour the surface under the dough. Then roll it back onto the floured surface. With your fingers, carefully press down on the dough to flatten it a bit. Or roll over it with a rolling pin until it is 3 inches wide and still 15 inches long. The edges should not be thicker than the rest, but they do not have to be perfectly straight.

You have a generous cup of filling. Therefore, you will use a slightly generous ¼ cup for each piece of dough. Measure it in a graded ¼-cup measuring cup.

To make a narrow strip of the filling down the length of the rolled-out dough, use a small spoon and spoon out scant ½ teaspoons just barely touching each other down the middle of the dough. If you use too much filling in any one spot you will not be able to close the sides of the dough over the filling, and you will not have enough to go around. It is not necessary to stay away from the ends; the filling does not run very much.

Now, to raise the long sides of the dough and have them meet over the top of the filling, here are a few hints. First, work quickly before the dough becomes too soft to handle. Second, use either a long, narrow spatula or a wide metal pancake turner to help lift the dough. The aim is to get the two sides to meet on the top and overlap about ½ inch. It is not necessary to wet the dough to make it stick to itself. And it is a waste of time to fuss too much to try to make this very neat, because it runs a bit (just enough to camouflage any irregularities) during baking. Don't worry about little cracks in the dough.

With a ruler, score the strip into 1½-inch lengths. With a sharp knife, cut the strip at the scored lines and, using a metal pancake turner, transfer the cookies to an unbuttered cookie sheet, placing them, seam up or down, about 1½ inches apart.

Bake one sheet at a time for 15 minutes, reversing the sheets top to bottom and back to front once to ensure even browning. When they are done they will just barely begin to darken and the tops will crack a bit. (Everything's under control.)

Use a wide metal spatula to transfer the cookies to a rack to cool.

Shape and bake the remaining dough and filling.

Store airtight.

FUDGE MALLOWS

28 cookies **Semisoft chocolate cookies with a pecan hidden underneath, a marshmallow on top, and then a thick chocolate icing.**

- 1¾ cups *sifted* all-purpose flour
- 1 teaspoon baking soda
- ¼ teaspoon salt
- ½ cup unsweetened cocoa powder (preferably Dutch-process), strained or *sifted*
- 4 ounces (1 stick) unsalted butter
- 1 teaspoon vanilla extract
- 1 cup granulated sugar
- 2 large eggs
- 28 large pecan halves (see Notes)
- 14 large marshmallows (see Notes)

CHOCOLATE ICING

- ½ cup unsweetened cocoa powder (preferably Dutch-process)
- Pinch of salt
- 1½ cups confectioners' sugar
- 5⅓ tablespoons unsalted butter
- About 3 tablespoons boiling water

NOTES

If you do not have large pecan halves, you may use several small pieces—just put them on the bottom of the cookies any which way.

If you use your own homemade marshmallows (page 248), they will be smaller than the regular-size commercial ones. Don't cut them in half; use them whole.

Adjust two racks to divide the oven into thirds and preheat oven to 350 degrees. Line cookie sheets with baking parchment or foil.

Sift together the flour, baking soda, salt, and cocoa and set aside.

In the large bowl of an electric mixer, cream the butter. Add the vanilla and granulated sugar and beat to mix well. Add the eggs one at a time and beat until smooth. On low speed, gradually add the sifted dry ingredients, scraping the bowl with a rubber spatula and beating only until thoroughly mixed.

Place a large piece of wax paper on the work surface. Use a heaping spoonful of dough to form each cookie and place them on the wax paper, making about 28 mounds.

Wet your hands under cold running water and shake off excess water—your hands should be damp but not too wet. Pick up a mound of dough and roll it between your hands into a round ball. Press a pecan half into the ball of dough, placing the curved side (top) of the nut into the dough. Do not enclose it completely. Place the cookie on the sheet so that the flat side of the pecan is on the bottom.

Continue to wet your hands as necessary while you shape the remaining cookies, placing them 2 inches apart on two sheets.

continues ↘

Bake for 16 to 18 minutes, reversing sheets top to bottom and front to back once to ensure even baking. Bake until cookies are barely done—not quite firm to the touch. Do not overbake.

While cookies are baking, cut the marshmallows in half crosswise. (Easier done with scissors.)

Remove the cookie sheets from the oven. Quickly place a marshmallow half, cut side down, on each cookie. Return to the oven for 1 to 1½ minutes. Watch the clock! If the marshmallows bake any longer, they will melt and run off the sides of the cookies—they should not melt and they should stay on top. These should not actually melt at all—only soften very slightly—and not get soft enough to change shape.

Let the cookies stand for a few seconds until they are firm enough to be moved and then, with a wide metal spatula, transfer to racks to cool.

FOR THE ICING

Place the cocoa, salt, and confectioners' sugar in the small bowl of an electric mixer. Melt the butter. Pour the hot butter and 3 tablespoons boiling water into the bowl and beat until completely smooth. The icing should be a thick, semifluid mixture. It should not be so thin that it will run off the cookies. It might be necessary to add a little more hot water, but add it very gradually—only a few drops at a time. (If the sugar has not been strained or sifted before measuring, you might need as much as 2 or 3 additional teaspoons of water.) If you add too much water and the icing becomes too thin, thicken it with additional sugar. If the icing thickens too much while you are icing the cookies, thin it carefully with a few drops of water.

Transfer the icing to a small bowl for ease in handling. Lift a cookie and hold it while you partially frost it with a generous teaspoon of the icing. Allow some of the marshmallow to show through—preferably one side of the marshmallow—the contrast of black and white is what you want. Also, don't try to cover the entire top of the cookie itself or you will not have enough for all the cookies. Replace cookie on rack. Ice all the cookies and then let them stand for a few hours to set.

CHOCOLATE PEPPER PRETZELS

24 pretzel cookies Pretzel superstitions go back to the time of the Romans. People wore pretzels made of flour and water around their necks to ward off evil spirits. They hung them on fruit trees in the belief that the pretzels would cause the trees to have a prolific yield. And they believed that if you broke a pretzel with someone else (like breaking a wishbone) and made a wish at the same time, your wish would come true. (Imagine—all that and chocolate too.)

All of these reasons have made it a popular custom to hang pretzels on Christmas trees. And also, it is so easy to thread a ribbon through a pretzel. These particular pretzel cookies are best when they are not too fresh—another reason to make them for the Christmas tree.

But Christmas aside, these are delicious and adorable. But they aren't as sweet as cookies usually are. They are peppery, but not sharp or harsh. The wonderful dough handles like ceramicist's clay and is just as much fun, if not more, because you get to eat these. A lovely and unusual way to serve these is with wine.

- ¼ cup unsweetened cocoa powder (preferably Dutch-process)
- 1 teaspoon instant coffee powder
- 3 tablespoons boiling water
- 4 ounces (1 stick) unsalted butter
- 1 teaspoon vanilla extract
- ½ teaspoon salt
- ⅛ teaspoon ground allspice
- ¼ teaspoon ground ginger
- 1 teaspoon finely ground black pepper
- ¼ cup granulated sugar
- 1 large egg
- 2 cups *unsifted* all-purpose flour

GLAZE AND TOPPING

- 1 large egg yolk
- 1 teaspoon water
- Coarse or sanding sugar, or granulated sugar

Place the cocoa and coffee in a small bowl; add the water and stir to dissolve. Set aside to cool slightly.

In the large bowl of an electric mixer, cream the butter. Add the vanilla, salt, allspice, ginger, pepper, and granulated sugar, and beat to mix well. Beat in the egg, then the chocolate mixture, and then, on low speed, gradually add the flour and beat until smooth.

Turn the mixture out onto a large board or work surface and shape it into a thick cylinder 6 inches long. Wrap it in plastic wrap and refrigerate for at least half an hour or for as long as a few days.

continues ↘

Before baking, adjust two racks to divide the oven into thirds and preheat oven to 350 degrees. Line cookie sheets with baking parchment.

With a sharp and heavy knife, cut the dough into six 1-inch slices. Then cut each slice into equal quarters, making 24 pieces. (You can cut the six slices but do not separate them; then quarter the whole cylinder.)

To shape pretzels: Roll a piece of the dough on a board or work surface (do not flour the work surface) under the fingers of both hands. As you go, spread your fingers slightly and move them back and forth and gradually out toward the ends of the roll. Each time you do this the roll will increase in length and become thinner. Continue until you have shaped a thin snake 10 inches long.

Form it into a simple pretzel shape by forming a U shape with the dough, then crossing the ends and placing the tips on the bottom right and left sides of the U. Place the pretzel on a cookie sheet.

Continue rolling the dough and forming pretzels.

FOR THE GLAZE AND TOPPING

Beat the yolk and water lightly just to mix and then strain. With a small, soft brush (I use an artist's watercolor brush), brush the glaze over about 4 pretzels at a time. Be careful not to allow the glaze to run down on the sheet or the cookies will stick. (If just a very little runs down, it is OK.)

Using your thumb and forefinger, carefully and slowly sprinkle the coarse, sanding, or granulated sugar generously over the pretzels.

Bake for about 25 minutes, until the cookies are thoroughly dry, reversing the sheets top to bottom and front to back once during baking to ensure even baking. Do not underbake. If you are not sure, break one to see.

With a wide metal spatula, transfer the cookies to racks to cool.

Store airtight. Let stand for at least a day or two before serving.

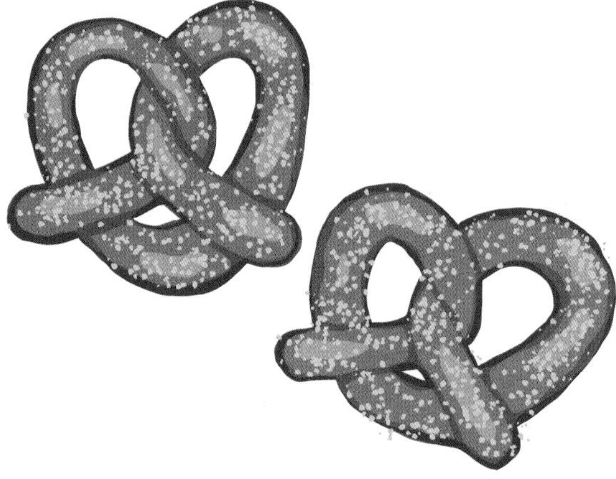

CHOCOLATE AGGIES

40 to 45 cookies **These are dense, chocolaty, rather thick, and semisoft. They are mixed in a saucepan, then rolled in confectioners' sugar before baking.**

- 2 cups *sifted* all-purpose flour
- 2 teaspoons baking powder
- ¼ teaspoon salt
- 2 ounces (½ stick) unsalted butter
- 4 ounces unsweetened chocolate
- 2 cups granulated sugar
- 4 extra-large or jumbo eggs
- 2 ounces (generous ½ cup) walnuts, cut medium fine
- About 1 cup confectioners' sugar or a bit more (to be used when cookies are shaped)

Sift together the flour, baking powder, and salt and set aside.

In a heavy 3-quart saucepan over low heat, melt the butter and chocolate. Stir occasionally until smooth and then remove from the heat. With a heavy wooden spoon, stir the granulated sugar into the warm chocolate mixture. Then stir in the eggs one at a time. Add the sifted dry ingredients and stir until smooth. Stir in the nuts.

It will be a soft dough and must be refrigerated. It may be left in the saucepan or transferred to a bowl. Either way, cover and refrigerate, preferably for 1½ hours (but the dough may be refrigerated longer or overnight if you wish).

Before baking, adjust two racks to divide the oven into thirds and preheat oven to 300 degrees. Line cookie sheets with baking parchment or foil.

Press the confectioners' sugar through a strainer and spread it out on a large piece of wax paper. Sugar the palms of your hands with some of the confectioners' sugar. Roll the dough into 1- to 1¼-inch balls, using a heaping spoonful of dough for each cookie. Roll the balls around in the confectioners' sugar and place them 2 inches apart on the cookie sheets. (If the dough was refrigerated overnight and if the cookies are not baked immediately after being shaped, the confectioners' sugar will become wet. If this happens, the cookies should be rolled around in the sugar again and then rolled between your hands again—the cookies will be more attractive if the confectioners' sugar coats them heavily.)

continues ↘

Bake the cookies for 20 to 22 minutes, until the tops are barely semi-firm to the touch. (If you bake only one sheet at a time, bake it high in the oven.) Reverse the position of the sheets top to bottom and front to back once during baking to ensure even baking. Do not overbake — these should be slightly soft in the centers.

With a wide metal spatula, transfer the cookies to racks to cool.

SEÑORITAS

48 cookies **These are crisp, crunchy, and chewy with toasted chopped almonds and a butterscotch flavor.**

- **5 ounces (1 cup) blanched almonds, coarsely chopped or diced (they must not be fine)**
- **3 cups *sifted* all-purpose flour**
- **1 teaspoon baking soda**
- **½ teaspoon cream of tartar**
- **½ teaspoon salt**
- **6 ounces (1½ sticks) unsalted butter**
- **½ teaspoon vanilla extract**
- **Scant ½ teaspoon almond extract**
- **1 cup granulated sugar**
- **1 cup firmly packed dark brown sugar**
- **2 large eggs**

Adjust two racks to divide the oven into thirds and preheat oven to 400 degrees. Line cookie sheets with baking parchment or foil.

Place the almonds in a small, shallow pan and toast them in the preheated oven, shaking the pan frequently, for about 8 minutes, until they are golden brown. Set aside to cool.

Sift together the flour, baking soda, cream of tartar, and salt and set aside.

In the large bowl of an electric mixer, cream the butter. Add the vanilla and almond extracts, and then gradually add both sugars and beat well. Add the eggs and beat well. On low speed, gradually add the sifted dry ingredients, scraping the bowl with a rubber spatula and beating only until thoroughly mixed. With a wooden spoon, stir in the cooled toasted almonds.

Place a large piece of wax paper in front of you. Use a heaping spoonful of the dough for each cookie and place the mounds on the wax paper, forming 48 mounds.

Roll the mounds of dough between your hands, forming them into balls and placing them at least 2 inches apart (no closer) on the cookie sheets.

It is very important to time the baking of these cookies exactly. Bake for 10 minutes (no longer), reversing the position of the sheets top to bottom and front to back once to ensure even baking. When the 10 minutes are up, the cookies will still feel soft, but they will harden as they cool and if they are baked any longer they will become too hard—they should remain slightly soft and chewy in the centers.

With a wide metal spatula, transfer the cookies to racks to cool.

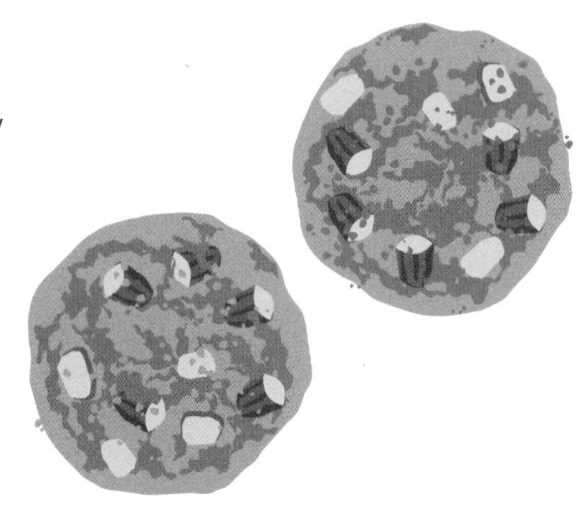

FRENCH FILBERT MACAROONS

24 macaroons **These are traditional Christmas holiday cookies in France. They are made extra soft and chewy with chopped cherries and a bit of jam. You will not need an electric mixer.**

8	**ounces (1⅔ cups) blanched or unblanched hazelnuts (filberts) (see Notes)**
1	**cup granulated sugar**
	Pinch of salt
1	**tablespoon smooth jam or preserves (see Notes)**
	About ¼ cup egg whites (1½ to 2 eggs, depending on size)
12	**glacéed cherries, finely chopped**
	Confectioners' sugar, for powdering your hands and sprinkling over the baked cookies

NOTES

Using unblanched nuts (nuts from which the skins have not been removed) will only affect the color, not the taste.

Any jam or preserves (like black raspberry) may be used but it must be smooth. If it is chunky, strain it.

If the macaroons have baked too long and are hard or dry instead of moist and chewy, place them (before sugaring the tops) in an airtight container with a slice of bread, a lemon, an orange, or half an apple (placed cut side up on top of the macaroons). Let stand for a day or two until they soften.

Adjust a rack to the center of the oven and preheat oven to 325 degrees. Line cookie sheets with baking parchment.

Grind the nuts to a fine powder in a nut grinder, blender, or food processor (see page 19).

Place the ground nuts in a bowl with the sugar and salt and stir to mix thoroughly. Add the jam or preserves and the egg whites. Stir, and then in order to mix the dough thoroughly, squeeze it between your hands until it is smooth. The mixture should be slightly moist but not wet—if it is crumbly and too dry to hold together easily, add a few drops of additional egg white as necessary. Add the cherries and work the dough again with your hands until they are evenly distributed.

Spread out a large piece of wax paper. Using a slightly rounded measuring tablespoon of dough for each cookie, make 24 mounds of dough and place them on the wax paper.

If necessary, powder your hands lightly with confectioners' sugar, then roll each mound of dough into a smooth, round ball. Place them 1 inch apart on the cookie sheets.

Bake for 20 minutes, reversing the position of the sheets top to bottom and front to back once to ensure even baking. Do not overbake—these should remain chewy-soft in the centers. Let the macaroons stand for 5 to 10 minutes.

With a wide metal spatula, carefully transfer the macaroons to a rack to finish cooling.

When cool, place the rack over wax paper. Sprinkle the tops generously with confectioners' sugar, pressing the sugar with your fingers through a strainer held over the macaroons.

DANISH BUTTER SANDWICHES

NOTE

Without the filling, these are delicious plain butter cookies.

24 sandwich cookies **These are crisp, brown-sugar butter cookies sandwiched together with a browned-butter filling.**

- 8 ounces (2 sticks) unsalted butter
- ¾ cup firmly packed light brown sugar
- 1 large egg yolk
- 2¼ cups *sifted* all-purpose flour

BROWNED-BUTTER FILLING

- 2 tablespoons unsalted butter
- 1¼ cups strained or *sifted* confectioners' sugar
- ½ teaspoon vanilla extract
- About 5 to 6 teaspoons heavy cream

Adjust two racks to divide the oven into thirds and preheat oven to 325 degrees. Line cookie sheets with baking parchment or foil.

In the large mixing bowl of an electric mixer, cream the butter. Add the brown sugar and beat to mix. Add the egg yolk and beat to mix. On low speed, gradually add the flour, scraping the bowl with a rubber spatula and beating until the mixture holds together.

Place a long piece of wax paper in front of you. Use a slightly rounded spoonful of the dough for each cookie, and place the mounds of dough on the wax paper, making 48 mounds.

Roll the mounds between your hands into round balls and place them 1½ to 2 inches apart on the lined cookie sheets. With the heel of your hand, or with your fingertips, flatten each mound into a round cookie about ¼ inch thick.

Have a little extra flour in a cup or on a piece of wax paper. Dip a fork into the flour and then press the back of the tines firmly onto the top of a cookie, forming deep indentations in one direction only. Reflour the fork each time you use it, and make the indentations on all of the cookies.

Bake for 15 to 20 minutes (depending on the thickness of the cookies), reversing the cookie sheets top to bottom and front to back once to ensure even baking. Do not allow the cookies to brown — when done they should be a pale golden color.

With a wide metal spatula, transfer the cookies to racks to cool.

Since these cookies are shaped by hand, they will not all be exactly the same size. They should be matched into even pairs before they are filled.

After matching them, place each pair, open, flat side up, on a long piece of wax paper.

continues ↘

FOR THE FILLING

Melt the butter in a small saucepan over moderate heat. Bring it to a boil and let boil until it browns slightly, shaking the pan gently during the last part of heating to prevent the sediment from burning. Remove from the heat when the butter has a rich golden color and immediately add the confectioners' sugar, vanilla, and 5 teaspoons cream. Stir until completely smooth. If necessary, add another teaspoon or so of the cream to make a thick filling.

Transfer the filling to a small custard cup or bowl for ease in handling.

Place a scant spoonful of the filling in the center of a cookie. Repeat with 4 or 5 cookies. Cover each cookie with its matching cookie and, as you do so, press the cookies gently together to spread the filling just to the edges of the sandwich. It is best to hold the cookies in your hands while you do this, and turn the cookies around so that you can see just where the filling is going.

Repeat, filling the remaining cookies, 4 or 5 at a time. While working with the filling, you will find it will thicken and will need to have a few drops of additional cream stirred in. Add only a few drops at a time in order not to make the filling too thin. Let the sandwiches stand for a few hours for the filling to set.

COCONUT WASHBOARDS

24 extra-large cookies **Years ago when we lived on a dairy farm in Brookfield Center, Connecticut, the local general store sold these by the pound from a large wooden barrel. They are extra-large, plain, semisoft, and nostalgic. The dough must be well chilled before the cookies are baked.**

- 2 cups *sifted* all-purpose flour
- ¾ teaspoon baking powder
- ¼ teaspoon baking soda
- ⅛ teaspoon salt
- 4 ounces (1 stick) unsalted butter
- ½ teaspoon vanilla extract
- 1 cup firmly packed light brown sugar
- 1 large egg
- 2 tablespoons water
- 3½ ounces (1 firmly packed cup) shredded coconut

Sift together the flour, baking powder, baking soda, and salt and set aside.

In the large bowl of an electric mixer, cream the butter. Beat in the vanilla. Add the brown sugar and beat to mix. Add the egg and the water and beat to mix well (the mixture will appear curdled — it's OK). On low speed, gradually add the sifted dry ingredients, scraping the bowl with a rubber spatula and beating only until incorporated. Stir in the coconut.

Cut a piece of wax paper to fit a cookie sheet. Use a heaping spoonful of the dough for each cookie (remember these are large). Place them close to each other on the wax paper, forming 24 mounds.

Slide a cookie sheet under the wax paper and transfer the mounds of dough to the freezer or refrigerator to chill until they are firm enough to be handled. (If they are in the freezer, watch them carefully — they should not be frozen solid.)

In the meantime, adjust two racks to divide the oven into thirds and preheat oven to 375 degrees. Line cookie sheets with baking parchment or foil. Have some flour handy for flouring your hands and a fork.

Flour your hands. Pick up a mound of the dough and roll it between your palms into a sausage shape about 3 inches long. Place it on a cookie sheet. Continue shaping the remaining mounds and placing them 3 inches apart (no closer).

Flour the fingertips of one hand and, with your fingertips, flatten each sausage-shaped roll of dough until it is only ¼ inch thick, 3½ inches long, and 2 inches wide.

Now, to form the traditional ridges that give these cookies their name, dip a fork into the flour and press the back of the tines

continues ↘

lengthwise onto the cookies, forming deep indentations. Since the cookies are so large, it will be necessary to press the fork onto each cookie four times, once for each quarter of the cookie surface. The ridges should be parallel and should go lengthwise with the shape of the cookie.

Bake the cookies for about 12 minutes, reversing the sheets top to bottom and front to back once to ensure even browning. (If you bake only one sheet at a time, use the higher rack.) Bake until the cookies are golden brown all over — do not underbake.

Let the cookies stand for a few seconds and then, with a wide metal spatula, transfer them to racks to cool.

SOUR-CREAM AND PECAN DREAMS

48 cookies **These are rather fancy. They are semisoft brown-sugar cookies with a baked-on sour cream and pecan topping.**

- 2 cups *sifted* all-purpose flour
- ½ teaspoon baking soda
- ¼ teaspoon salt
- 4 ounces (1 stick) unsalted butter
- 1 teaspoon vanilla extract
- 1 cup firmly packed dark brown sugar
- 1 large egg

SOUR-CREAM AND PECAN TOPPING

- ½ cup firmly packed dark brown sugar
- ½ teaspoon ground cinnamon
- ¼ cup sour cream
- 4 ounces (generous 1 cup) pecans, finely chopped (these should not be ground or chopped so fine that they are powdery)

Adjust two racks to divide the oven into thirds and preheat oven to 350 degrees. Line cookie sheets with baking parchment or foil.

Sift together the flour, baking soda, and salt and set aside.

In the large bowl of an electric mixer, cream the butter. Add the vanilla and sugar and beat well. Add the egg and continue to beat for a few minutes, scraping the bowl with a rubber spatula and beating until the mixture lightens in color. On low speed, gradually add the sifted dry ingredients, scraping the bowl with the spatula and beating only until the mixture is smooth.

Use a slightly rounded spoonful of dough for each cookie—make these a little smaller than average. (To be sure that you are not making the cookies too large, before rolling any of the dough into balls you may divide the dough into 48 equal mounds on wax paper.) Roll the dough between your hands into round balls and place them 2 inches apart—no closer—on the cookie sheets.

With your fingertip or with the handle end of a large wooden spoon, make a wide, round depression in the center of each cookie—reaching almost to the edges and leaving a rim.

FOR THE TOPPING

Place the sugar, cinnamon, and sour cream in a small mixing bowl. With a rubber spatula, stir until smooth. Stir in the nuts.

With a demitasse spoon or a small measuring spoon, place some of the topping on each cookie. The topping should be mounded fairly high above the rims of the cookies.

Bake for 13 to 15 minutes, reversing the cookie sheets top to bottom and front to back once to ensure even baking. If you bake only one sheet at a time, use the higher rack.

With a wide metal spatula, transfer the cookies to racks to cool.

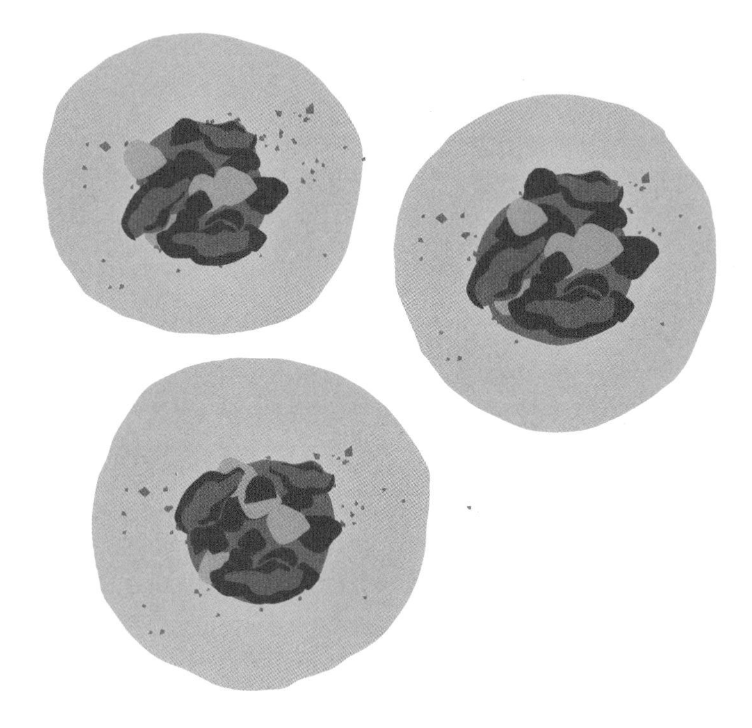

CHARLIE BROWN'S PEANUT COOKIES

36 cookies **These are coated with chopped peanuts and have a baked-on topping of peanut butter and chocolate morsels. They are fancy and take a little longer to make than many other cookies, but they are worth the time and are fun to make.**

NOTES

In place of the semisweet chocolate morsels you may, if you wish, use butterscotch morsels. Or use chocolate on half of the cookies and butterscotch on the others. Or you may use mini morsels, in which case use as many as it takes to cover the peanut butter.

Don't worry about placing the morsels exactly in position because as the cookies spread in baking, the morsels will slide out over the tops and won't stay where you put them anyhow.

- 2 cups *sifted* all-purpose flour
- 1 teaspoon baking powder
- ½ teaspoon ground cinnamon
- 8 ounces (2 sticks) unsalted butter
- 1 cup firmly packed dark brown sugar
- 2 large eggs (leave 1 egg whole and separate the other)
- 1 teaspoon water
- 10 ounces (2¼ cups) salted peanuts (preferably dry-roasted), chopped medium fine
- Scant ¾ cup smooth (not chunky) peanut butter (it is not necessary to measure this; you may use it right from the jar)
- 4 ounces (⅔ cup) semisweet chocolate morsels (see Notes)

Sift together the flour, baking powder, and cinnamon and set aside.

In the large bowl of an electric mixer, cream the butter. Add the sugar and beat to mix. Beat in 1 whole egg and 1 egg yolk (reserve the second white). On low speed, gradually add the sifted dry ingredients, scraping the bowl with a rubber spatula and beating only until thoroughly mixed.

Place one long piece of wax paper on the work surface. Divide the dough into 36 equal mounds on the wax paper, using a heaping spoonful for each. Flour your hands and roll each mound into a round ball, continuing to flour your hands before rolling each ball. As you roll the balls, replace them on the wax paper.

Adjust two racks to divide the oven into thirds and preheat oven to 375 degrees. Line cookie sheets with baking parchment or foil.

In a small, shallow bowl, beat the reserved egg white with the water, beating only until mixed and barely foamy. Place the chopped peanuts on a long piece of aluminum foil or wax paper. Pick up a

continues ↘

cookie and use your fingers to roll it around in the egg white. Place it on the chopped nuts and roll around in the nuts to coat thoroughly. Coat 4 or 5 cookies at a time. Place the nut-covered cookies 2 inches apart on the cookie sheets. Continue to prepare all of the cookies the same way.

Now, form a depression in the top of each cookie. Either do it with the handle end of a large wooden spoon or with your thumb to keep the dough from sticking. Make the depression rather deep and wide but not so deep that you make the bottom of the cookie too thin.

With a small demitasse spoon or a ½-teaspoon measuring spoon, place a generous ½ teaspoon of the peanut butter into each indentation. Place 5 or 6 chocolate morsels on the top of each cookie, pressing them slightly into the peanut butter.

Bake the cookies for 12 to 13 minutes, reversing the sheets top to bottom and front to back once to ensure even browning.

Let the cookies cool for a minute or two before removing them with a wide metal spatula to racks to cool.

When the cookies have reached room temperature, place them in the refrigerator very briefly—only long enough to set the chocolate morsels.

ENGLISH GINGERSNAPS #1

22 large cookies **This is a classic recipe for large, dark semisoft gingersnaps.**

- **2¼ cups *sifted* all-purpose flour**
- **2 teaspoons baking soda**
- **½ teaspoon salt**
- **1 teaspoon ground cinnamon**
- **1 teaspoon ground ginger**
- **½ teaspoon ground cloves**
- **¼ teaspoon ground allspice**
- **¼ teaspoon finely ground black pepper**
- **6 ounces (1½ sticks) unsalted butter**
- **1 cup firmly packed dark brown sugar**
- **1 large egg**
- **¼ cup molasses**
- **Granulated sugar, for rolling the cookies**

Sift together the flour, baking soda, salt, cinnamon, ginger, cloves, allspice, and black pepper and set aside.

In the large bowl of an electric mixer, cream the butter. Add the brown sugar and beat well. Add the egg and the molasses and beat for a few minutes, until the mixture is light in color. On low speed, gradually add the sifted dry ingredients, scraping the bowl with a rubber spatula and beating only until incorporated.

Refrigerate the dough briefly (in the mixing bowl if you wish) until it can be handled; 10 to 15 minutes might be enough.

Adjust two racks to divide the oven into thirds and preheat oven to 375 degrees. Line cookie sheets with baking parchment or foil.

Spread some granulated sugar on a large piece of wax paper. Use a rounded large spoonful of dough for each cookie. Roll it into a ball between your hands, then roll it around in the granulated sugar. Place the balls 2½ to 3 inches apart on the cookie sheets.

Bake the cookies for about 13 minutes, reversing the sheets top to bottom and front to back once to ensure even browning. The cookies are done when they feel semi-firm to the touch.

With a wide metal spatula, transfer the cookies to racks to cool.

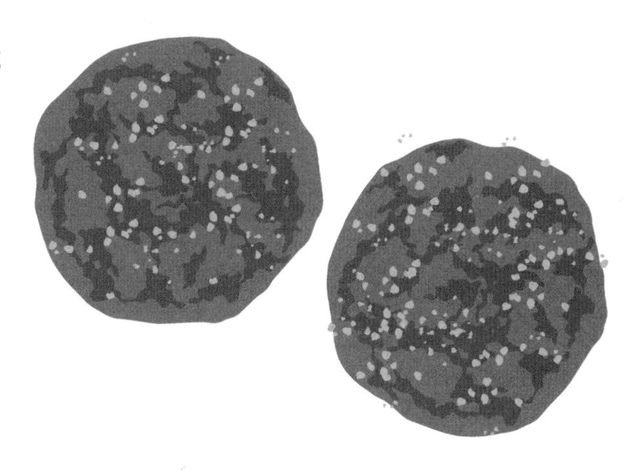

continues ↘

VARIATION

English Gingersnaps #2: These are made smaller, and are more crisp and gingery. Use only 2 cups plus 2 tablespoons flour, increase the ginger to 2 teaspoons, use light brown sugar instead of dark brown, and stir the finely grated zest of 1 small lemon and 1 orange into the dough.

Because of the slightly smaller amount of flour, this dough will need a bit more chilling time, and then it is best to work with one-fourth of the dough at a time and keep the remainder refrigerated.

Use one very slightly rounded spoonful of dough for each cookie, roll into balls, roll in sugar as above, and place the cookies about 1½ inches apart. Bake for 10 to 12 minutes. (Makes 70 to 80 cookies.)

"Eating in bed is my favorite pastime.

I eat anything and everything there.

I love, love, love it."

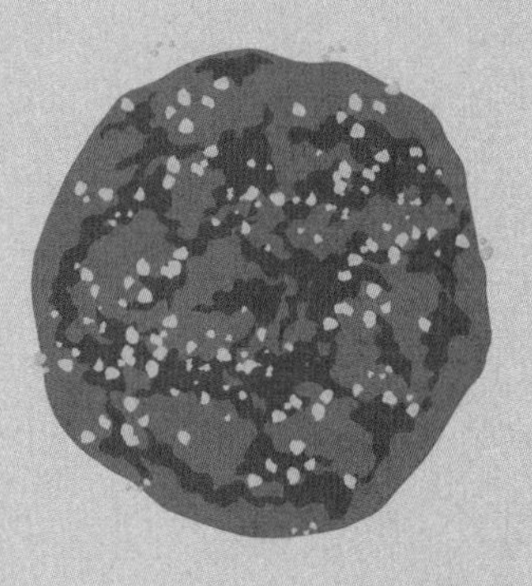

MORE!

A variety of recipes that do not fit into any of the previous categories. Some of these might call for special equipment.

ALMOND TARTLETS

NOTE

If you do not have enough molds to bake these all at once, the remaining pastry and filling may wait at room temperature. The molds do not have to be washed and dried if they are to be reused right away, but they must be cool.

60 to 70 tiny tartlets **To make these fancy petit-four-type cookies, it is necessary to use shallow, very small individual tartlet molds; they may be plain or fluted. Mine are French; they are assorted shapes and they vary in diameter from about 1 to 2 inches. Or you may use plain round, shallow French tartlet pans about 2 to 2½ inches in diameter and ½ inch deep. These little pans should be washed with only hot soapy water; anything rougher would cause future cookies to stick.**

FILLING

- **5 ounces (1 cup) blanched almonds**
- **2 large eggs**
- **½ teaspoon almond extract**
- **½ cup sugar**

PASTRY

- **8 ounces (2 sticks) unsalted butter**
- **⅛ teaspoon salt**
- **1 teaspoon vanilla extract**
- **½ cup sugar**
- **1 large egg**
- **2 cups *sifted* all-purpose flour**

FOR THE FILLING

In a nut grinder, blender, or food processor, grind the almonds (see page 19). They must be dry and powdery. If you use a blender, the nuts might form oily lumps. If so, with your fingertips press the ground nuts through a large strainer set over a large bowl in order to aerate the nuts and break up any oily lumps. Any pieces too large to go through the strainer should be stirred into the strained nuts. Set aside.

In the small bowl of an electric mixer, beat the eggs until foamy. Add the almond extract and then gradually add the sugar. Beat at high speed for about 7 minutes, until the mixture is almost white and forms ribbons when the beaters are raised. On low speed, stir in the ground almonds. Set aside at room temperature.

FOR THE PASTRY

In the large bowl of an electric mixer, cream the butter. Add the salt, vanilla, and sugar and beat well. Beat in the egg. On low speed, add the flour, scraping the bowl with a rubber spatula and beating until the mixture is smooth and holds together.

Adjust a rack one-third up from the bottom of the oven and preheat oven to 350 degrees.

continues ↘

To line the molds with the dough (do not butter them), use a demitasse spoon or a small measuring spoon to place some of the dough in a mold. With the back of the spoon or your fingertips, spread the dough to make a layer ¼ to ⅓ inch thick. Don't worry about making the thickness exactly even but do make the top edge level with the top of the mold. Line all of the molds and place them on a cookie sheet or rimmed baking sheet.

Now, with a small spoon, put the filling into the lined molds, mounding it slightly higher than the rims. If the almonds in the filling have sunk to the bottom, stir lightly to mix before spooning into the molds.

Bake for 20 to 25 minutes, until the crust is golden and the filling is well browned. Carefully reverse the position of the pan front to back once to ensure even browning.

Remove from the oven and let stand for 5 minutes. Then, with your fingertips, carefully remove the cookies from the molds and place them on racks to finish cooling.

VARIATIONS

Coarsely chop about ⅓ cup candied cherries or pineapple and place a few pieces in each pastry-lined form before adding the filling.

Place the racks of baked cookies over a large piece of wax paper. With your fingertips, press confectioners' sugar through a fine strainer held over the cookies to coat them generously.

CHOCOLATE CHIP COCONUT MACAROONS

NOTE

If you use a compound chocolate (see page 15) for the glaze, it will dry quickly without refrigeration; the finished cookies may stand at room temperature; and the chocolate will not discolor. Otherwise, any real semisweet chocolate may be used, with the directions for refrigerating (see page 218).

36 cookies **These are white cookies with chocolate chips and a layer of melted chocolate on the bottom. They are easy to make and keep well.**

- **⅓ cup *sifted* all-purpose flour**
- **¼ teaspoon baking powder**
- **⅛ teaspoon salt**
- **1 tablespoon unsalted butter**
- **¾ cup granulated sugar**
- **2 large eggs**
- **1 teaspoon vanilla extract**
- **10½ ounces (4 loosely packed cups) shredded coconut**
- **6 ounces (1 cup) semisweet chocolate morsels**
- **6 ounces semisweet chocolate or compound chocolate (see Note)**

Adjust two racks to divide the oven into thirds and preheat oven to 325 degrees. Line cookie sheets with aluminum foil.

Sift together the flour, baking powder, and salt and set aside.

Place the butter in a small pan over low heat to melt. Then set it aside to cool but do not let it harden—it must stay liquid.

Meanwhile, in the small bowl of an electric mixer, beat the sugar and eggs at high speed for 5 minutes, until the mixture is almost white.

On lowest speed, add the sifted dry ingredients, scraping the bowl with a rubber spatula and beating only until incorporated.

Remove from the mixer and fold in the liquid butter and then the vanilla. Then fold in the coconut and finally the chocolate morsels.

Use a well-rounded spoonful of the mixture for each cookie and place them 1½ inches apart on the aluminum foil.

Bake two sheets at a time, reversing the sheets top to bottom and front to back once during baking to ensure even browning. (If you bake one sheet at a time, bake it on the lower rack.) Bake for about 18 minutes, or until some parts of the tops of the cookies are lightly golden-colored—some parts of the cookies will still be white.

With a wide metal spatula, transfer the cookies to racks to cool.

While the cookies are baking or cooling prepare the glaze: Break up the semisweet or compound chocolate and place it in the top of a small double boiler over warm

continues ↘

water on low heat to melt slowly. Cover until partially melted, then uncover and stir until completely smooth. Remove the top of the double boiler from the hot water.

Cover one or two cookie sheets with wax paper or aluminum foil.

With a small metal spatula, spread some of the chocolate on the bottoms of the cookies, spreading it smoothly all the way to the edges in a rather thin layer. After you spread the chocolate on a cookie, place it chocolate side down on the lined cookie sheet.

Refrigerate until the chocolate is firm and the cookies can be lifted easily. Place them in an airtight box.

These are best if they are stored in the refrigerator and served cold if you have used regular semisweet chocolate (see Note).

ALMOND MACAROONS

28 macaroons **These are classic French macaroons—soft and chewy. They are formed with a pastry bag and a large star-shaped tube. They may be made without an electric mixer.**

- **8 ounces (1⅔ cups) blanched almonds**
- **⅔ cup sugar**
- **½ cup egg whites (3 to 4 eggs, depending on size)**
- **½ teaspoon almond extract**
- **14 glacéed cherries, cut into halves, or about 3 tablespoons slivered (julienne-shaped) blanched almonds**

Adjust two racks to divide the oven into thirds and preheat oven to 350 degrees. Line two cookie sheets with aluminum foil and set aside.

The almonds must be ground to a very fine powder. They may be ground in a nut grinder, blender, or food processor (see page 19). If they are ground in a blender they will probably become oily and lumpy—if so they must be strained to aerate them; place a large strainer over a large bowl and, with your fingertips, force the nuts through the strainer.

Place the ground nuts and sugar in a medium-size mixing bowl and stir together until thoroughly mixed.

Beat the egg whites until they hold a firm shape and are stiff but not dry, adding the almond extract toward the end of the beating. Fold the whites into the ground almond and sugar mixture.

Fit a 12-inch pastry bag with a #8 star-shaped tube. Fold down a deep cuff on the outside of the bag. Support the bag by placing it in a tall, narrow glass or jar. Place the macaroon mixture in the bag and, quickly, before the mixture runs out through the tube, unfold the cuff, twist the top of the bag closed, and turn the bag tube end up.

Hold the bag at a right angle to a foil-lined sheet. Press from the top of the bag to press out rosettes of the dough 1½ to 1¾ inches in diameter, placing them 1 inch apart.

Top each macaroon with a glacéed cherry half or a few pieces of slivered almonds.

Bake for about 20 minutes, until the macaroons are lightly colored. Reverse the sheets top to bottom and front to back as necessary to ensure even browning. These are more attractive if they are not too pale, but do not overbake. They should be a golden color on the ridges and the edges, but they may still be pale between the ridges.

Slide the foil off the cookie sheets and let stand for about 5 minutes. Then peel the foil away from the backs of the macaroons and transfer them to racks to finish cooling.

CONNECTICUT STRIPPERS

40 to 48 strips **These are soft, moist fruit-and-nut strips, traditionally a Christmas treat.**

DOUGH

- 2 cups *sifted* all-purpose flour
- ½ teaspoon baking soda
- ½ teaspoon salt
- 1½ teaspoons ground cinnamon
- ½ teaspoon ground nutmeg
- 5⅓ ounces (10⅔ tablespoons) unsalted butter
- 1 teaspoon vanilla extract
- 1 cup firmly packed dark or light brown sugar
- 1 large egg plus 1 egg yolk (reserve the white for the topping)
- 3½ ounces (1 cup) walnuts, cut into medium-size pieces
- 7½ ounces (1½ cups) currants

TOPPING

- 2 tablespoons granulated sugar
- ½ teaspoon ground cinnamon
- ⅓ cup walnuts, finely chopped
- 1 large egg white (reserved from the dough)

FOR THE DOUGH

Sift together the flour, baking soda, salt, cinnamon, and nutmeg and set aside.

In the large bowl of an electric mixer, cream the butter. Add the vanilla and brown sugar and beat to mix well. Add the whole egg and egg yolk and beat until smooth. On low speed, add the sifted dry ingredients, scraping the bowl with a rubber spatula and beating only until incorporated. Mix in the nuts and currants.

Place the bowl of dough in the refrigerator for about half an hour, or until it is firm enough to handle.

Adjust two racks to divide the oven into thirds and preheat oven to 400 degrees. Line two 12 x 15½-inch cookie sheets with aluminum foil.

Generously flour a large board or smooth work surface. Divide the dough into quarters and work with one piece at a time. Flour your hands, form the piece of dough into a ball, and turn it over several times on the board to flour it on all sides. Then, with your hands, form the dough into a roll 13 inches long and place it lengthwise on one of the lined cookie sheets. Repeat with the remaining pieces of dough, placing two rolls about 4 inches apart on each sheet.

With floured fingertips, press each roll of dough to flatten to ½- to ¾-inch thickness.

FOR THE TOPPING

Stir the granulated sugar and cinnamon together to mix thoroughly. Stir in the nuts. In a small bowl, beat the egg white until it is foamy, not stiff. Use a pastry brush to brush some of the beaten white generously over one strip of the dough. Sprinkle with one-fourth of the topping. Repeat the process with the remaining three strips of dough.

Bake for 12 to 15 minutes, reversing the cookie sheets top to bottom and front to back as necessary to ensure even browning. Bake until the tops of the strips spring back when lightly pressed with a fingertip.

Slide the foil and strips off the cookie sheets and let the strips stand for about 10 minutes. Then, with a wide metal spatula, release but do not remove the strips from the foil. Let them stand until completely cool. Then use a cookie sheet as a spatula to transfer the strips to a large cutting board.

With a sharp knife, cut the strips at an angle into 1- to 1¼-inch slices.

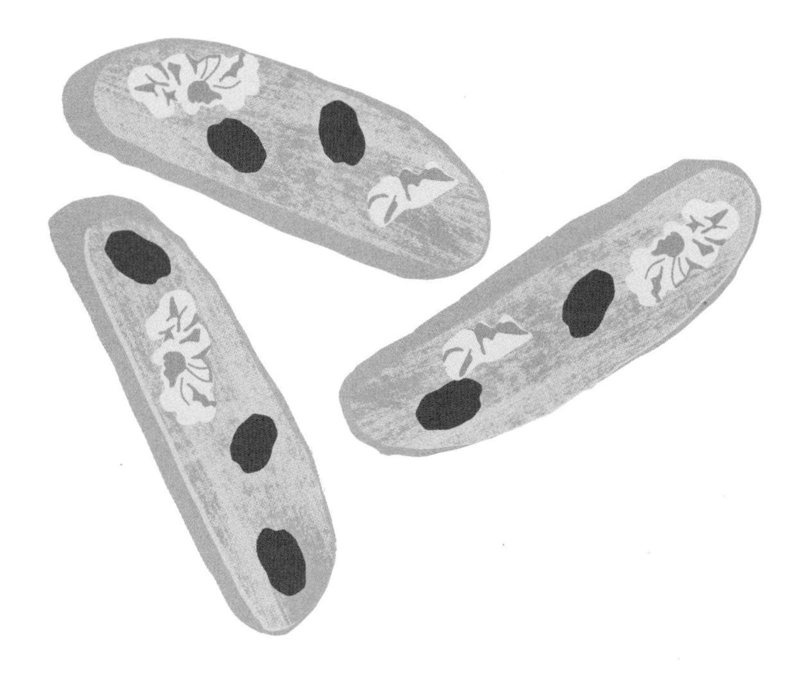

FRENCH SUGAR FANS

36 fans **These wafers may be served as plain sugar cookies, or place two of them, points down, at angles into a portion of ice cream. The dough must chill for at least an hour before baking.**

- **2 cups *sifted* all-purpose flour**
- **1½ teaspoons baking powder**
- **¼ teaspoon salt**
- **5⅓ ounces (10⅔ tablespoons) unsalted butter**
- **½ teaspoon vanilla extract**
- **¾ cup sugar**
- **1 large egg**
- **4 teaspoons milk**
- **Finely grated zest of 1 lemon**
- **Additional sugar for sprinkling over the cookies**

Sift together the flour, baking powder, and salt and set aside.

In the large bowl of an electric mixer, cream the butter. Beat in the vanilla and sugar. Add the egg and then the milk and lemon zest and beat well. On low speed, gradually add the sifted dry ingredients, scraping the bowl with a rubber spatula and beating until the dough holds together.

Tear off four pieces of wax paper. Place one-fourth of the dough on each piece of paper. Wrap the dough and flatten it slightly. Refrigerate (do not chill in the freezer) for at least 1 hour.

Before baking, adjust two racks to divide the oven into thirds and preheat oven to 375 degrees. Line cookie sheets with baking parchment or foil.

Flour a pastry cloth and rolling pin very well. Work with one piece of the dough at a time, keeping the rest refrigerated. Work quickly before the dough softens. Place it on the floured cloth and turn it over several times to flour both sides. With the floured rolling pin, roll the dough into a circle ⅓ inch thick and slightly larger than 8 inches in diameter (reflour the pin as necessary).

Now you will need something as a pattern for cutting an 8-inch circle of dough; use a flan ring, a canister cover, or a cake pan turned upside down. Place the pattern on the dough and cut around it with a plain or fluted pastry wheel (the fluted wheel will give a rippled, fanlike appearance). Or, in place of the pastry wheel, a small, sharp knife may be used to cut a plain edge.

With a long knife, cut the circle into eight pie-shaped wedges. If the blade sticks to the dough, flour it as necessary.

With the back (dull side) of a knife or the edge of a metal spatula, mark each cookie with five or six lines that radiate from the point to the outside curve—the lines should be deep but not deep enough to cut through the dough. Flour the knife or spatula as necessary to keep it from sticking.

continues ↘

With a wide metal spatula, transfer the fans to the cookie sheets, placing them 1 inch apart. Sprinkle the fans with sugar.

Bake for 7 to 10 minutes, reversing the sheets top to bottom and front to back as necessary to ensure even cooking. The fans should bake only until they are slightly colored. They should not be brown, but if they are underbaked they will be too soft.

With a wide metal spatula, transfer the fans to racks to cool.

SWEDISH FRIED TWISTS

NOTE

These directions are for very large twists. I do it that way because it is fun—and they look wild. But they may be made smaller, ¾ inch x 3 inches, if you wish.

36 very large twists **Most European countries have their own version of these sweet crackers. In Poland, they are called Favorki and are traditionally made around Eastertime. In America they are known as Bow Ties, Knots, Christmas Crullers, etc. Light, dry, airy, and extremely plain, they are generally served with coffee or wine, more commonly between meals than as an after-dinner sweet. You will need a deep-fry thermometer and a pastry wheel.**

- Vegetable oil (for deep frying)
- 4 large egg yolks (reserve 1 white to use later)
- 1/3 cup confectioners' sugar
- 1 teaspoon ground cardamom
- Pinch of salt
- 1/4 cup plus 1 tablespoon heavy cream
- 2 tablespoons cognac, brandy, or whiskey
- 1 large egg white
- About 2 1/4 cups *sifted* all-purpose flour
- Additional confectioners' sugar, for sprinkling over the twists

You will need a wide saucepan or a large deep-frying pan. Heat at least 2 inches of oil in the pan over moderate heat. Insert a deep-fry thermometer and slowly bring the temperature to 365 degrees.

Meanwhile, prepare the dough: In the small bowl of an electric mixer, beat the egg yolks with the sugar, cardamom, and salt at high speed for 4 or 5 minutes, until the mixture is very thick and light lemon-colored. On low speed, gradually add the cream and cognac, brandy, or whiskey, scraping the bowl with a rubber spatula and beating only until mixed.

Beat the egg white until it holds a firm shape and is stiff but not dry. On low speed, add the beaten white to the yolk mixture. Then, on low speed, gradually add most of the flour, scraping the bowl with the spatula. When you have added enough flour to make a very thick mixture, remove the bowl from the mixer.

Spread the remaining flour out on a large board. Turn the dough out onto the flour. Using only as much flour as necessary to make a dough that is firm enough to knead, knead it on the floured board until it is very smooth and not sticky.

Cover the dough lightly with plastic wrap or with a kitchen towel and let stand for 15 minutes.

Cut the dough in half. Work with one piece at a time, setting the other piece aside and covering it lightly. On the floured board

continues

(using no more flour than necessary), with a lightly floured rolling pin, roll the dough into a rectangle ⅛ inch thick.

Using a ruler and a plain or zigzag pastry wheel, cut the dough into strips 2 inches wide. Then cut across all the strips at once, so that each piece of dough is about 5 inches long, or a little less (see Note). Don't worry about any different-size pieces on the corners or ends — use them as they are.

Now, with the pastry wheel, cut a slit 3 to 4 inches long lengthwise down the middle of each piece of dough. Slip one end of the dough through the slit. (You may prepare them all before frying, or you may pull the end through each one just before you fry it.)

Adjust the heat as necessary to maintain the oil at 365 degrees. Fry only a few twists at a time; the number depends on the size of the pan — don't crowd them. Place a few of the twists in the oil and fry until golden brown on the bottoms. Then, with two flat wire whisks or slotted spoons or spatulas, turn them and fry until the cookies are golden brown on both sides. Drain on heavy brown paper.

When the twists are cool, sprinkle the tops generously with confectioners' sugar, pressing it with your fingertips through a strainer held over the twists. Transfer them to a large platter or a deep bowl for serving.

BLACK-AND-WHITE RUSKS

About 78 rusks **This is German *mandelbrot,* or "almond bread," although it is not bread and there are no almonds in the recipe. The rusks are hard, plain, and dry.**

- **3 cups *sifted* all-purpose flour**
- **2 teaspoons baking powder**
- **⅛ teaspoon baking soda**
- **¼ teaspoon salt**
- **1 ounce unsweetened chocolate**
- **2 large eggs**
- **1 cup sugar**
- **1 teaspoon vanilla extract**
- **¾ teaspoon almond extract**
- **½ cup vegetable oil (not olive oil)**
- **Finely grated zest of 1 large, deep-colored orange**

Adjust two racks to divide the oven into thirds and preheat oven to 350 degrees. Line two cookie sheets with aluminum foil.

Sift together the flour, baking powder, baking soda, and salt and set aside.

Melt the chocolate either in the top of a small double boiler or in a small, heat-proof cup set in shallow hot water over moderate heat, and then set the melted chocolate aside to cool.

In the large bowl of an electric mixer, beat the eggs at high speed until foamy. Gradually add the sugar and continue to beat at high speed for a few minutes, until pale in color. Beat in the vanilla and almond extracts. On low speed, mix in one-third of the sifted dry ingredients, then all of the oil, and a second third of the dry ingredients. The mixture will be stiff; remove it from the mixer and use a wooden spatula to stir in the orange zest and the remaining third of the dry ingredients. Stir until thoroughly mixed.

Transfer ⅔ cup of the mixture to a mixing bowl and, with a wooden spatula, stir in the melted chocolate.

On a board, form the chocolate dough with your hands into a thick roll 8 inches long. Cut the roll into quarters. On the board (it does not have to be floured), with your fingers, form each quarter into a thin roll 12 inches long. Set the chocolate rolls aside.

Now flour the board lightly (the white dough is a little sticky). Work with one-quarter (½ cup) of the white dough at a time. Flour your hands lightly and form the dough with your fingers into a roll 12 inches long. Then, on the floured board, using your fingers and the palms of your hands, flatten the dough until it is 2½ inches wide. Place one of the chocolate rolls lengthwise in the center of the white dough. With your fingers, bring up both sides of the white dough to enclose the chocolate. Pinch the edges of the white dough together to seal.

Place the roll, seam down, lengthwise on one of the foil-lined cookie sheets. Continue making the rolls, four altogether, allowing for two rolls on each sheet. With your hands, straighten and shape them evenly.

Bake for 20 to 25 minutes, until lightly browned. Reverse the cookie sheets top to

continues ↘

bottom and front to back once to ensure even browning. Don't worry about the tops of the rolls cracking—that's OK.

With a wide metal spatula, transfer the baked rolls to a large cutting board. Do not turn off the oven.

Do not wait for the rolls to cool—slice the hot rolls at a sharp angle into ½-inch slices. (Try different knives to see which works best; I use a finely serrated knife.)

Return the slices, cut side down, to the foil-lined sheets. Then return the sheets to the 350-degree oven to bake the rusks until they are dry. Reverse the positions of the cookie sheets occasionally so that the cookies will dry evenly. Bake for about 15 minutes, or until the rusks are only lightly colored—do not allow them to brown too much. They will become crisp as they cool.

Transfer the rusks to racks to cool.

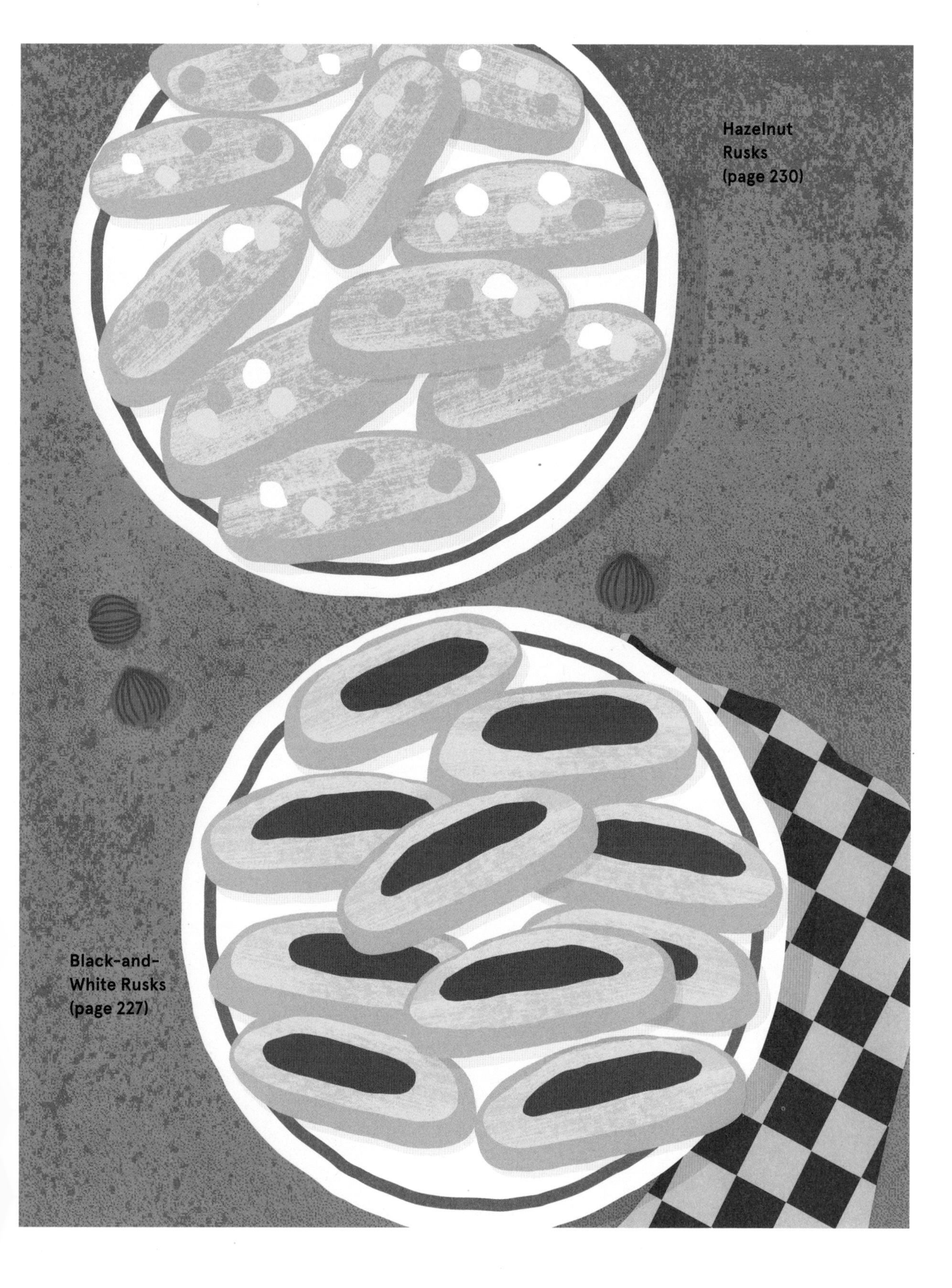
Hazelnut
Rusks
(page 230)
Black-and-
White Rusks
(page 227)

HAZELNUT RUSKS

About 78 rusks **This is an old German recipe. The rusks are hard, plain, dry, and crunchy.**

- **3 cups *sifted* all-purpose flour**
- **1 teaspoon baking powder**
- **¼ teaspoon salt**
- **3 extra-large eggs**
- **1¼ cups sugar**
- **½ teaspoon almond extract**
- **12 ounces (2 generous cups) blanched hazelnuts (see page 18), coarsely chopped (see Note)**

NOTE

Blanched almonds may be substituted for the hazelnuts, but do try the rusks sometime with hazelnuts—they're so good. The nuts should be coarsely cut. For this recipe I find that chopping them on a board or in a bowl creates too many fine, small pieces. I prefer to cut them individually with a small paring knife, cutting each nut into halves or thirds.

Adjust two racks to divide the oven into thirds and preheat oven to 350 degrees. Line two 12 x 15½-inch cookie sheets with aluminum foil.

Sift together the flour, baking powder, and salt and set aside.

In the small bowl of an electric mixer, beat the eggs with the sugar at high speed for 12 to 15 minutes, until the mixture is almost white and forms a ribbon when the beaters are lifted. Beat in the almond extract.

Transfer the mixture to the large bowl of the electric mixer. On low speed, add the sifted dry ingredients, scraping the bowl with a rubber spatula and beating only until smooth. Fold in the nuts.

To make three strips of dough, two on one sheet and one on the other, place the dough in large spoonfuls, touching each other, lengthwise on the foil. The strips should be 13 inches long, 2 to 3 inches wide, and about 1½ inches thick. The two strips on one piece of foil should be about 3 inches apart. Place the dough carefully to make the strips rather even in shape but do not smooth over the tops or sides—they will run a bit in baking and will level themselves enough.

Bake the strips for 25 to 30 minutes, reversing them top to bottom and front to back to ensure even browning. Bake until the strips are firm to the touch—they will remain pale in color. Remove the strips from the oven but do not turn off the oven.

Slide the foil off the cookie sheets. Let stand for 2 or 3 minutes. Place a folded towel or a pot holder in your left hand and invert a strip onto it. Peel away the foil and then turn the strip over and place it top side up on a cutting board. The strip will be hot and a little delicate, so handle with care. Repeat with remaining strips and let stand for a few minutes.

While the strips are still slightly warm, cut them crosswise into ½-inch slices with a finely serrated knife or a long, thin, very sharp slicing knife. These are best if they are not thicker than ½ inch.

Transfer the slices back to the cookie sheets and place them, top side up, with space between them.

Bake again at 350 degrees for 10 minutes, reversing the position of the sheets halfway through, to dry. They will feel soft while hot but will become crisp when cool. If they are not crisp they should be baked longer — if they are thicker than ½ inch they might need a bit more baking — but do not overbake them or they might become too hard and dry.

SHORTBREAD DOUGHNUT COOKIES

NOTE

If you don't have a doughnut cutter, you can use two round cutters, one larger than the other, to cut doughnut shapes.

24 large cookies **These are delicious, very simple shortbread cookies, cut into a doughnut shape.**

- **8 ounces (2 sticks) unsalted butter**
- **1 cup confectioners' sugar**
- **2 cups *sifted* all-purpose flour**

Adjust rack to center of oven and preheat oven to 375 degrees.

In large bowl of electric mixer, beat the butter a bit to soften. Add the sugar and beat until blended. On lowest speed, gradually add the flour, scraping the bowl with a rubber spatula as necessary to keep the mixture smooth.

(If necessary, chill the dough slightly only until it can be rolled. Do not let it get too firm. If it does, let it soften slightly at room temperature and then beat again.)

On a lightly floured cloth with a floured rolling pin, roll the dough to a ¼-inch thickness. Cut with a floured 3-inch doughnut cutter (or see Note). Save all the scraps and reroll and cut them together. Place ¾ inch apart on unbuttered cookie sheets.

Bake, one sheet at a time, for 13 minutes, reversing the position of the cookie sheet during baking, or until the cookies are lightly colored on the edges and barely sandy-colored on top. These should not brown. Do not overbake.

Let cool briefly on cookie sheets. Transfer with wide metal spatula to cool on a rack.

LADYFINGERS

About 30 (4-inch) ladyfingers **Making ladyfingers is great fun. It's quick—but you have to beat egg whites correctly, fold them in correctly, and use a pastry bag correctly. Then the satisfaction is tremendous. And the ladyfingers are delicious.**

If you have extra-large cookie sheets (17 x 14 inches), use them for this recipe. And you will need a 15-inch pastry bag and a plain tube with a ⅝-inch opening (#8).

NOTE

If you do not have superfine sugar, place plain granulated sugar in the bowl of a food processor fitted with the metal chopping blade and process for 30 seconds.

- **1 cup *sifted* unbleached flour**
- **4 large eggs, separated**
- **1 teaspoon vanilla extract**
- **¼ teaspoon salt**
- **⅛ teaspoon cream of tartar**
- **½ cup plus 3 tablespoons superfine sugar (see Note)**
- **Confectioners' sugar, for sifting over the tops before baking**

Adjust two racks to divide the oven into thirds and preheat the oven to 325 degrees. Lightly butter two cookie sheets (see above), dust them with flour through a sifter, and shake off excess over the sink. Set aside.

Have ready a 15-inch pastry bag fitted with a plain round tube that has a ⅝-inch opening (#8): Fold down a cuff about 2 inches wide on the outside of the bag. Twist the tube end of the bag and push it up a bit into the bag to prevent the batter from leaking out. Place the bag in a tall glass or jar to support it while you fill it. Set aside.

Resift the flour two or three times and set it aside in the sifter on a piece of paper.

In a small bowl, beat the yolks and vanilla with an eggbeater to mix well. Set aside.

Place the egg whites and salt in a clean small bowl of an electric mixer and, with clean beaters, beat on medium speed until foamy. Add the cream of tartar and beat on high speed until the whites hold a soft point when the beaters are raised. On moderate speed, add the superfine sugar 1 rounded spoonful at a time. Then beat on high speed again until the whites are stiff but not dry. Remove the bowl from the mixer.

Add the beaten yolks all at once to the whites and fold together without being thorough about it. Turn into a large mixing bowl. In three additions, sift the flour over the top, folding it in with a rubber spatula. At first do not be completely thorough with the folding, and even at the end, fold only until you do not see any dry ingredients. Even if the mixture looks lumpy and not smooth, do not fold any more.

continues ↘

Turn the mixture into the pastry bag. Unfold the cuff, gather the top of the bag closed, and untwist the tube end.

Press out one 4-inch-long ladyfinger onto a prepared sheet. At the end of the ladyfinger, lift the pastry bag slowly toward the other end to prevent leaving a tail of the batter. Continue pressing out ladyfingers, allowing ½ to ¾ inch space between each.

Through a fine strainer, quickly strain confectioners' sugar generously onto the ladyfingers. Bake immediately for 15 to 18 minutes, reversing the sheets once, top to bottom and front to back, to ensure even baking. Bake until the ladyfingers are lightly colored and feel dry and springy when gently pressed with a fingertip.

Remove the ladyfingers with a wide metal spatula.

Ladyfingers are best when they are very fresh (the day they are made) — but they are also very good when they have been only loosely covered for a day or two and have become dry and almost crisp. But for lining a container (as for an icebox cake) they should be very fresh.

MADELEINES

12 (3-inch) madeleines **Plain, buttery, and spongy—traditionally baked in madeleine pans with shell-shaped cups, which are generally available in kitchen equipment shops. This recipe is for one pan with twelve cups for cookies 3 inches long.**

Madeleines became famous in French literature because it was the taste of a madeleine dipped in a cup of tea that Marcel Proust used as the starting point of his literary journey into the past. They are delicious when just baked, but Proust's might well have been stale—when dry and stale they are great for dunking.

NOTES

Never clean madeleine pans with anything rough or anything other than soap and water—it might make future cookies stick.

This recipe may be doubled for two madeleine pans if they will both fit on the same oven rack. The madeleines must not be baked on two racks at one time or they will not brown properly. Therefore, to make a large number, repeat the directions—the prepared batter should not stand.

- **2 ounces (½ stick) unsalted butter**
- **1 large egg plus 2 egg yolks, at room temperature**
- **¼ cup sugar**
- **½ teaspoon vanilla extract**
- **½ cup *sifted* all-purpose flour**
- **Finely grated zest of 1 large lemon**

Adjust rack one-third up from bottom of oven and preheat oven to 375 degrees.

To prepare the pan: Bring about 1½ tablespoons butter (this is in addition to that called for in recipe) to room temperature to soften. Do not use melted butter. With a pastry brush, brush the butter on the cups, brushing from the top to the bottom the long way and then reversing and brushing from the bottom to the top. Examine the cups carefully to make sure that you haven't missed any spots and also that the butter is not too thick anywhere. Now, over wax paper, sprinkle the cups with fine, dry bread crumbs. Tilt and shake the pan to coat the cups thoroughly. Invert the pan and tap it firmly, leaving a very light coating of crumbs.

Cut up the 2 ounces of butter and, in a small pan over low heat, melt it, stirring occasionally. Set aside to cool but do not let it harden.

In small bowl of an electric mixer, beat the egg, egg yolks, sugar, and vanilla at high speed for about 15 minutes, until the mixture barely flows when beaters are lifted. On lowest speed, gradually add the flour, scraping the bowl with a rubber spatula as necessary and beating only until the flour is incorporated—do not overbeat. Remove from mixer. (Use your fingertips to remove the batter from the beaters.)

continues ↘

Fold in the lemon zest and then, in four or five additions, the cooled melted butter, folding only until no butter shows. Bake immediately—do not let the batter stand.

Spoon the batter into the prepared cups. The batter will be mounded slightly above the tops. Do not smooth; the batter will level itself.

Bake for 18 minutes, or until the tops are golden brown and spring back firmly when lightly touched. If necessary, reverse the position of the pan for the last few minutes of baking to ensure even browning.

Madeleines must be removed from the pan immediately. Quickly cover the pan with a rack or a cookie sheet and invert. Remove the pan. Cool the madeleines on a rack.

MACADAMIA AND MILK CHOCOLATE BISCOTTI

About 24 large biscotti **These are very large and divinely and deliciously crisp-crunchy. They are loaded with whole, voluptuous macadamias and extra-large chunks of creamy and dreamy milk chocolate and have a hint of toasted almonds. They involve a little more work—and a little more expense—than most other biscotti. And they are worth it all. Fantabulous! Get the best milk chocolate you can find.**

- **1½ ounces (⅓ cup) blanched (skinned) whole almonds**
- **12 ounces milk chocolate**
- **2 cups *sifted* all-purpose flour**
- **½ teaspoon baking powder**
- **½ teaspoon baking soda**
- **¼ teaspoon salt**
- **1 cup sugar**
- **7 ounces (1½ cups) roasted and salted whole macadamia nuts (I use Mauna Loa brand)**
- **2 large eggs**
- **1 teaspoon vanilla extract**
- **¼ teaspoon almond extract**
- **2 tablespoons whiskey or brandy**

First toast the almonds in a shallow pan in a preheated 350-degree oven for 12 to 15 minutes, shaking the pan a few times, until the nuts are lightly colored and have a delicious smell of toasted almonds when you open the oven door. Set aside to cool.

Adjust rack to the middle of the oven and preheat the oven to 375 degrees. Line a large, flat cookie sheet (preferably 17 x 14 inches) with heavy-duty aluminum foil. Set the sheet aside.

To cut the chocolate into chunks, I use an ice pick. However you do it, cut the chocolate into uneven pieces no more than about ½ inch in any direction. Set aside.

Into a large bowl (preferably one with flared rather than straight sides), sift together the flour, baking powder, baking soda, salt, and sugar.

Place about ⅓ cup of the sifted dry ingredients in the bowl of a food processor fitted with the metal chopping blade. Add the toasted almonds. Process for about 45 seconds, until the nuts are very fine and powdery.

Add the processed mixture to the sifted ingredients in the large bowl. Add the macadamia nuts and the cut-up chocolate. Stir to mix.

In a small bowl, beat the eggs, vanilla and almond extracts, and whiskey or brandy, beating until well mixed.

Add the egg mixture to the dry ingredients and stir—and stir—until the dry ingredients are all moistened. I stir with a large rubber spatula—and a lot of patience. You will think there is not enough liquid; just keep on stirring. (Actually, stir and then turn the ingredients over and over and press down on them firmly with the spatula until the dry ingredients are incorporated.)

Generously spray the lined cookie sheet with nonstick cooking oil spray.

Turn the dough out onto the lined sheet. Wet your hands with cold water — do not dry them. With your wet hands, press the dough together to form a mound, then shape it into an oval and flatten it a bit. With a dough scraper or a large metal spatula, cut the dough lengthwise into equal halves. Continue to wet your hands and shape into two strips with rounded ends, each one about 12 inches long, 3 inches wide, and 1 inch thick. There should be 2 or 3 inches of space between the two strips, and the strips should be pressed firmly so that they are compact.

Bake for 28 minutes, reversing the sheet front to back once during baking.

Remove the sheet from the oven, slide the foil off the sheet onto a large cutting board, and let stand for 20 minutes.

Reduce the oven temperature to 275 degrees and adjust two racks to divide the oven into thirds.

With a wide metal spatula, transfer the baked strips to the cutting board.

Now, to cut these into biscotti, you must be careful. Use a serrated bread knife and cut with a sawing motion. (Actually, I find it is best to cut through the top crust with a serrated knife, and then finish the cut with a very sharp, straight-bladed knife. Or, you might use only one knife — try different knives.) Cut biscotti on an angle about a scant ¾ inch wide. The sharper the angle, the larger the biscotti will be, so unless you want very large biscotti, do not cut at too sharp an angle.

At this stage, the biscotti are very fragile; use a large metal spatula or pancake turner to carefully transfer them to two unlined cookie sheets, placing them cut side down. Bake the two sheets for 35 minutes. Once during baking, turn the slices over and reverse the sheets top to bottom and front to back.

When finished, turn the oven off, open the oven door, and let the biscotti cool in the oven.

When they are cool, the chunks of chocolate might still be soft. If so, let the biscotti stand for about an hour, and then store them airtight.

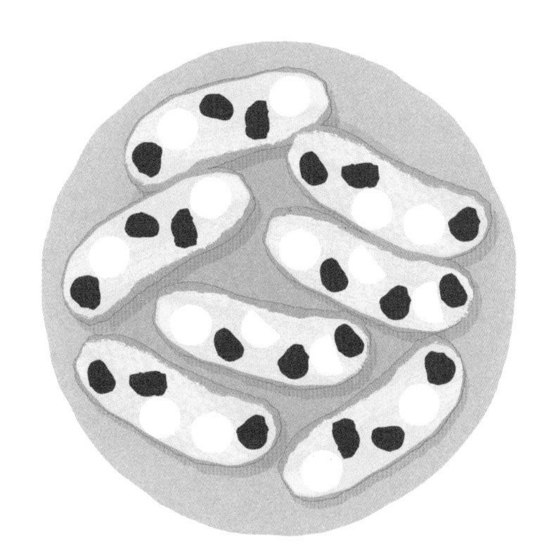

HONEY GRAHAM CRACKERS

24 to 30 double crackers **These are almost like the store-bought ones — plain, dry, crunchy squares.**

- 1 cup *sifted* all-purpose white flour
- 1 teaspoon baking powder
- ½ teaspoon baking soda
- ½ teaspoon salt
- ½ teaspoon ground cinnamon
- 4 ounces (1 stick) unsalted butter
- 1 teaspoon vanilla extract
- ½ cup firmly packed dark brown sugar
- ¼ cup honey
- 2 cups *unsifted* all-purpose whole-wheat flour (stir lightly to aerate before measuring)
- ½ cup milk

Sift together the white flour, baking powder, baking soda, salt, and cinnamon and set aside.

In the large bowl of an electric mixer, cream the butter. Add the vanilla, brown sugar, and honey and beat well. On low speed, add the whole-wheat flour and the sifted ingredients in three additions, alternating with the milk in two additions. Scrape the bowl as necessary with a rubber spatula and beat only until smooth after each addition. If the mixture is not completely smooth, turn it out onto a large board or a smooth surface and knead it briefly with the heel of your hand.

Form the dough into an even, flattened oblong. Wrap it airtight and refrigerate for 2 to 3 hours or longer, overnight if you wish.

Before baking, adjust two racks to divide the oven into thirds and preheat oven to 350 degrees. Line cookie sheets with baking parchment or foil.

Cut the chilled dough into equal quarters and work with one piece at a time.

On a well-floured pastry cloth with a floured rolling pin, roll the dough into an even 15 x 5-inch rectangle. With a long, sharp knife, trim the edges. (The trimmings should be reserved, pressed together, and rerolled all at once in order not to incorporate any more flour than necessary.) Use a ruler as a guide and cut crosswise into six 5 x 2½-inch rectangles. With the back (or dull) side of a knife, lightly score across the center of each cracker, dividing it into two halves, each 2½ inches square.

With a wide metal spatula, transfer the crackers to the cookie sheets, placing them ½ to 1 inch apart. With a fork, prick the crackers evenly in parallel rows at ½-inch intervals.

Bake for 12 to 14 minutes, until the crackers are lightly colored, reversing the sheets top to bottom and front to back as necessary to ensure even browning. (If you bake only one sheet at a time, bake it high in the oven.)

Crackers

The next three recipes are not cookies, but I cannot resist including them. They are crackers — to serve with a meal, or with cheese, or just to nibble on, plain, with tea or coffee or wine. They are unusual (some of the directions are strange) and delicious (I don't know of anything that I make that people rave about more than they rave about Corn Melba) and fun to make, and I love them.

CORN MELBA

96 crackers Many years ago the dining room of the Hampshire House in New York City always had a basket of these on each table. They were unbelievable! They were surely the thinnest (as though they had been made by a special machine — not by a person), crispest, flakiest, most buttery, most exciting . . . the flavor was bland and mild and simply buttery and simply delicious and I simply had to have the recipe. The hotel would not give it to me. That was the beginning of a hunt that lasted for many years and involved almost everyone I knew from coast to coast. I was getting nowhere.

Sometime before I started my Corn Melba hunt, I had sent 25¢ for a small pamphlet called "Menus and Recipes of Famous Hostesses," published in July 1955 by *Vogue* magazine. I made a few things from it and put it away in a desk drawer and forgot about it. Years later I came across it, and as soon as I opened it I saw Corn Melba; it even had the same name. The recipe was from Mrs. Robert Sherwin of Edgartown, Massachusetts, and her luncheon menu included "Corn-Meal Melba Toast" served with fish mousse.

Serve Corn Melba anytime, anyplace, with or without anything.

Making these is a most unusual experience, different from any other baking I have done. And fun all the way.

NOTE

When a friend of mine had trouble with this recipe, we talked long distance for hours. We finally found the trouble. She was buttering the pans with melted butter and a pastry brush, and was using much more butter than you use when you spread the butter (not melted) with crumpled wax paper. The excess butter prevented the crackers from baking as they should. The pans should be buttered normally, not extra heavy and not extra thin.

continues ↘

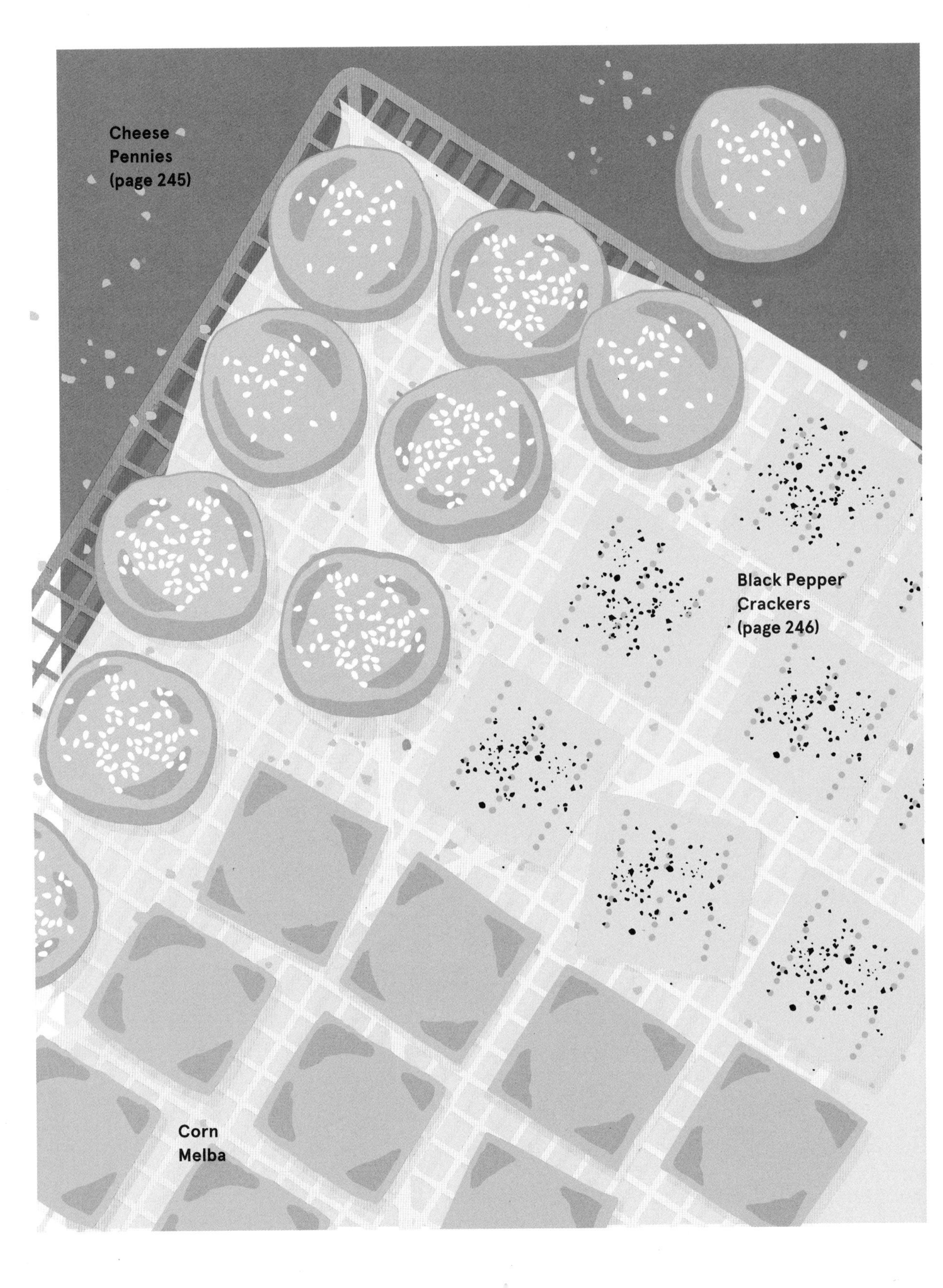
Cheese
Pennies
(page 245)
Black Pepper
Crackers
(page 246)
Corn
Melba

Corn Melba keeps well for a week or more. What I mean is, it does not spoil. But it is hard to keep it around.

This is baked in rimmed baking sheets. The recipe makes six panfuls. If you have only one pan, and therefore bake only one pan at a time, be prepared to spend several hours near the oven. But if you bake three or four pans of it at one time, it can all be completed in about 1½ hours.

- **2 cups *double- or triple-sifted* all-purpose flour (if your sifter has only one screen, resift the flour before measuring; if it is sifted only once, you will be using a little more flour, and the mixture will be a little too thick)**
- **2 teaspoons baking powder**
- **½ teaspoon salt**
- **4 ounces (1 stick) unsalted butter, at room temperature**
- **2 tablespoons sugar**
- **2 large eggs**
- **1 cup milk, at room temperature**
- **1 cup water, at room temperature**
- **½ cup cornmeal (the cornmeal may be white or yellow—I have used both many times—but I think that the Melba is slightly thinner and crisper with white water-ground cornmeal)**

This is made in rimmed baking sheets that measure 10½ x 15½ x 1 inch. The crackers will be cut into squares in the pans; therefore you should not use pans that have a nonstick finish or you will cut through the finish. You can bake six pans at a time if you have that many pans and oven racks, or you can bake only one or more at a time (the remaining batter should stand at room temperature). Adjust oven racks for as many pans as you have, or adjust a rack to the center for only one pan. Preheat oven to 375 degrees. Butter the pans (see Note).

Sift together the flour, baking powder, and salt and set aside.

In the large bowl of an electric mixer, beat the butter until it is soft. Beat in the sugar and then the eggs, one at a time. On low speed, add the sifted dry ingredients in three additions, alternating with the milk and water in two additions, scraping the bowl with a rubber spatula and beating until well mixed after each addition. Add the cornmeal last and beat only until mixed. The mixture will look curdled during the mixing and might still be lumpy after the mixing. Strain it through a coarse strainer set over a bowl to remove any lumps. It will be a thin mixture.

You will have 4 cups of batter with which to make 6 panfuls of Melba. As closely as I can figure it, that means that for each panful you should use ⅔ cup of batter. Measure it in a glass measuring cup.

Pour the measured amount along one long side of the buttered pan, scraping out the

continues ↘

cup with a rubber spatula. Tilt the pan as necessary for the batter to run into a thin, thin layer completely covering the bottom of the pan. Hold the pan almost vertically, turn it one way and then another, and have patience—the batter might run slowly. If, after a reasonable length of time, you see that you simply cannot get the batter to cover the pan, use an extra spoonful or so as necessary.

Bake one or more pans at a time—you can put a second pan in after the first one has started baking. After 5 to 7 minutes, the batter should be firm enough to be cut; remove it from the oven and, with a small, sharp knife, cut the long way to make 4 strips, and then cut crossways to make 16 rectangles.

Return the pan to the oven and continue to bake for about 25 minutes more, until the Melba is crisp all over—part of it might be golden brown or even darker, and part of it may be lighter (although it is best when it is all an even golden color). During baking, reverse the pans top to bottom and front to back as necessary to ensure even browning. The crackers will shrink as they bake, and some of the crackers may still look wet and buttery in places, but they will dry and crisp as they cool if they have been baked enough.

The crackers will not all be done at the same time; some may be done in 20 to 25 minutes, others might take as long as 45 minutes. Remove them from the oven as they are done.

With a wide metal spatula, transfer the baked crackers to a paper towel to cool. When you run out of room, it is all right to place some of them on top of others.

Wash, dry, and butter the pans each time you use them.

Corn Melba is fragile—handle with care. (Before I knew how to make this, we ordered it by mail from New York; when it arrived in Florida it was pretty well broken up—but we were happy to have it anyway.) Store it airtight but don't worry about this getting limp—it stays crisp. It may be frozen if you want to keep it for many weeks or months.

VARIATION

Ralph's Corn Melba: For many years my husband asked me to add some cayenne pepper to this recipe. I don't know why it took me years to do it. I finally did, and Ralph loved it. If you want to try it, add ¼ teaspoon of cayenne to ⅔ cup of the batter and make one panful.

CHEESE PENNIES

55 to 60 crackers **This is a cheese cracker to serve with cocktails, or at the table with soup or salad. They are thin, light, and crisp, and I make them quite sharp with cayenne. The procedure is the same as for making icebox cookies—the dough must be refrigerated for several hours or longer.**

- **1 cup *sifted* all-purpose flour**
- **½ teaspoon salt**
- **⅛ to ½ teaspoon cayenne pepper (see Notes)**
- **8 ounces extra-sharp cheddar cheese**
- **4 ounces (1 stick) unsalted butter**
- **3 tablespoons sesame seeds (see Notes)**

NOTES

I like these crackers sharp and spicy—I use ½ teaspoon cayenne. With ⅛ teaspoon they will have a good flavor but will be mild, ¼ teaspoon will make them warm, ½ teaspoon will make them hot, but for hot-hot, you may want to use even more. Be your own judge about how much to use.

There are white sesame seeds (hulled) and grayish-tan ones (unhulled)—use the white ones.

Sift together the flour, salt, and cayenne pepper and set aside.

Grate the cheese as fine as possible. In the large bowl of an electric mixer, cream the butter. Add the grated cheese and beat until thoroughly blended. On low speed, gradually add the sifted dry ingredients and beat, scraping the bowl with a rubber spatula, until thoroughly incorporated.

Spread a bit of flour lightly on a board and turn the dough out onto the floured board. Flour your hands lightly. With your hands, shape the dough as for icebox cookies into a round or square log about 8 inches long and 1¾ inches in diameter.

Wrap the roll in plastic wrap or wax paper and place in the refrigerator (not the freezer—if the dough is frozen it will be difficult to slice). Let stand in the refrigerator for at least several hours, or several days if you wish.

Any time before baking the crackers, toast the sesame seeds as follows: Spread them in a small, shallow pan and place the pan in the middle of a preheated 350-degree oven. Bake, shaking the pan occasionally, until the seeds have turned golden brown—it will take 15 to 20 minutes. Set aside to cool. (Toasting brings out the flavor of the seeds.)

Before baking, adjust two racks to divide the oven into thirds and preheat oven to 350 degrees.

Unwrap the roll of dough and place on a cutting board. With a very thin, sharp knife, cut slices ⅛ to ¼ inch thick (I like these thin) and place them 1½ to 2 inches apart on unbuttered cookie sheets.

Sprinkle the tops of the slices generously with the toasted sesame seeds.

Bake for 12 to 15 minutes, until the pennies are lightly colored. Reverse the sheets top

continues ↘

to bottom and front to back as necessary to ensure even browning. They must bake long enough to be very crisp, but overbaking will burn the cheese and spoil the flavor.

The crackers must be removed from the sheets as soon as they are taken out of the oven. Use a wide metal spatula to loosen all the crackers from the sheet quickly and then transfer them to racks to cool.

Store airtight.

BLACK PEPPER CRACKERS

About 24 crackers **Delicate, tender, delicious, thin, and crisp—serve these all-purpose crackers with soup or salad, or with cheese. I use a generous amount of pepper—enough so you can really taste it—but you may use less for a more subtle flavor, or omit it entirely. Or you can substitute chili powder, or caraway or sesame seeds. Or garlic or onion powder. Or whatever.**

- 2 cups *sifted* all-purpose flour
- 1 tablespoon sugar
- ¾ teaspoon salt
- ¼ teaspoon baking powder
- 2 ounces (½ stick) unsalted butter, cold and firm, cut into ¼-inch pieces (it is best to cut it ahead of time and refrigerate)
- ½ cup milk or light cream
- Additional milk or light cream, for brushing
- Black pepper (preferably use whole peppercorns and a mill, or use ground pepper)

Adjust two racks to divide the oven into thirds and preheat oven to 425 degrees. You will use unbuttered and unlined cookie sheets, which may be plain or nonstick.

This may be put together in a food processor or in a bowl with a pastry blender.

In a processor (fitted with the steel blade): Sift together the flour, sugar, salt, and baking powder and place in the bowl of the processor. Add the butter and process very briefly with quick on-and-off pulses for about 10 seconds or less, only until the mixture resembles coarse meal. Then, through the feed tube, quickly add the milk or cream and process only until the mixture barely holds together.

With a pastry blender: Into a large bowl, sift together the flour, sugar, salt, and baking powder. Add the butter and, with a pastry blender, cut it in until the mixture resembles coarse meal. Add the milk or cream and stir with a fork to make a stiff dough.

Work with half of the dough at a time. Press it into a square shape, place it on a floured pastry cloth, and roll it with a floured rolling pin. Keep the shape squarish and roll the dough until it is very, very thin, or as thin as you can make it. (The crackers will be good if the dough is not that thin, but they will be better if it is.)

With a pizza cutter, pastry cutter, or long, sharp knife, trim the edges square. With a fork, prick the dough all over at ½-inch intervals. Then brush it all lightly with milk or cream. Now grind the black pepper over the dough. Or sprinkle with whatever topping or combination you wish. I use black pepper, and I use enough so you can really taste it (it is delicious) but not enough to make it really harsh. But it is up to you. (It is a good idea to bake one as a sample; it is too bad to bake them all and then say, "They should have had more pepper.")

Now, with the cutter or knife, cut the entire piece of dough into even squares or rectangles. (I make them about the size of store-bought graham cracker rectangles and, with the edge of a wide metal spatula, lightly score each cracker through the middle into halves like graham crackers.)

Place the crackers on unbuttered, unlined cookie sheets. Bake for 18 to 20 minutes, until the crackers are golden colored, reversing the sheets top to bottom and front to back as necessary to ensure even browning. Be sure to bake them long enough for them to be crisp.

Cool on a rack and then store airtight.

MARSHMALLOWS

About 1¾ pounds marshmallows **These are candy — not cookies. But homemade marshmallows are so very popular and such fun to make that I want to share the recipe with you. You will need a candy thermometer and an electric mixer. And the cooked marshmallow mixture must stand for 8 to 12 hours (or a little longer if it is more convenient) before it is cut into individual pieces.**

NOTE

An interesting little aside about marshmallows: I gave this recipe to a friend who is a high school home economics teacher. She was ecstatic about it and taught it in all of her classes. She started each class by asking her students to write down the ingredients they thought were in marshmallows. No one knew. The guesses included egg whites, milk, cream, flour, cornstarch, and some said "marsh" or "mallow," which they thought was a natural substance that grows on trees. But they soon found out, and my friend tells me that it is the single most popular recipe she has ever taught, and that now there are hundreds of girls in Miami Beach who make marshmallows regularly.

- Vegetable shortening (such as Crisco), for preparing the pan
- 1 cup cold water
- 3 tablespoons (3 envelopes) unflavored gelatin
- 2 cups granulated sugar
- ¾ cup light corn syrup
- ¼ teaspoon salt
- 1½ teaspoons vanilla extract
- Confectioners' sugar, for coating the marshmallows

Prepare a 9 x 13 x 2-inch pan as follows: Invert the pan. Cut a piece of aluminum foil long enough to cover the bottom and sides of the pan. Place the foil, shiny side down, over the inverted pan and fold down the sides and corners just to shape. Remove the foil and turn the pan right side up. Place the foil in the pan and press it gently into place. With a pastry brush or crumpled wax paper, coat the foil thoroughly but lightly with vegetable shortening. Set aside.

Place half of the cold water (reserve remaining ½ cup) in the large bowl of an electric mixer. Sprinkle the gelatin over the surface of the water and set aside.

Place the sugar, corn syrup, salt, and reserved ½ cup water in a heavy 1½- to 2-quart saucepan over moderately low heat. Stir until the sugar is dissolved and the mixture comes to a boil. Cover for 3 minutes to allow any sugar crystals on the sides of the saucepan to dissolve. Uncover, raise the heat to high, insert a candy thermometer, and let the syrup boil without stirring until temperature reaches 240 degrees. Do not overcook. Remove from heat.

Beating constantly at medium speed, pour the syrup slowly into the gelatin mixture. After all the syrup has been added, increase the speed to high and beat for

continues ↘

15 minutes, until the mixture is lukewarm, snowy white, and the consistency of whipped marshmallow, adding the vanilla a few minutes before the end of the beating. (During the beating, occasionally scrape the bowl with a rubber spatula. The marshmallow will thicken and become sticky — if the mixture crawls up on the beaters as it thickens, carefully wipe it down with a rubber spatula.)

Pour the slightly warm and thick marshmallow mixture into the prepared pan and, with your forefinger, scrape all the mixture off the beaters. Smooth the top of the marshmallow. Let stand uncovered at room temperature for 8 to 12 hours or a little longer if it is more convenient.

Then, sift or strain confectioners' sugar generously onto a large cutting board to cover a surface larger than the 9 x 13-inch pan. Invert the marshmallow over the sugared surface. Remove the pan and peel off the foil. Strain confectioners' sugar generously over the top of the marshmallow.

To cut the marshmallow into even 1-inch strips, use a ruler and toothpicks to mark it every 1 inch. Prepare a long, heavy, sharp knife by brushing the blade lightly with vegetable shortening. Cutting down firmly with the full length of the blade, cut the marshmallow into 1-inch strips. (After cutting the first slice, just keep the blade sugared to keep it from sticking.)

Dip the cut sides of each strip into confectioners' sugar to coat them thoroughly — you should have enough excess sugar on the board to do this.

Now cut each strip into 1-inch squares. (You may place three strips together and cut through them all at once.) Roll the marshmallows in the sugar to coat the remaining cut sides. Shake off excess sugar.

Store in a plastic box or any airtight container — or in a plastic bag like the commercial marshmallows.

SWEDISH JELLY SLICES

42 to 48 bars **These are rolls of cookie dough, baked and filled with thick, tart jam and ground almonds, then topped with a glaze. They are interesting, rustic cookies.**

- **2¼ cups *sifted* all-purpose flour**
- **½ teaspoon baking powder**
- **¼ teaspoon salt**
- **6 ounces (1½ sticks) unsalted butter**
- **2 teaspoons vanilla extract**
- **⅔ cup granulated sugar**
- **1 large egg**
- **¾ to 1 cup apricot preserves (or any thick, tart jam or jelly)**
- **2½ ounces (¾ cup) almonds, blanched and sliced thin**

GLAZE

- **1¼ cups confectioners' sugar**
- **2 tablespoons boiling water (approximately)**

Adjust rack one-third down from top of oven and preheat oven to 375 degrees.

Sift together flour, baking powder, and salt and set aside.

In large bowl of an electric mixer, beat the butter to soften a bit. Add the vanilla and granulated sugar and beat well. Beat in the egg. On lowest speed, add the sifted dry ingredients, scraping the bowl with a rubber spatula and beating until the dry ingredients are thoroughly incorporated. Turn out onto a lightly floured board, shape into a ball, and cut into four equal parts.

Working on the board with your fingers (flour them if dough sticks), work each piece into a roll about 12 inches long and 1 inch in diameter.

Place the rolls crossways on a large, unbuttered cookie sheet, about 14 x 16 inches, leaving 2 to 3 inches between them. The rolls will spread a bit as they bake.

Make a narrow, shallow trench down the length of each roll by pressing gently with a fingertip. Leaving a little space at the ends, work the full length in one direction, and then work in the opposite direction. The ends and the sides should be higher. Do not make the trench too deep or the cookies will not hold together after they are baked and sliced.

To fill the trench with the preserves, use a pastry bag without a tube; or, if the opening of the bag is too large, use a plain, round tube about ½ inch in diameter. Or use a very small spoon. The filling should be level with the sides or very slightly higher (if the preserves are thick enough they will not run over the sides). With your fingertips, generously sprinkle the sliced almonds over the preserves.

Bake for about 25 minutes, until the cookies are sandy-colored on top and golden brown around the edges, reversing position of pan during baking to ensure an even color.

Shortly before removing cookies from oven, mix the glaze.

continues ↘

FOR THE GLAZE

Mix the confectioners' sugar and boiling water until smooth, using enough water to make the consistency similar to heavy cream. Cover airtight when not in use.

Remove the cookie sheet from oven and apply the glaze by pouring it or spooning it down the length of each roll, over the preserves and nuts.

Using a flat-sided cookie sheet as a spatula, carefully slide the rolls onto a large rack to cool for about 5 minutes. Then carefully transfer them to a cutting board. With a very sharp, heavy knife, cut each warm roll on an angle into slices 1 to 1¼ inches wide. Replace cookies on the rack to finish cooling.

PALM ISLAND BRANDY SNAPS

40 cookies **These brittle ginger wafers are rolled, after baking, around the handle of a wooden spoon into a tube shape. The original recipe is from England. In old English books, the directions are to fill the tubes with whipped cream and tie a thin satin ribbon around each tube. With the whipped-cream filling, these cookies become an elegant dinner party dessert. But with or without the whipped cream and the ribbon, they are decorative cookies and fun to make. They are made without a mixer and are very easy, though time-consuming, since they are baked only five at a time.**

NOTE

If you plan to serve these filled with whipped cream and would like a wider tube to make room for more cream, the cookies may be rolled around something about 1 inch in diameter. Metal tubes made for cannoli (Italian pastries) are about 1 inch in diameter and generally available in specialty kitchen equipment shops and online. Or you can use a piece of wooden doweling cut 6 to 7 inches long.

- ½ cup *sifted* all-purpose flour
- 1½ teaspoons ground ginger
- ⅓ cup light molasses
- 4 ounces (1 stick) unsalted butter, cut into small bits
- ½ cup granulated sugar
- 1½ teaspoons brandy

OPTIONAL WHIPPED CREAM FILLING

- 2 cups heavy cream
- ½ cup confectioners' sugar
- 2 teaspoons vanilla extract

Adjust a rack to the center of the oven and preheat oven to 325 degrees. Butter a 12 x 15½-inch cookie sheet.

Sift together the flour and ginger and set aside.

Place the molasses, butter, and granulated sugar in a heavy 2-quart saucepan over moderate heat. Stir until the butter is melted and the mixture is only warm, not hot. Remove from the heat. Add the sifted dry ingredients and stir well until completely smooth—if necessary, beat with a wire whisk. Stir in the brandy. Transfer the mixture to a small bowl for ease in handling. (The mixture will be thin; it will thicken slightly as it stands.)

Use 1 level spoonful of the mixture for each cookie. Spoon portions onto the buttered sheet, placing only 5 per sheet—these spread and they need plenty of room. Bake, only one sheet at a time, for about 8 minutes, or until the cookies are lightly browned and have a mottled texture. Reverse the sheet front to back once during baking to ensure even browning.

Remove the sheet from the oven and let stand for 1½ to 2 minutes, until a cookie

continues ↘

can be removed without losing its shape. If the cookies have run together, use a small, sharp knife to cut them apart before removing them from the sheet. Now work quickly before the cookies cool and harden. With a wide metal spatula, loosen one side of a cookie and then, with your fingers, quickly but carefully peel the cookie away from the sheet and place it facedown on a board or smooth work surface. Immediately place the handle of a wooden spoon (it must be round) at the closest edge of the cookie and roll the cookie loosely around the handle to form a tube. (If you roll the cookie too tightly around the spoon handle it will be difficult to slide it off.) Immediately slide the cookie off the handle, place it on the board or work surface to cool, and continue to shape the remaining cookies while they are warm. (If the tubes collapse and do not hold their round hollow shapes, they were removed from the cookie sheet too soon — they may be opened and rerolled while they are still warm. Or, if they have already become crisp, they may be replaced briefly in the oven to soften so they can be opened and rerolled. If the cookies cool and harden before they are rolled, replace them in the oven briefly — only until they soften. If they are not completely crisp when cool, they were not baked long enough.)

It is not necessary to cool, wash or wipe, or rebutter the cookie sheet before placing another batch of cookies on it.

As soon as the cookies have cooled, store them airtight or they may become sticky.

TO FILL THE BRANDY SNAPS WITH WHIPPED CREAM

You will need a pastry bag (preferably a canvas bag with a waterproof or plastic coating on the inside) and a star-shaped tube with about a ½-inch opening. Insert the tube in the bag. Set aside.

The bowl and beaters for whipping the cream should be chilled ahead of time. Place the cream, confectioners' sugar, and vanilla in the chilled bowl and, with the chilled beaters, whip the cream only until it holds a shape — if it is too stiff it will curdle as it is pressed through the pastry bag and tube.

Fill the pastry bag with the whipped cream. Hold a Brandy Snap in one hand and with the other hand hold the pastry bag, inserting the tube a little way into the opening of the Brandy Snap. Press gently from the top of the pastry bag to fill one side of the cookie, forming a rosette at the opening. Then turn the cookie around and fill the other side, form a rosette, and carefully place the cookie on a tray. Continue filling the other Brandy Snaps.

These may be refrigerated for a very short time (no more than 1 hour), but as the filled cookies stand in the refrigerator they will become less crisp. It is best to freeze them if they must stand for even a short time, and then serve them directly from the freezer. (The unfilled cookies may be made way ahead of time and stored airtight or frozen — if they are frozen they must not be exposed to the air until completely thawed. Then, if they are filled shortly before dinner and refrozen for only an hour or so, they will be at their best for serving.)

index

C

G

H

R

about the author

Maida Heatter, dubbed the Queen of Cake by *Saveur,* was the author of several classic books on dessert and baking. Heatter was also the recipient of three James Beard Foundation awards and was inducted into the organization's Hall of Fame.